Analyzing Global Environmental Issues

The existence of environmental dilemmas and political conflicts leads us to appreciate the need for individuals and groups to behave strategically in order to achieve their goals and maintain their well-being. Global issues such as climate change, resource depletion, and pollution, as well as revolts and protests against corporations, regimes, and other central authorities, are the result of increased levels of externalities among individuals and nations. These all require policy intervention at international and global levels.

This book includes chapters by experts proposing game theoretical solutions and applying experimental design to a variety of social issues related to global and international conflicts over natural resources and the environment. The focus of the book is on applications that have policy implications and relevance and, consequently, could lead to the establishment of policy dialogue. The chapters in the book address issues that are global in nature, such as international environmental agreements over climate change, international water management, common pool resources, public goods, international fisheries, international trade, and collective action, protest, and revolt.

The book's main objective is to illustrate the usefulness of game theory and experimental economics in policy making at multiple levels and for various aspects related to global and international issues. The subject area of this book is already widely taught and researched, but it continues to gain popularity, given growing recognition that the environment and natural resources have become more strategic in human behavior.

Ariel Dinar is Professor of Environmental Economics and Policy, and Director of the Water Science and Policy Center at the University of California, Riverside, USA. His teaching and research focus on environmental and resource economics and strategic behavior, and the environment at local and international levels. He publishes on issues related to the economics and politics of natural resources and the environment, with emphasis on water.

Amnon Rapoport is Distinguished Professor of Management at the University of California, Riverside, USA. His research interests are in individual and interactive decision making. He has published several books and more than 200 book chapters and articles on sequential choice behavior, coalition behavior, dynamic pricing, route choice in networks, and bargaining.

Routledge Explorations in Environmental Economics
Edited by Nick Hanley
University of Stirling, UK

Analyzing Global Environmental Issues

Theoretical and experimental applications and their policy implications

Edited by Ariel Dinar and
Amnon Rapoport

Routledge
Taylor & Francis Group

NEW YORK AND LONDON

First published 2013
by Routledge
711 Third Avenue, New York, NY 10017

Simultaneously published in the UK
by Routledge
2 Park Square, Milton Park, Abingdon, Oxon OX14 4RN

Routledge is an imprint of the Taylor & Francis Group, an informa business

British Library Cataloguing in Publication Data
A catalogue record for this book is available from the British Library

Library of Congress Cataloging in Publication Data
Analyzing global environmental issues : theoretical and experimental applications and their policy implications / edited by Ariel Dinar and Amnon Rapoport.
    p. cm.
Includes bibliographical references and index.
1. Environmental policy–Economic aspects. 2. Environmental policy–International cooperation. 3. Globalization–Environmental aspects.
I. Dinar, Ariel, 1947– II. Rapoport, Amnon.
HC79.E5A495 2013
333.7–dc23   2012035530

ISBN: 978-0-415-62718-4 (hbk)
ISBN: 978-0-203-10219-0 (ebk)

Typeset in Times New Roman
by Wearset Ltd, Boldon, Tyne and Wear

Printed and bound in the United States of America by Publishers Graphics, LLC on sustainably sourced paper.

This book is dedicated to Roy Gardner, a friend, a colleague, and a big fan of the Game Theory Practice meetings. Roy was the first one to submit his paper for the GTP8 (the meeting leading to this book) in Riverside, California, but was not able to make it to the meeting. He passed away on January 10, 2011 at the age of 63.

Contents

PART II
Game theory and political economy applications

Figures

Tables

Contributors

Astrid Dannenberg is a Research Fellow at Columbia University and Gothenburg University. Her research interests lie primarily in global sustainable development issues, especially climate change. Her research uses game theoretic models and economic experiments, but also integrates other disciplines such as natural sciences and psychology. In particular, the research focuses on human decision making and how institutions can be designed to promote cooperation and to identify and remove barriers to cooperation.

Bouwe R. Dijkstra is Associate Professor with the School of Economics, University of Nottingham (UK). Before joining Nottingham in 2001, he held positions at the Interdisciplinary Institute for Environmental Economics, University of Heidelberg (Germany) and the Department of Economics and Public Finance, University of Groningen (the Netherlands). He holds a M.Sc. in Economics and a Ph.D. in Law and Economics from the University of Groningen. His main interest is in environmental economics, particularly instruments of environmental policy and political as well as international dimensions.

Ariel Dinar is a Professor of Environmental Economics and Policy and Director of the Water Science and Policy Center, Department of Environmental Economics, University of California, Riverside, USA. He teaches, conducts research, and publishes on water economics, economics of climate change, strategic behavior and the environment, and regional cooperation over natural resources.

Ana Espinola-Arredondo has been an Assistant Professor in the School of Economic Sciences at Washington State University since 2009. She specializes in the areas of environmental economics and industrial organization. She received a Ph.D. in Economics from the University of Pittsburgh and was awarded the Research Medal Award of the Global Development Network. She has recently published, among others, in the *Journal of Environmental Economics and Management*, *Ecological Economics*, and *Environment and Development Economics*.

Kenji Fujiwara is Associate Professor at the School of Economics, Kwansei Gakuin University, Japan. He completed his Ph.D. in Economics at Kobe University in 2006. His main areas of research are international trade and dynamic games.

Roy Gardner (1947–2011) was a Professor Emeritus of Economics at Indiana University, as well as Academic Director of the Kyiv School of Economics, Kyiv, Ukraine. He specialized in the theory of games and economic behavior, with applications to class struggle, spoils systems, draft resistance, alliance formation, monetary union, corruption, and especially the human dimension of global environmental change. His research was funded by NSF (1987–2000; 2008–2011), USDA, CNRS, the German Science Foundation, and the Alexander von Humboldt Foundation, among others. He served as Associate Editor of the *European Economic Review* and a member of the editorial council of the *Journal of Environmental Economics and Management*.

Mario Gilli is a Professor of Economics in the Department of Economics, University of Milano-Bicocca since 2002. He is founder of the Center for Interdisciplinary Studies in Economics, Psychology, and Social Sciences at the University of Milano-Bicocca (http://dipeco.economia.unimib.it/ciseps/) and he is director of the Ph.D. Program in Economics at Bicocca-University. He received his Ph.D. in Economics at Cambridge University in 1996. His fields of interest include: learning and evolutionary theories in game theory; cross fertilizations among economics, psychology and social sciences; analysis of organizations and institutions; conflict theories with particular focus on suicide terrorism; and political economics.

Kim Hang Pham-Do is a Senior Lecturer at the School of Economics and Finance, Massey University in Palmerston North, New Zealand. She earned a Ph.D. in Economics from the University of Tilburg, the Netherlands. Her specialization is coalitional games and its application for analyzing international environmental problems and transboundary resource management.

Harold Houba is Associate Professor at the Department of Econometrics of the VU University Amsterdam. He obtained his Ph.D. in economics from Tilburg University in 1994. Houba has been affiliated with the VU since 1992. His specialization is bargaining theory, with applications to environmental economics including international rivers. He has published a great number of papers in international journals, including *European Economic Review, Games and Economic Behavior*, and *Journal of Environmental Economics and Management*.

Jérémy Laurent-Lucchetti holds a Ph.D. in Economics from HEC Montréal (Canada). He is currently a Researcher in the Department of Economics at the University of Bern (Switzerland) and at the Oeschger Center for Climate Change. He is particularly interested in the issue of common resource management, especially when criteria of efficiency and fairness cannot be achieved by the usual market mechanisms.

Justin Leroux is an Associate Professor at the Institute of Applied Economics at HEC Montréal (Canada) and a Fellow at CIRANO and CIRPÉE (Montréal, Canada). He holds a Ph.D. in Economics from Rice University (2005) and was a laureate of the nationwide French competition for tenured professorship in economics in 2010. His research focuses on normative and mechanism design approaches to managing externalities. He consults for the government of Québec on setting rates for public services, like road networks and water services.

Antonio Lloret earned his Ph.D. at the Bren School of Environmental Science and Management at the University of California, Santa Barbara, in 2007. Currently, he is an Assistant Professor at the Business School of the Instituto Tecnológico Autónomo de México, a private research university in Mexico City. His work focuses on the link between institutions and the environment at multiple levels. His current projects address the relationship between sustainability and competitiveness in Latin America.

Ngo Van Long is James McGill Professor of Economics at the Department of Economics, McGill University, Canada. Long completed his Ph.D. in Economics at the Australian National University in 1975. His main areas of research are natural resources and environmental economics, dynamic games and inter-temporal optimization, and international economics.

Felix Munoz-Garcia has been an Assistant Professor in the School of Economic Sciences at Washington State University since 2008. His research focuses on the areas of industrial organization and game theory. He received a M.Sc. in Economics from the Universitat de Barcelona and a Ph.D. in Economics from the University of Pittsburgh. He has recently published, among others, in the *International Journal of Industrial Organization, Economics Letters*, and the *Journal of Environmental Economics and Management*.

Gordon R. Munro is a Professor Emeritus with the Department of Economics and the Fisheries Centre, University of British Columbia, and Visiting Professor with the Centre for the Economics and Management of Aquatic Resources, University of Portsmouth, UK. He has done research on the economics of fisheries management at both the theoretical and the policy level, since the early 1970s, giving particular attention to the management of internationally shared capture fishery resources. He was the first to introduce game theory to the fisheries economics literature in his analysis of the management of these shared resources. From 2000 to 2002, he worked with the FAO of the UN in organizing, and then participating in, the 2002 Norway-FAO Expert Consultation on the Management of Shared Fish Stocks. In 2006–2007, he served as a member of the six-person Independent Panel to Develop a Model for Improved Governance by Regional Fisheries Management Organizations, based at the Royal Institute of International Affairs, London.

Andries Nentjes is Emeritus Professor in Economics and Public Finance at the University of Groningen in the Netherlands. He has published on history of economic thought, in particular the economics of Keynes, and on the economics of environmental policy, in particular the use of market-based instruments. In the 1990s, he was a regular visiting scholar at IIASA (Laxenburg, Austria).

Nentjes has served as a member on the Dutch Advisory Board on Energy, the Advisory Board on Environmental Policy, the board of the Dutch Royal Association for Economics, and as chairman of the Dutch Society for Post-Keynesian Economics. He is Officer in the Order of Orange Nassau.

Svetlana Pevnitskaya is an Associate Professor of Economics at Florida State University. Her research interests are in the areas of applied microeconomic theory and experimental economics with the focus on individual decision making in strategic environments. Dr. Pevnitskaya's specific interests include behavior in auctions, decisions under risk and uncertainty, learning, the effect of beliefs on decision making, rewards and punishment in strategic behavior, and games with dynamic externalities. She holds a Ph.D. in Economics from the University of Southern California, and worked at Caltech and Ohio State University prior to joining FSU.

Amnon Rapoport is a Distinguished Professor of Management and Marketing at the Anderson Graduate School of Management, University of California, Riverside. He is the author of eight books and more than 200 refereed papers and book chapters. He has served as associate editor or member of the editorial board of the *Journal of Mathematical Psychology, Experimental Economics, Organizational Behavior and Human Decision Processes*, and *Games and Economic Behavior*. He has received numerous grants from such agencies as the National Science Foundation, the Hong Kong Research Grants Council, United States – Israel Binational Science Foundation, and the United States Air Force. His current research focuses on individual and interactive decision making.

Dmitry Ryvkin is an Associate Professor of Economics at Florida State University. He received his Ph.D. in Economics from the Center for Economic Research and Graduate Education – Economics Institute (CERGE-EI) in Prague, and Ph.D. in Physics from Michigan State University in East Lansing in 2006. Dr. Ryvkin's research is mainly in the areas of microeconomic theory, experimental economics, and economic psychology. His topics of interest include tournament theory, corruption, overconfidence, and games with dynamic externalities.

Bernard Sinclair-Desgagné is the International Economics and Governance Chair at HEC Montréal. His main research areas are the economics of incentives and organization, environmental economics, and risk management. His publications can be found in journals such as *Econometrica, Management Science*, the *Journal of Environmental Economics and Management*, and *the Journal of Regulatory Economics*. He is a Fellow of the European Economic Association, and an Associate Editor of *Resource and Energy Economics* and the *International Review of Environmental and Resource Economics*.

Alessandro Tavoni is a Research Fellow at the London School of Economics, which he joined late in 2010 to work at the Grantham Research Institute on

Climate Change and the Environment. He investigates the obstacles and the drivers of cooperative behavior in the global and local commons (e.g., coping with climate change, or avoiding overharvesting resources at a local scale). This is tackled through a combination of game theory models, experiments, and simulations, in an effort to shed light on how norms and diverging interests among stakeholders affect the success of environmental management.

Frans P. de Vries is a Reader in Economics at the Management School, University of Stirling, Scotland. Before joining Stirling in 2007, he held academic positions at the University of Groningen and Tilburg University, the Netherlands. He holds a M.Sc. in Agricultural and Environmental Economics from Wageningen University (The Netherlands) and a Ph.D. in Law and Economics from the University of Groningen. His main interest is in the domain of environmental economics, with specific expertise in environmental policy and technological innovation. He has been a consultant for the OECD Environment Directorate and the UK Department for International Development (DFID).

Paloma Zapata-Lillo is a Professor of Game Theory and Mathematical Economics at Science School of the Universidad Nacional Autónoma de México. Her areas of interest are the theories of repeated games and evolutionary games. She has written the books *Fundamentación Matemática de los Algoritmos Simpliciales* (Mathematical Foundation of the Simplicial Algorithms), *Economía, Política y Otros Juegos: Una Introducción a los Juegos no Cooperativos* (Economics, Politics, and Other Games: An Introduction to Non Cooperative Games). Another book, *Los Juegos del Comportamiento Social* (Social Behavior Games), will be published soon. A fourth book, *Infinite Extensive Games with Continuous Normal Form*, is in preparation.

Dmytro Zhosan is an Associate Professor of Business and Economics at Ripon College, Ripon, WI. He focuses his teaching in the areas of theoretical and applied microeconomics and business management. His primary research interests include experimental economics, game theory, and industrial organization. His research focuses on factors that can aid in solving the problem of the commons. His research has been funded by NSF (2008–2011), Bates College, and Ripon College. He received his Ph.D. in economics at Indiana University in 2009. He spent several years in Maine teaching at Bates College and at Colby College and working on his research involving Maine lobstermen and ground fishermen.

Xueqin Zhu is Assistant Professor at Environmental Economics and Natural Resources Group of Wageningen University. She obtained a M.Sc. degree with distinction in 2000, and a Ph.D. degree in environmental economics in 2004 from Wageningen University. Her main research interest is in the field of applied general equilibrium modeling and welfare economics for environmental problems. She has published a number of papers in journals including *Ecological Economics*, *Environmental and Resource Economics*, and *Water Resources Management*.

1 Global and environmental issues

Theoretical applications and policy implications

Ariel Dinar and Amnon Rapoport

1.1 Introduction

A growing number of environmental dilemmas and political conflicts have led us to examine the need for individuals, institutions, and nations to behave strategically in order to achieve their goals and maintain their well-being. Global issues such as climate change, migration, resource depletion, and pollution, as well as revolts and protests against corporations, regimes, and other central authorities, are the result of increased levels of negative externalities among individuals and nations that jointly mandate policy intervention at international and global levels.

Game theory and experimental economics have become the main analytical tools for addressing strategic issues in the field of economics and have gained considerable influence in other disciplines, including political science, sociology, and law, as well as computer science and evolutionary biology. With globalization and the growing openness of our societies, and with the growing level of communication and analytical capacity, game theory and experimental economics are perceived as major tools for policy makers and not only for theory construction.

This book contains chapters by experts proposing game theoretical solutions to a variety of social issues related to global and international conflicts over natural resources and the environment. The focus of the book is on applications that have policy implications and may consequently lead to the establishment of policy dialogues. A main objective of the book is to illustrate the usefulness of game theory in policy making at multiple levels and for various aspects related to global and international issues.

The book constitutes a collection of papers that were originally presented at a conference dedicated to game theory and practice in global and international issues that took place in Riverside, California, in July 2011. The meeting in Riverside was the eighth in a series of biennial meetings on game theory and practice commencing in 1998.[1]

1.2 Content of the book

The book includes 13 chapters focusing on a variety of issues related to climate change, management of common pool resources, negotiations over international or global resources, international fishery management, prevention of regional ecological damages, globalization and environmental protection, management of international water, the Arab Spring, and pollution and international trade. It is divided into two parts: (1) experimental economics applications to global and international issues, and (2) game theory and political economy applications to global and international issues. Brief descriptions of the chapters are presented below.

1.2.1 Part I: Experimental economics applications

Part I includes five chapters that are concerned with management of common pool resources and public bad under uncertainty and asymmetry of information.

Chapter 2, by Tavoni and Dannenberg, starts with the observation that efforts to protect global climate often face the challenge of coordinating national contributions and distributing costs equitably in the face of different notions that countries might have of equity and strong incentives for free-riding. Using experimental methods, the authors study the drivers of cooperation among autonomous agents who are faced with a cooperative game requiring multilateral efforts in order to reach a pre-specified threshold and thereby avoid a collective risk. Their design differs from the standard linear public good game by requesting sequential, rather than simultaneous, contributions; imposing the common objective of avoiding loss, rather than creating surplus; and introducing uncertain, rather than deterministic losses. Communication modes are also experimentally manipulated. The chapter reports that asymmetry in endowments undermined coordination, particularly when the subjects had no signaling mechanism beyond their own contributions, with 80 percent of all groups failing to reach the target sum. On the other hand, pledges significantly decreased the percentage of failure. There seems to be no evidence that "wealthy" agents, who bear more responsibility for reaching the target threshold, contribute more.

Chapter 3 by Munoz-Garcia and Espinola-Arredondo shifts the emphasis from the management of resources and communication opportunities to the management of information about the size of the initial stock of a common pool resource (CPR). This issue is studied experimentally in a two-person, two-period entry deterrence game between an incumbent player, who is perfectly informed about the size of the CPR, and an uninformed potential entrant. The initial stock of the CPR is set to be either high or low. In the complete information condition, both agents are accurately informed about the initial stock sizes, whereas, in the incomplete information condition, the incumbent is privately informed about the stock size, but the entrant only observes the incumbent's first-period appropriation level. The results suggest important links between stock size and information. Under incomplete information and high-stock level, the incumbent over-exploits the CPR during the first period. Both agents exploit the CPR in the second period. Under incomplete information and high-stock level, the incumbent under-exploits the CPR in order to signal the presence of low stock to potential entrants. However, if the stock level is high, the incumbent also under-exploits the CPR but for a different reason, namely, to conceal its type from potential entrants and thereby deter entry. The implications of these inefficiencies to the conservation or destruction of the CPR are clearly explored.

In Chapter 4, Espinola-Arredondo and Munoz-Garcia start with the observation that negotiations of environmental agreements generally involve uncertainty because no accurate assessments may be made on whether or not other countries have the technical ability to fully comply with the terms of the treaty. Incomplete information about other countries' ability to comply with the terms of the treaty is experimentally manipulated in a two-player, two-stage signaling game, which in the first stage – the negotiation stage of the international environmental agreement (IEA) – the leader announces its participation decision, accepting a given set of non-binding commitment levels. In the second stage, the follower chooses whether or not to participate in the IEA. Two layers of uncertainty are considered – namely, unilateral uncertainty and bilateral uncertainty. Using the calculus of game theory, the analysis shows that, relative to complete information, unilateral uncertainty may facilitate the emergence of successful treaties. However, the introduction of bilateral uncertainty may entail equilibrium outcomes in which the IEA is signed under the same conditions as in complete information. The chapter also demonstrates that, under complete information, both welfare improvements and welfare losses may be reached, depending on the type (high or low) of the negotiating parties.

Ample empirical evidence shows that, under certain circumstances, the "tragedy of the commons" may be avoidable (see the work of Elinor Ostrom and her collaborators). Group size, group homogeneity, and the type of game that appropriators play contribute to the efficiency of CPR appropriation. In Chapter 5, Zhosan and Gardner examine the potential effects of dividing the common into smaller areas on appropriation efficiency. They propose a simple model that incorporates geographic separation, rules of cooperation, and norms into a standard game of the commons setup and then analyze the conditions under which the game results in efficient equilibrium. The authors summarize the results of a previous experiment and then conclude that, under simple assumptions, enforcing geographical separation may prove to be another effective tool in successfully managing the commons.

Pevnitskaya and Ryvkin (Chapter 6) explore the joint effects of environmental context and termination uncertainty on decisions in a dynamic game with a public bad. This context is relevant for situations known for regulation of polluting agents such as CO_2 pollution by states that benefit from economic revenue (private good), but at the same time the production process creates pollution (private bad), which accumulates over time. On every period of the game, subjects are instructed to choose a production level that generates private revenue. It also generates "emissions" that accumulate over time and serve as public bad. Using the Markov perfect equilibrium solution and social optimum as two alternative benchmarks in a dynamic experimental setting, the observed individual decisions are shown to fall between these two benchmarks. An interesting result of the experiment is that subjects allocate their entire endowment to production under termination uncertainty in the last stages of the game.

1.2.2 Part II: Game theory and political economy applications

The eight chapters that comprise Part II address various global and international issues, such as pollution, climate change, social unrest, trade, and natural resources including fisheries and water.

Chapter 7 by Munro reviews the role of game theory in instigating policy decisions confronting Regional Fisheries Management Organizations (RFMOs). RFMOs were designed to manage fish stocks to be found within both the coastal state Exclusive Economic Zone (EEZ) (see also Zhosan and Gardner, Chapter 5) and the adjacent high seas. RFMOs face the "new member" problem, in which states included in the RFMOs are obligated to consider membership of states expressing a desire to be included in the RFMOs' fishery resources after the RFMOs have been established. The chapter demonstrates the role game theory plays in developing solutions to "new member" problems, now being discussed within the Organization for Economic Co-operation and Development (OECD).

Human societies rely on indispensable ecological services that give rise to the "tragedy of the commons," including water purification, livestock support, and climate stability. These services are provided by wetlands, forests, and oceans, to mention just a few. Chapter 8 by Laurent-Lucchetti, Leroux, and Sinclair-Desgangé is built on two observations. The first is that the provision of ecological services is subject to discontinuities (threshold effects) following the abuse of the involved ecosystems. The second and related observation is that the inherent complexity of ecosystems usually renders it difficult to assess threshold values with certainty. The authors establish that a strategic environment, in which the total resource to be divided between the agents follows a multinomial distribution, contains multiple equilibria. They focus on "cautious equilibria" in which agents collectively avoid the worst outcome, "dangerous equilibria" in which the total demand may be unsustainable, and "dreadful equilibria." Their analysis of the equilibria gives rise to a major insight, namely, that allowing agents to cooperate and form deviating coalitions would eliminate all the "dreadful equilibria" and some of the "dangerous equilibria," while keeping "cautious equilibria," which are robust to such deviations.

Globalization and the resulting fierce competition over natural resources have dramatically enhanced the over-exploitation of water, land, and forests. Some of the deteriorating effects of over-exploitation have been environmental pollution, deforestation, and climate change. Another serious consequence, which is the focus of Chapter 9 by Zapata-Lillo, is the breaking of both the social bonds and the virtuous interaction between the communities and their environment. The author proposes a model of collective action in which the players are the social groups forming the communities. Players have to decide independently whether to act collectively to protect the common natural resources or stay indifferent. A payoff structure is then imposed on this game, and the equilibria of the game are constructed. The emergence of certain patterns of social organization of these communities and the role that protective stock accumulation plays in the formation of these patterns are then investigated. Analysis of the model supports the opinion that communities maintaining close contact with natural resources may be the main actors in facing environmental and natural resource catastrophes.

Governance of international water resources requires understanding of the interplay of formal and informal agreements. Cooperation in the form of formal agreements enhances the welfare of the river basin and prevents potential conflicts. However, uncertain conditions (e.g., variability in water flow) that could not be anticipated when the agreement was signed may change the initial conditions and thereby render the agreements unsustainable. Chapter 10 by Lloret models the potential welfare gains associated with informal agreements, whether or not formal agreements are in place. The model is parameterized with a bargaining power parameter and the benefit functions of the countries sharing the basin. Theoretical analysis of the parameter space shows that establishing informal agreements provides maximum gains, and subsequent empirical investigation of 39 bilateral basins estimates the mean gain at 6.5 percent.

Zhu, Houba, and Pham-Do (Chapter 11) address another problem in the management of international water. They propose a joint management approach for international water that is claimed to be efficient and stable, and apply it to the case of the Mekong River, which recently has become a hot spot in terms of unilateral activities by its riparians. The authors observe that the Mekong River Commission (MRC) that regulates the Lower Mekong region has a great potential for welfare improvements from cooperation. But the MRC faces uncertainty in reaching an agreement with China, which is at present not a signatory to the 1995 Mekong Treaty. Welfare gains would increase significantly if China is part of the agreement. The chapter describes the gains from a joint management that includes all upper and lower Mekong riparian states.

The so-called "Arab Spring" is still unfolding. Chapter 12 by Gilli proposes a new point of view on the protests, none of them peaceful, that have characterized Tunisia, Libya, Egypt, Bahrain, Yemen, and more recently Syria from December 2010 to about May 2012. The chapter proposes a simple game theoretical model to describe the relationship between the disenfranchised (the citizens) and the enfranchised (the selectorate) segments of the population. It focuses on the role of the country's wealth and on the size of its selectorate. It is characterized by asymmetric information on the likelihood of establishing a working democratic rule through protests and revolts. The model is admittedly simplistic, but some of its implications are testable. Thus, the model implies that if the country is poor, but the regime is strong, then the autocracy will remain in power. If the country possesses intermediate wealth, then the citizens will protest and the selectorate will appease, leading to reforms. And if the country is sufficiently wealthy and the selectorate is large, then the citizens will revolt. Clearly, the model is too simple to consider all the important aspects of real events of the

Arab Spring that vary from one country to another (e.g., conflicts between religious sects), but it offers a specific point of view that merits consideration.

Fujiwara and Van Long (Chapter 13) propose a model to explain possible solutions to the trade of an exhaustible resource between exporting and importing states. The chapter provides dynamic and static settings and then compares the Nash and Stackelberg equilibrium solutions under leadership by the importing or exporting country. Its findings suggest that, as compared to the static Nash equilibrium for normal form games, both countries are better off in equilibrium if the importing country is the leader, but that the follower is worse off if the exporting country is the leader. The world welfare is highest under the importing country's leadership and lowest under the exporting country's leadership.

Nentjes, Dijkstra, and De Vries (Chapter 14) address the objective of efficiency and equity in international environmental agreements that aim at reducing damages caused by negative externalities and common pool problems. The Nash Bargaining Solution (NBS) has been used to address such objectives, but it requires perfect information. An alternative concept, the Market Exchange Solution (MES), is proposed. The authors demonstrate how each approach performs and suggest that MES is a more suitable model than the NBS for describing and predicting allocation of effort and the distribution of payoffs resulting from international negotiations between self-interested sovereign states.

1.3 Policy messages

Not surprisingly, the policy messages are both general and chapter-specific. We start with the chapter-specific policy messages and then synthesize them.

The policy message in the chapter by Tavoni and Dannenberg, which deals with coordination and protection of the global climate, is that coordination-promoting institutions, early action, and redistribution from richer to poorer nations are essential for the avoidance of collective risk. The next chapter by Munoz-Garcia and Espinola-Arredondo, which deals with information and the tragedy of the commons, suggests that policy makers may use incentive-driven regulations such as quotas that specify significant penalties to signal users the cost of over-exploitation under various states of stock and information setting. Chapter 4 by Espinola-Arredondo and Munoz-Garcia focuses on uncertainty and environmental negotiations. It suggests that international agencies could provide incentives to either strategically distribute or conceal information in order to promote successful treaties. Zhosan and Gardner, who test the effectiveness of geographic restrictions on common pool resources, imply that, in creating the smaller geographical areas, a policy maker should always analyze the equilibrium number of appropriators in each area to allow for small manageable groups. However, creating too many areas may increase management costs, thus negating potential benefits of co-management. Dealing with public bad impacts on growth and welfare, Pevnitskaya and Ryvkin recommend that pollution-mitigating institutions are necessary to solve the social dilemma between private economic growth and global environmental sustainability. In order for states to sacrifice profits from production to reduce pollution that imposes costs on everyone, they have to face severe costs of pollution and climate change either through taxing policies or as direct losses.

In the first chapter of Part II, Munro concludes that there is now increasing evidence that the results of game theoretic analysis conducted in relation to the RNFOs has begun to have an impact in the realm of policy. The evidence cited is a document by OECD that recognizes the need for a policy goal that allows for a stable cooperative agreement that is time consistent and adjustable to external shocks. Laurent-Lucchetti *et al.* address the question of whether to adopt precautionary measures in order to avoid claiming natural capital beyond the lowest possible threshold leading to its collapse. From a policy point of view, a desirable outcome in terms of the resource can actually be achieved in a decentralized way, corresponding to what they named "cautious equilibrium." Zapata-Lillo, who investigates the link between globalization, natural resources, and dependent-community sustainability, finds that not all economic and political activities that are introduced to prevent harm on the community are valid, and that relevant international treaties should be enforced. Lloret shows that, when water supply is variable, there always are gains to the riparian states from establishing informal agreements in addition to the existing treaty, regardless of the bargaining power. An important finding, which is in agreement with previous work, is a positive correlation between the water flow variability and the net gains of informal agreements (Dinar *et al.* 2011). Zhu *et al.*, who developed a model to estimate the gains from a joint mode of management of a river basin such as the Mekong, suggest several policy-relevant results. They stress the importance of demonstrating the value of cooperation to all riparian states, rather than only the lower Mekong states. They further suggest that cooperation should start with a common perception of the status quo, including a mutual acceptance of aspects such as the presence of claims to water, perceived property rights, and official water use data. Attempting to explain the likely democratization in Arab revolt, Gilli arrives at surprising policy implications. The results suggest that being a poor country is not conducive to revolt or protest. However, an intermediate or a big national wealth is a precondition for massive revolts. The chapter by Fujiwara and Van Long, which deals with trade of an exhaustible resource between exporting and importing states, provides important policy implications. It suggests that, if both trading countries have market powers and the resource exporting country uses quantity-setting strategies, it would be in their interest to agree on the order of moves, compared with making their moves simultaneously. This will render everyone better off; therefore, it is in the best interest of a supra agency to intervene and establish an institution to coordinate the moves. Nentjes *et al.* suggest that when agents, such as countries dealing with possible cooperation, are self-interested, Market Exchange Solution (MES) is better equipped than Nash Bargaining Solution (NBS) to predict the allocation of effort and the distribution of gains from cooperation in the case of an international or global public good. The main reason for that is that, in MES, the allocation of contributed shares is based on individual gains expected from the public good, whereas, in NBS, contributed shares are calculated by a planner. Therefore, NBS is less suitable as a model of cooperation between sovereign states.

1.4 Conclusion

This collection of studies on application of game theory and experimental economic models to issues of global and international nature is a second contribution from the biennial game theory practice. The first publication (Dinar *et al.* 2008) focused on game theory and policy making as applied to natural resources and the environment. This book focuses on global and international issues, most of which are environmental in nature. Another difference is that this book includes experimental economic applications, which, together with the game theory applications, provide meaningful results that could be used by policy makers in each of the issues analyzed.

As was already indicated in the introductory section, with globalization and the increase in openness of societies, and with the growing level of communication ability and analytical capacity, game theory and experimental economics demonstrated their usefulness as tools for policy makers and not only for theory construction or analysis. The various chapters in this book support such conclusion.

Note

1 The 8th meeting on Game Theory Practice dedicated to global and international issues was co-funded by the Water Science and Policy Center and the Anderson Graduate School of Management at the University of California, Riverside. Previous meetings of Game Theory Practice took place in Genoa, Italy (1998), Valencia, Spain (2000), Hilvareenbeek, The Netherlands (2002), Elche, Spain (2004), Zaragoza, Spain (2006), and Montreal, Canada (2007).

References

Dinar, S., Dinar, A., and Kurukulasuriya, P. (2011) "Scarcity and cooperation along international rivers: An empirical assessment of bilateral treaties," *International Studies Quarterly*, 55: 809–833.

Dinar, A., Albiac, J., and Sanchez-Soriano, J. (eds) (2008) *Game Theory and Policy Making in Natural Resources and the Environment.* London: Routledge Publishing.

Part I

Experimental economics applications

2 Coordinating to protect the global climate

Inequality and communication in the experimental lab[1]

Alessandro Tavoni and Astrid Dannenberg

2.1 Introduction

The emission of greenhouse gases (GHG) and the associated change of the global climate has become a growing concern worldwide. The projected consequences include rising average surface temperature, sea level rise, melting glaciers, changing precipitation patterns, and more extreme weather events. Climate change mitigation, therefore, is universally desirable but suffers from particularly strong free-riding incentives, as argued below.

In game-theoretic models, climate change mitigation is usually modeled as an n-player prisoners' dilemma game. The players in the games are the countries represented by their national governments. What makes the game a dilemma is that the unique Nash equilibrium, in which no player can do better by deviating unilaterally, is socially inefficient. The models concerned with international environmental agreements (IEA) add more stages to the game. In the first stage, countries choose whether or not to be a signatory to an IEA while they decide on their emission abatement in later stages. Signatories to the IEA are typically assumed to cooperate with each other, while non-signatories act independently. The key finding of these models is that, if the potential gain from cooperation is large, only few countries form an IEA (Barrett 1994; Hoel 1992; Carraro and Siniscalco 1993). Thus, the analytical models mostly deliver pessimistic results for the prospect of international cooperation. Experimental studies have confirmed that, in the absence of strong monitoring and sanction institutions, human cooperation is difficult to sustain (for reviews, see Ledyard 1995 and Chaudhuri 2011).

The climate system furthermore involves threshold effects, so-called "tipping points." Triggering a tipping point can have disastrous consequences for the environment and human well-being (Alley *et al.* 2003; Lenton *et al.* 2008). Prominent examples are the dieback of the Amazon rainforest (Malhi *et al.* 2009), the collapse of the Atlantic Thermohaline Circulation (Zickfeld *et al.* 2007), and the decay of the Greenland ice sheet (Notz 2009). The existence of such thresholds can alter the "climate change game" and the incentives to cooperate fundamentally (Barrett forthcoming). The introduction of a threshold makes the benefit curve of the climate change game discontinuous, while it is traditionally modeled as continuous. As long as the threshold is known with precision, it may facilitate the problem of enforcement; in other words, the disastrous consequences of passing the threshold can help to solve the cooperation problem (Barrett and Dannenberg 2012).

Against this background, this chapter is concerned with the drivers of cooperation among groups of unrelated individuals faced with a coordination game requiring multilateral efforts in order to reach a known threshold and avoid losses to all members. Given the empirical nature of the problem, we address it by means of a controlled laboratory experiment. We thereby pay special attention to a salient feature of the ongoing climate debate: inequality between countries. Inequality and fairness considerations appear to have played a determinant role in the negotiation discourse. Developed countries are historically the main contributors to climate change, while in some newly industrializing economies, notably China, GHG emissions grow at an unprecedented rate. What is a fair way to share the responsibilities among developing and developed countries in the containment of global GHG emissions?

In international climate policy, different notions of equity have been proposed. For example, the egalitarian rule incorporates the principle of equal per capita emissions, the sovereignty rule postulates the principle of equal percentage reduction of current emissions, the polluter-pays rule incorporates the principle of equal ratio between abatement costs and emissions, and the ability-to-pay rule stipulates the principle of equal ratio between abatement costs and GDP (Lange *et al.* 2010). The lack of consensus on equity principles has been a major impediment to reaching an agreement between the United States and China over who is to be the first mover in the emission reduction game. Advocating the other country was to take the lead in terms of timing and magnitude of GHG reductions on the grounds of reciprocity considerations; the two largest emitters worldwide (each accounts for roughly one-fifth of energy-related global CO_2 emissions) have managed to stay clear of any binding commitments to date.

Our experiment, therefore, is designed with the objective of exploring the consequences of an asymmetric geometry for sharing the burdens of mitigation. Differences in endowments originating from computer-generated contributions (or lack thereof) in the initial rounds of play are introduced in two treatments to convey the idea of differential wealth and responsibilities to players. Such asymmetries in wealth and carbon responsibilities among the actors, and the ensuing issues of equity referred to in the Framework Convention on Climate Change (UNFCCC 1992), might impede coordination. Furthermore, we empower players with the ability to make non-binding pledges before the actions are chosen. This is reminiscent of the current climate negotiations in which individual nations can make pledges in an uncoordinated manner. While these announcements do not carry any enforceable commitments with them, we postulate that they establish an important communication possibility that facilitates the coordination among players.

2.2 Experimental design

Most experiments on public goods utilize linear public goods games in which participants have the option to invest a fraction of their endowments in a public good by means of a voluntary contributions mechanism (for reviews, see Ledyard 1995 and Chaudhuri 2011). Typically, the returns on the investment are equally shared among the participants according to the marginal per capita return. We depart from this standard formulation in many ways. First, the provision of the public good is sequential, as multiple stages of contributions (ten rounds) are performed before the assessment of the group effectiveness in preventing simulated catastrophic climate change. Second, the objective of the game is to avoid a loss rather than creating a surplus by contributing to a public good (with higher group contributions leading to higher returns to the players). Here players' contributions to the public good make them collectively better off only insofar as they are sufficient to reach a threshold (€120). All contributions below (or above) it are wasted, as they fail to secure the private accounts (what is left of the initial €40 endowment after contributions to the public good) by the participants, or have no additional benefit if above the threshold. This feature leads to the next salient point, concerning the probabilistic nature of the losses. To account for the uncertainty involved in climatic change, the actions of the six players forming the groups taking part in the game have consequences that are not deterministic. If groups collectively fail to reach the target required to provide the climate protection public good, they will lose their savings on the private account with a probability of 50 percent.

The probability of the climate catastrophe was chosen in light of the results of the experiment by Milinski *et al.* (2008), which shares with ours the above departures from standard public good games, and which we enriched with features that will be discussed below. It is therefore worth taking a closer look at their experiment. In a nutshell, Milinski and his co-authors implemented the above setup, with individuals deciding in each of the ten rounds of the game whether to contribute €0, €2, or €4 to the climate account (these values are meant to represent the costs of reducing emissions by various levels). Each group was presented with one of three different treatments corresponding to three probabilities of loss in savings: 90 percent, 50 percent, and 10 percent, respectively. These yielded the following levels of success in avoiding simulated climate change: 50 percent, 10 percent, and 0 percent. That is, with the highest stakes, due to the larger gains in expected value from reaching the target, cooperation was highest and half of the participating groups where successful in collecting at least €120, while only one group out of ten succeeded in the 50 percent treatment and none from the one in which failing groups had only a small probability of incurring the loss.

In keeping with the above, we had groups of six individuals playing together, and each individual was initially endowed with €40. The players decided in each of the active rounds of the game whether to contribute €0, €2, or €4 to the climate account. All groups were presented with a 50 percent probability of loss in savings. Expecting that our introduction of a communication channel among subjects would facilitate coordination, we chose the intermediate probability of loss to avoid trivial results. Moreover, a 50 percent probability more strongly conveys the uncertainty regarding the consequences of passing the tipping point than a close-to-certain 90 percent loss probability (see section 2.3 for a discussion of the ensuing equilibria). After each round, the players were informed about all individual contributions and the aggregate group contribution in that round, as well as the cumulative past contribution of each player and the group. Players were assigned nicknames in order to keep their identities private. Since the focus of this study is to test in the lab for the role of inequalities in informing the debate on climate change, we introduced different treatments aimed at capturing features of asymmetry among participants in terms of wealth, past contributions, and future commitment announcements.

In order to induce subjects to perceive the inequalities among them as the result of past actions, we modified the game described above by replacing the first three rounds with three inactive ones in which half of the group had only the option of choosing a €4/round contribution, while the remaining three players could only select a €0/round contribution. That is, rather than externally imposing different endowments from the beginning of the experiment, players were all told they had the full €40 endowment before the start, but witnessed through the first three rounds a growing divergence between high and low contributors. As a result of these three inactive rounds, the players began the active play consisting of seven rounds with substantial "inherited" differences: Those who contributed €12 prior to round four had €28 left in their private accounts, while those who previously did not contribute anything to the public good found themselves with the entire endowment available for the ensuing seven rounds. We call this treatment "Base-Unequal," and we expect that this setup conveys a sense of responsibility to the relatively wealthy players, as their advantageous position is due to past free-riding. This situation is reminiscent of that of global GHG emissions, with developed countries owing much of their prosperity to past energy-intensive industrialization, relative to developing countries with historically smaller carbon footprints and wealth.

In order to single out the effect on coordination of the introduced asymmetry, a "Base" treatment was performed without such unequalizing redistribution. In it, subjects went through three inactive rounds in which they all had no other option than to choose the intermediate contribution of €2 per round. Finally, we implemented two treatments in which the subjects had the opportunity to make future commitment announcements. The "Pledge" treatment introduced two pledge stages to the symmetric case, while the "Pledge-Unequal" treatment implemented two pledge stages in the asymmetric case. In both pledge treatments, it was common knowledge that the pledges were non-binding and merely a possibility to communicate. The first pledge stage was after the (inactive) first three rounds. The subjects simultaneously and independently announced their intended contributions for the subsequent seven rounds. Afterwards the players saw the intended climate account, which contained the individual contributions from the first three (inactive) rounds plus the individual pledges. Thereby they immediately detected whether the intended contributions would be sufficient to avoid catastrophic climate change. The second pledge stage took place after round seven. Similar to the first pledge, the players simultaneously and independently announced their intended contributions for the last three rounds and were subsequently informed about the new intended climate account that included past contributions and the pledges. Table 2.1 summarizes the key features of our experimental design and the number of participants in each session.

The experiment was run in May 2010 at the MaxLab laboratory at the University of Magdeburg, Germany. In total, 240 students, equally split between the four treatments, participated in the experiment. No subject participated in more than one treatment. Sessions lasted about 60 minutes. For each session, we recruited either 12 or 18 subjects using the ORSEE software (Greiner 2004). Each subject was seated at linked computer terminals that were used to transmit all decision and payoff information. We used the Z-tree software (Fischbacher 2007) for programming. Once the individuals were seated and logged into the terminals, a set of written instructions was handed out. Experimental instructions included a numerical example and control questions in order to ensure that all subjects understood the games. At the beginning of the experiment, subjects were randomly assigned to groups of six. The subjects were not aware with whom they were grouped, but they did know that they remained within the same group of players throughout the ten rounds. After the final round, the players were informed whether the group had successfully reached the threshold of €120. Afterwards they were asked to fill in a short questionnaire. The questionnaire was designed to elicit the players' impressions and motivation during the game (see Table 2.2 on page 23). At the end of the experiment, one of two ping-pong balls was publicly drawn from a bag by a volunteer student to determine the "fate" of the groups that had not reached the threshold. Out of the 20 groups that did not reach the threshold, 11 groups were lucky and kept their money, while nine groups lost their money. No show-up fee was administered. On average, a subject earned €17.23 in the games; the maximum payoff was €40 and the minimum was €0.

Table 2.1 Summary of experimental design

Treatment	Asymmetric players	Pledge stages	Probability of climate damage (%)	No. of subjects
Base	no	no	50	60
Pledge	no	yes	50	60
Base-Unequal	yes	no	50	60
Pledge-Unequal	yes	yes	50	60

2.3 Equilibria

The game is characterized by a multiplicity of equilibria. It is a modified six-person stochastic threshold public goods game, with a total of ten rounds, of which only seven allow freedom of choice over the three possible actions.

Both contributing nothing and contributing €2 in each active round are symmetrical pure strategy Nash equilibria, because unilateral deviations are nonprofitable. Depending on the round and the path that led to it, a contribution of €4, bringing the individual investment above €20, may still be optimal if successful in guaranteeing that past investments are not wasted. Conversely, if at a certain stage the target becomes out of reach because of insufficient members' contributions up to that point, one's best response is to stop contributing and play the odds. In the symmetrical treatments, each group trajectory leading to a cumulative contribution of €120, irrespective of individual contributions provided that each subject invests at most €22 overall, is a Nash equilibrium. This is the case because the latter investment translates into a payoff of €18, which is above the €17 that is expected when all players choose not to contribute to the public good. Therefore, individuals can maximize the payoff of the game by choosing the intermediate level of contribution, investing a further €14 over rounds four through ten, and securing the €20. In the asymmetrical treatments, as a result of the different disposable endowments of rich and poor players, the former gain the most when the climate is protected with equal burden sharing in the active rounds (€26, resulting from an investment of €14). Relative to the no-contribution equilibrium, it is more appealing because the rich will be at least as well off when investing €20 at most. The poor, on the other hand, do not stand to gain from the equal burden-sharing equilibrium in the active rounds, assuming risk neutrality. Given the early round contributions of €12, only by investing less than €14 in the active rounds (with the group still reaching the threshold) can these players have a higher expectation than by not investing in the public good. The game design allows for such redistribution. The rich have a surplus of €12 in the €2 per active round equilibrium relative to the poor and can, in principle, forego part or all of it by investing more and allowing the poor to decrease their investment correspondingly. An average of €3 per round for the rich and €1 per round for the poor almost equalizes contributions (and payoffs) among the players. With full redistribution, rich and poor have a final payoff of €20, which, for the rich, is still rational in the sense of not being welfare diminishing, relative to not contributing anything.

To grasp the trade-offs in the simplest treatments (the symmetric ones, Base and Pledge), assume for the time being that behaviors are independent of the actions of others. The whole dynamic in the seven active rounds can then be collapsed into a one-round game, as in Figure 2.1. That is, every player has to decide on one-time contributions to the public good, as if the game was played in a single round. Given that (symmetric) provision requires all to invest an additional €14 relative to the inactive rounds, the choice is between contributing €0 and €14. The corresponding expected payoffs are indicated on the vertical axis

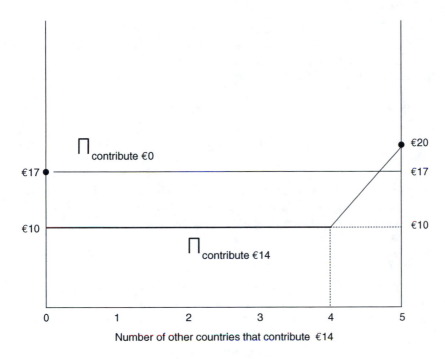

Figure 2.1 The symmetric treatments: equilibria in a one-round representation of the game (reproduced from Barrett 2011).

of Figure 2.1, while the horizontal axis shows the number of other players that choose to invest in climate mitigation. It is evident that the preferable outcome in terms of payoff (€20) is only achieved when all invest; however, if at least one player chooses not to invest, each has an incentive to also contribute €0 (and the worst equilibrium occurs yielding an expected payoff of €17).

In sum, since the welfare-maximizing outcome is supportable as Nash equilibrium, the players' task is merely to coordinate their effort toward this equilibrium. We hypothesize that inequality hampers coordination due to players' divergent incentives, while communication helps coordination. We derive the latter hypothesis from the broad experimental literature on the effects on communication. It has been known for a long time that communication among players can increase cooperation, although the effects generally depend on the nature of the game and the communication medium. In a nutshell, while communication often works in coordination games, it works much less reliably in dilemma games. As for the latter, communication is most likely to increase cooperation when it is face-to-face among small groups of players, allowing them to discuss the problem and to make and elicit ethically binding promises (see, for example, Dawes 1980; Sally 1995; Crawford 1998; Ostrom 2006).

2.4 Results

The bird's eye view of the cooperation level across treatments is provided in Figure 2.2. That is, for each treatment, it shows the percentage of groups who contributed at least €120 to the climate account.

   Inspection of Figure 2.2 suggests that:

a   the pledges are effective tools to ease coordination among group members; and
b   inequality disrupts coordination, but less severely so in the presence of the pledges.

In the following three sections, we take a closer look at between- and within-treatment differences, and find supporting evidence for the above claims, as well as offering explanations based on the underlying patterns.

2.4.1 Success rate

Both Pledge treatments were well above the corresponding ones without pledges. Income inequality, on the other hand, reduced the prospects of success: Five of ten groups succeeded in the Base treatment, versus two of ten in the Base-Unequal

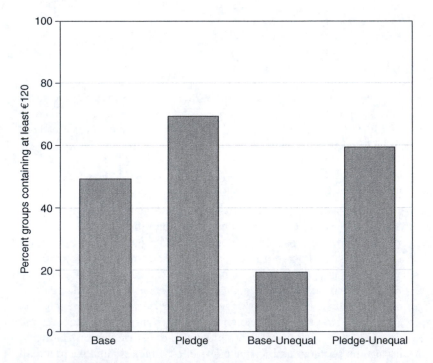

Figure 2.2 Percentage of groups that reached the threshold.

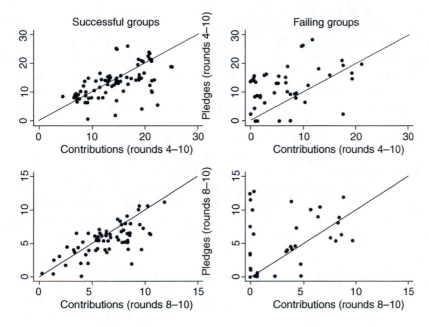

Figure 2.3 Contribution–pledge gap.

treatment. The Pledge option had more effect under conditions of inequality: Success rates tripled from two of ten in the Base-Unequal treatment to six of ten in the Pledge-Unequal treatment ($n=20$, $P=0.085$, Fisher's exact test). The latter success rate (six of ten) is not significantly different from the seven of ten achieved by participants of the symmetrical Pledge treatment ($P=0.500$), indicating that inequality is a less serious threat once a better coordination mechanism is introduced.

Although non-binding, players generally respected pledges. Following the second pledge, average cumulative contributions in rounds eight through ten were €31.8 and €30 in Pledge-Unequal and Pledge, respectively, and the stated amounts were €32.6 and €29.6. The closer the pledges were to actual contributions, the higher the probability of group success. The probability that a player belongs to a successful group decreases with the contribution–pledge gap – that is, with the differences between cumulative contributions and the corresponding amounts pledged both early (rounds four through ten, Probit, $P=0.002$) and later (rounds eight through ten, Probit, $P=0.032$) in the game. The link between success and adherence to the initial pledge is visually confirmed in Figure 2.3. For the groups that provided the public good (left panels), the contribution–pledge gap is tighter than for the unsuccessful ones (right panels), as indicated by the dispersion around the bisector. This positive effect of communication is remarkable, given the fact that the incentives needed to coordinate toward a high contribution level are relatively weak. Going for the €2 per round strategy provides only moderate benefits compared with zero contribution, and, unlike the latter, it requires the cooperation of the remaining group members.

The contributions in both successful and failing groups shed light on the motivation (or lack thereof) to provide the public good of climate protection. While in Base and Pledge, failing groups provided €70 and €62.7, respectively, failing groups participating in Base-Unequal and Pledge-Unequal contributed a remarkable €95.5 and €88. This finding suggests that the role of the asymmetric endowments is twofold: It disrupts cooperation by rendering more complex coordination, but the increased failure rate is not simply the result of a decision by a larger proportion of group members to opt for a no contribution strategy in the hope of high earnings. Many groups in these two treatments clearly tried to reach the €120 threshold, therefore increasing the average contribution relative to the failing groups in Base and Pledge. In other words, the inequality undermined the groups' ability to combat simulated climate change damage, but not their motivation, which is actually higher than in symmetric treatments.

2.4.2 *Inequality and early signaling*

We have already seen that inequality impeded coordination among the players. Now we will analyze in more detail how the groups in the asymmetric treatments Base-Unequal and Pledge-Unequal handled the inequality, and we will compare the handling of groups that successfully reached the threshold and groups that did not. Successful groups were strikingly effective in eliminating the inherited inequality. Both the rich players and the poor players contributed on average precisely €20 to the climate account, including the contributions made in the inactive rounds (see Figure 2.4a, $n=16$, $P=0.820$, Mann–Whitney–Wilcoxon test). Thereby, 92 percent of the rich players and also 92 percent of the poor players gave €20 or more. Even in the absence of communication, participants in successful groups tacitly coordinated on an equalizing redistribution that offset the original endowment asymmetry. Conversely, the difference in contributions between rich and poor is significant in failing groups (see Figure 2.4b, $n=24$, $P=0.014$), indicating that such redistribution did not take place. Poor players paid, on average, €18.17 into the climate account; whereas the rich players gave only €12.83. Thereby, 47 percent of the poor players but only 17 percent of the rich players paid €20 or more. However, the rich players did not completely refuse to invest. The majority (53 percent) invested €14 or more. That means they were willing to reduce but not to eliminate inequality. The poor players, on the other hand, were not willing to accept inequality. Obviously, the rich and the poor had different views of what the appropriate contribution was for each type of player. In the end, the persistence in their different viewpoints was crucial and caused the shipwreck of the group. The pledges appeared to be of great help in mitigating these differences because, in the Pledge-Unequal treatment, 75 percent of the groups managed to eliminate inequality and reach the target; whereas, in the Base-Unequal treatment, only 33 percent of the groups managed to do so. We come back to this point in the next section, which discusses the questionnaire data.

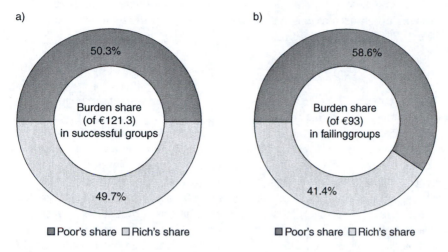

a)

50.3%

Burden share
(of €121.3)
in successful groups

49.7%

■ Poor's share □ Rich's share

b)

58.6%

Burden share
(of €93)
in failinggroups

41.4%

■ Poor's share □ Rich's share

Figure 2.4 Burden sharing.

Another interesting aspect is whether or not there were marked differences in contributions in the first active round (round four) between failing groups and successful ones – that is, whether "early action" mattered. The answer is yes: In all treatments, success in the entire game was highly linked to contributions in round four. The 20 groups that were able to coordinate to protect the climate had average individual contributions of €1.92, while the remaining 20 groups had initial individual provisions of only €1.25 ($n=40$, $P=0.000$, Mann–Whitney–Wilcoxon test). We therefore speculate that early action carried an important weight as it signaled the members' commitment in taking quantifiable efforts early on. In terms of feasible trajectories to reach the €120 target, this difference was a small burden, as it only took slightly more than one altruistic act in the ensuing six rounds to compensate the gap accumulated in round four between successful and unsuccessful groups. Yet, we argue that this lack of early initiative had deep symbolic value and could help to explain the resulting differences in success rate.

Early signals by the rich of their willingness to redistribute were decisive in the asymmetrical games. On average, rich players in successful groups contributed €3.17 in round four; whereas the rich in failing groups contributed only €2.06 ($n=20$, $P=0.005$, Mann–Whitney–Wilcoxon test). Cumulative contributions by the rich over rounds four through six were €9.83 in successful groups; whereas the rich in failing groups appeared to be unwilling to commit to early redistribution and invested only €6.67 ($n=20$, $P=0.004$). The poor, on the other hand, were not willing to compensate for the rich's inaction, so the rich's action became decisive for the group's performance. Hence, early leadership by the rich, in addition to appropriate coordination mechanisms, was instrumental in the avoidance of simulated disastrous climate change. Such insight is of relevance for the current climate negotiations and reinforces the importance of following up on declarations with tangible action, especially among developed nations with higher responsibilities.

2.4.3 Fairness perceptions

After the game, subjects were asked to fill in a questionnaire about their motivation and impression during the game (see Table 2.2). The qualitative categorization of responses reveals that the majority of players were primarily motivated by the achievement of the threshold (43 percent), fairness considerations (18 percent), material self-interest (15 percent), and the past group performance (14 percent). Understandably, the poor players in the asymmetric treatments Base-Unequal and Pledge-Unequal cared more about fairness than the rich players (22 percent versus 15 percent) and more about the past group performance (27 percent versus 14 percent). In the final round, the players were primarily motivated by the achievement of the threshold (42 percent), material self-interest (18 percent), the hopelessness to reach the threshold (14 percent), and fairness considerations (11 percent). The self-reported motives were in line with the actual behavior in the game – for example, people stating that fairness was the most important reason often contributed €20 to the climate account, while people stating that self-interest was their primary motive mostly gave less than €20. The self-reported motives furthermore help to understand why some groups did not manage to reach the threshold. Comparing the successful groups that reached the threshold and the groups that did not, fairness considerations were more important for the successful groups (23 percent versus 13 percent) as well as the achievement of the target (52 percent versus 35 percent), while self-interest (9 percent versus 20 percent) and the past group performance (8 percent versus 21 percent) were less important.

In order to elicit players' fairness perceptions during the game, subjects in the asymmetric treatments were asked whether they agreed with the following statement: "Those who began in round four with a starting capital of €40 should pay more into the climate account in the following seven rounds than the other players." Seventy-five percent of the rich in successful groups but only 53 percent of the rich in failing groups agreed with that claim. Therefore, the rich's opinion in that question and the group's success are significantly correlated ($n=60$, $P=0.086$, Spearman's correlation test).

Moreover, there are significant differences between poor and rich subjects regarding their support of the above claim: Of the poor players, 90 percent agree, 5 percent disagree, and 5 percent do neither of them, while of the rich players only 62 percent agree, 15 percent disagree, and 23 percent do neither of them. Thus, the acceptance of this claim is highly dependent on the player's wealth ($n=120$, $P=0.000$, Spearman's correlation test). In another question, subjects were asked, "What would you consider a fair average investment for the last seven (active) rounds for those beginning with €40 and for those beginning with €28?" Possible answers included €0, €1, €2, €3, and €4. Almost all of the poor

Table 2.2 Ex-post questionnaire and responses

Question	Answer		No.	%
(1) Do you agree with the following statement? "Those who began in round four with a starting capital of €40 should pay more into the climate account in the following seven rounds than the other players."	Agree		91	75.83
	Disagree		12	10.00
	Neither		17	14.17
(2) Please assume that three players of a group begin in round 4 with a starting capital of EUR 40 (because they have not paid anything into the climate account yet) whereas the other three players begin with a starting capital of EUR 28 (because they have paid EUR 4 into the climate account in each of the first three rounds).	What would you consider a fair average investment for the following seven rounds for those beginning with EUR 40?	0	2	0.83
		1	2	0.83
		2	30	12.50
		3	190	79.17
		4	16	6.67
	What would you consider a fair investment for the following seven rounds for those beginning with €28?	0	9	3.75
		1	143	59.58
		2	85	35.42
		3	3	1.25
		4	0	0.00
(3) Please imagine the following situation: You have €40. With a probability of 50%, you will lose all €40. You could avoid the risk by giving away €20 of the €40. Would you pay €20 to avoid the risk?	Yes		165	68.75
	No		22	9.17
	Indifferent		53	22.08
(4) Please briefly describe the three most important reasons for your investment decisions in a descending order of importance.				
(5) What has been your motivation for your investment decision in the last round (round 10)? Please state your three most important reasons in a descending order of importance.				
(6) If you were to play the game again, would you make different decisions? Please state your three most significant changes in a descending order of importance.				
	Σ		240	100.0

Notes

Question 1 was asked in the asymmetric treatments *Base-Unequal* and *Pledge-Unequal* only. Question 2 was asked in all treatments; therefore, it was hypothetical in the symmetric treatments *Base* and *Pledge*, while it was real in the asymmetric treatments. No responses are provided for the open questions 4–6.

players (95 percent) perceived €3 as the fair amount for the rich players, while only 72 percent of the rich players shared this perception. Similarly, only 23 percent of the poor players perceived €2 as the fair average contribution for the poor players, while 42 percent of the rich players state that this would be the fair amount. These specific amounts (€3 for the rich and €2 for the poor) are particularly important because they reflect the application of the different equity principles. In our game, the egalitarian rule, the polluter-pays rule, and the ability-to-pay rule are equivalent. According to these principles, the rich (and responsible) players should compensate for the inactive rounds in which they gained their wealth without contributing to climate protection. In order to equalize the players' contributions and payments, the rich should contribute €20 in the active rounds – that is, on average €3 per round. As opposed, the sovereignty rule does not consider the players' wealth or responsibility but rather requires the same contribution during the active rounds – that is, €2 per round for the rich as well as for the poor players. In fact, a couple of rich subjects argued that the assignment of roles was just bad luck or good luck, and that the €2 contribution per (active) round and player was a fair burden sharing. Hence, our game as much as the real climate negotiations allow for different notions of fairness. The players tend to pick the notion that is in their best interest ("self-serving bias"), meaning that the implementation of that notion would generate the least costs for them. This self-serving bias in the perception of fairness has been also observed in the real climate negotiations (Lange *et al.* 2010), and it obviously deteriorates the chances for effective coordination.

2.5 Policy implications

The implications of our results for the ongoing climate policy discussions are important. The asymmetric geometry of global emissions introduces the possibility to argue in essentially opposite directions on the grounds of fairness motives. The lack of supranational institutions for establishing appropriate rights and duties to render credible punishment-based strategies means that implementing the socially desirable cooperative outcome has to rely on voluntary actions and is therefore exposed to the risk of disagreement over the distribution of the burdens.

This result is also found in a recent study by Kolstad (2011). By employing Charness-Rabin social preferences in a game of voluntary provision of public goods, he finds that "the window of wealth disparities that does not destroy the equilibrium is quite narrow. [...] This suggests that very little wealth inequality would be tolerated in an equilibrium." In the context of international environmental agreements, the above result and the findings outlined in section 2.4 clearly highlight the importance of addressing inequalities at the outset of the negotiation process. As Kolstad puts it, "It would not take very much wealth variation to destroy the stability of this coalition. An alternative way of looking at this is that coalitions are more likely to occur among the subset of agents which share similar endowments."

Developing countries may insist on the importance of past emissions to justify their unwillingness to take action, while developed countries can appeal to the relevance of current emissions, often higher in transitioning economies, to refute to take the lead in mitigation actions. These positions can be backed with different notions of equity. The egalitarian rule, for example, incorporates the principle of equal per capita emissions, which would demand drastic emission cuts in industrialized countries. On the other hand, the sovereignty rule, which postulates the principle of equal percentage reduction of current emissions, shifts more of the abatement burden to developing countries. Such asymmetries may lead to "political lock-ins" that are detrimental to the establishment of a global agreement to curb emissions. Moreover, unlike in our game, an equitable distribution of efforts is not obvious, as countries differ not only in their contributions to climate protection but also in many other aspects. It is difficult to compare countries' sacrifices. Therefore, if a fair distribution is decisive for success but at the same time difficult to implement, a practical implication of our study may be to reframe the climate negotiations in a way that makes the comparison easier (Barrett 2011).

If we want to be able to inform policy by means of controlled experiments, a crucial question is whether findings are replicable and robust to changing some of the features. In a related laboratory experiment (Dannenberg *et al.* 2011), we compared how coordination success in a threshold public goods game was affected by whether or not the threshold was known. In particular, we employed four different forms of threshold uncertainty. Whereas two experimental treatments involved risk, as the threshold was a random variable with known probability distribution, two other treatments involved ambiguity, as the probability distribution of the threshold was unknown. Results indicate that threshold uncertainty was detrimental for the provision of the public good. While all groups succeeded in preventing the public bad when the threshold was known, this result was not replicated in the presence of threshold uncertainty. Contributions were generally lower when players did not know ex-ante the exact threshold value, and were particularly low and erratic in the treatments involving ambiguity. As in the experiment discussed here, we found that early signaling of willingness to contribute and share the burden equitably made groups more likely to reach a high public good provision level.

Our analysis may apply not only to climate change, but more generally to many natural resource problems characterized by tipping points beyond which probabilistic destruction is imminent. Prominent examples include deep-sea fishery, tropical rainforests, groundwater basins, and biodiversity. Countries typically have the possibility to announce their intended use and to observe the actual use thereafter. Differences in historical use of these resources are likely to create tensions.

2.6 Conclusions

The climate change game presented in this chapter focuses on: (i) introducing asymmetries among players by means of a novel unequalizing mechanism in the first three rounds; (ii) allowing players to make non-binding pledges concerning future contributions. This game captures trade-offs that are salient for the issue of climate change mitigation. It is a promising tool for analyzing such tensions, notwithstanding its simplicity, as it provides insights into many aspects that are crucial to climate change and coordination more broadly. Given the lack of scientific consensus about who should bear the burden of mitigation costs, providing empirical evidence on the driving forces behind coordination in a setting designed to mimic inequalities and bargaining possibilities faced by actors involved with climate change should be fruitful also from a policy perspective.

While neither of the new features introduced in the climate game alters the game structure, in terms of the aggregate group contributions required to reach the threshold for climate protection, they both affect the success rate of the experimental groups. Asymmetries undermined coordination, especially in the treatment in which subjects had no signaling mechanism beyond contributions, and 80 percent of the groups failed to reach the target sum. Pledges, on the other hand, proved to be a very effective lubricant of coordination, halving the percentage of failures in the treatment with endowment inequalities. Both in the baseline and across all treatments, the rate of success was 50 percent, a remarkably high level considering the previous findings of 10 percent success by Milinski *et al.* (2008). The higher provision level arguably stems from design differences, most notably the communication mechanism (or lack thereof), and subject pool differences.

The main purpose of this study was to address the question, "Will the most responsible actors contribute more to combat climate change damage in a public goods game experiment in which players differ in wealth and responsibilities?" The empirical answer to this question is generally, "No." Initially, wealthier subjects were often unwilling to compensate for past "inherited" actions that had benefited them at the expense of the common good. Such resistance, much to the frustration of the remaining subjects who expected initiative on the part of the wealthy, accounted for the frequent coordination failures in the asymmetric treatments. In all 12 instances (out of 20 participating groups) where the target sum was not provided, there was an unfavorable contribution imbalance for those who had been bound to the altruistic act in the first three rounds, who ended up paying on average 60 percent of the bill. In contrast, the burden was shared evenly in the remaining eight successful groups, with both subgroups contributing 50 percent of the sum.

Although necessarily simple for the sake of control and tractability, the game presented here is designed to incorporate key real-world issues, such as equity and communication. Further salient aspects that are not captured by this game are those of uncertainty over the magnitude of the threshold and gradual climate change impacts. Future research is needed along these lines. Different games emphasizing mitigation cooperation over catastrophe avoidance coordination would complement the present analysis. Nevertheless, it is tempting to relate the basic structure of this game to the current stage of climate talks. Signaling commitment to contribute appears decisive for coordination, restoring confidence in the commitment of nations to take action rather than to gamble with the global climate. Unfortunately, the latest climate negotiations have delivered, at best, a very weak signal.

Note

1 The experiment presented in this chapter has been published in the *Proceedings of the National Academy of Sciences* (see Tavoni *et al.* 2011 for the methods and statistical means used to back the inference advanced in this chapter).

References

Alley, R.B., Marotzke, J., Nordhaus, W.D., Overpeck, J.T., Peteet, D.M., Pielke, R.A. Jr., Pierrehumbert, R.T., Rhines, P.B., Stocker, T.F., Talley, L.D., and Wallace, J.M. (2003) "Abrupt climate change," *Science*, 299(5615): 2005–2010.

Barrett, S. (1994) "Self-enforcing international environmental agreements," *Oxford Economic Papers*, 46: 878–894.

Barrett, S. (2011) "Avoiding disastrous climate change is possible but not inevitable," *Proceedings of the National Academy of Sciences*, 108(29): 11733–11734.

Barrett, S. (forthcoming) "Climate treaties and approaching catastrophes," *Journal of Environmental Economics and Management.*

Barrett, S. and Dannenberg, A. (2012) "Climate negotiations under scientific uncertainty," *Proceedings of the National Academy of Sciences*, 10(43): 17372–17376.

Carraro, C. and Siniscalco, D. (1993) "Strategies for the international protection of the environment," *Journal of Public Economics*, 52(3): 309–328.

Chaudhuri, A. (2011) "Sustaining cooperation in laboratory public goods experiments: A selective survey of the literature," *Experimental Economics*, 14(1): 47–83.

Crawford, V. (1998) "A survey of experiments on communication via cheap talk," *Journal of Economic Theory*, 78: 286–298.

Dannenberg, A., Löschel, A., Paolacci, G., Reif, C., and Tavoni, A. (2011) "Coordination under threshold uncertainty in a public goods game," Grantham Research Institute on Climate Change and the Environment, Working Paper No. 64, London School of Economics.

Dawes, R.M. (1980) "Social dilemmas," *Annual Review of Psychology*, 31(1): 169–193.

Fischbacher, U. (2007) "Z-Tree: Zurich toolbox for ready-made economic experiments," *Experimental Economics*, 10: 171–178.

Greiner, B. (2004) "An online recruitment system for economic experiments," in K. Kremer and V. Macho (eds), *Forschung und wissenschaftliches Rechnen 2003* (pp. 79–93), GWDG Bericht 63, Göttingen: Ges. für Wiss. Datenverarbeitung.

Hoel, M. (1992) "International environmental conventions: The case of uniform reductions of emissions," *Environmental and Resource Economics*, 2: 41–59.

Kolstad, C. (2011) "Public goods agreements with other-regarding preferences," University of California, Santa Barbara, available at: www.ckolstad.org/papers/PGAgreements.pdf (accessed January 2012).

Lange, A., Löschel, A., Vogt, C., and Ziegler, A. (2010) "On the self-interested use of equity in international climate negotiations," *European Economic Review*, 54(3): 359–375.

Ledyard, J.O. (1995) "Public goods: A survey of experimental research," in J.H. Kagel and A.E. Roth (eds), *The Handbook of Experimental Economics* (pp. 111–194), Princeton: Princeton University Press.

Lenton, T.M., Held, H., Kriegler, E., Hall, J.W., Lucht, W., Rahmstorf, S., and Schellnhuber, H.J. (2008) "Tipping elements in the Earth's climate system," *Proceedings of the National Academy of Sciences*, 105(6): 1786–1793.

Malhi, Y., Aragão, L.E.O.C., Galbraith, D., Huntingford, C., Fisher, R., Zelazowski, P., Sitch, S., McSweeney, C., and Meir, P. (2009) "Exploring the likelihood and mechanism of a climate-change-induced dieback of the Amazon rainforest," *Proceedings of the National Academy of Sciences*, 106(49): 20610–20615.

Milinski, M., Sommerfeld, R.D., Krambeck, H.-J., Reed, F.A., and Marotzke, J. (2008) "The collective risk social dilemma and the prevention of simulated dangerous climate change," *Proceedings of the National Academy of Sciences*, 105: 2291–2294.

Notz, D. (2009) "The future ice sheets and sea ice: Between reversible retreat and unstoppable loss," *Proceedings of the National Academy of Sciences*, 106(49): 20590–20595.

Ostrom, E. (2006) "The value-added of laboratory experiments for the study of institutions and common-pool resources," *Journal of Economic Behavior & Organization*, 61: 149–163.

Sally, D. (1995) "Conversation and cooperation in social dilemmas: A meta-analysis of experiments from 1958 to 1992," *Rationality and Society*, 7: 58–92.

Tavoni, A., Dannenberg, A., Kallis, G., and Loeschel, A. (2011) "Inequality, communication, and the avoidance of disastrous climate change in a public goods game," *Proceedings of the National Academy of Sciences*, 108(29): 11825–11829.

UNFCCC (1992) *United Nations Framework Convention on Climate Change*, text available at: http://unfccc.int/resource/docs/convkp/conveng.pdf (accessed January 2012).

Zickfeld, K., Levermann, A., Morgan, M., Kuhlbrodt, T., Rahmstorf, S., and Keith, D. (2007) "Expert judgements on the response of the Atlantic meridional overturning circulation to climate change," *Climatic Change*, 82(3): 235–265.

3 The role of information in the tragedy of the commons[1]

Felix Munoz-Garcia and Ana Espinola-Arredondo

3.1 Introduction

Many scholars have analyzed how to ameliorate the negative outcome that arises during the so-called "tragedy of the commons." Some studies have focused on the role of institutions as a tool to avoid the overuse of the common pool resource (CPR) and examine contexts in which all the agents have accurate information about the initial stock of the CPR (Ostrom 1990). Surprisingly, contexts in which one agent has access to more accurate information about the CPR, given its leading position exploiting the resource, have often been overlooked by the literature. Nonetheless, these settings arise in several commons. For instance, fisheries that have operated in specific areas of the Pacific Ocean for several years have more precise information about these fishing grounds than fisheries whose operations are confined to the Atlantic Ocean. Similarly, mining companies that have exploited diamonds in the remote north of Western Australia for several decades have more information about the mineral deposit than foreign firms. Of course, modern scanning techniques can help an initially uninformed firm to better assess the true level of the stock (e.g., mineral content of underground deposit, or available fish in a fishing ground). Such measurement, however, is not as accurate as the precise information that a firm operating the CPR has after decades of exploiting the resource, thus leading to a situation of asymmetric information. This chapter investigates under which conditions the presence of asymmetric information helps prevent the over-exploitation of a common resource, and in which cases the firms appropriating the CPR can strategically choose to under-exploit the commons below its socially optimal level.

We examine a setting in which an experienced agent – an incumbent who observes the state of the initial stock of the CPR – interacts with an uninformed firm which analyzes whether or not to enter into the CPR but does not have accurate information about the precise level of the stock. In particular, we consider that in the first period the incumbent is the only firm operating in the CPR, and the potential entrant evaluates whether or not to exploit the resource in the second period. The initial stock of the CPR can be either high (abundant) or low (scarce). In this information context, the incumbent's first-period appropriation can reveal information about the state of the stock to the potential entrant.

Specifically, we investigate the signaling role of the incumbent's exploitation of the resource and how its action conveys or conceals information to entrants. Moreover, we examine the incumbent's incentives to deter entry, and how those individual incentives serve as a tool to preserve the common pool resource without the need of government intervention.

As a benchmark for comparison, we first analyze a setting of complete information, in which both incumbent and entrant perfectly observe the initial stock of the CPR. In this context, the potential entrant prefers to stay out when the initial stock is low, which implies that the incumbent is the only agent exploiting the resource across time. Hence, the incumbent fully internalizes the negative effect that an increase in its first-period appropriation imposes on its future profits. As a consequence, the incumbent exploits the resource at the socially optimal level. On the contrary, when the initial stock is high, the entrant decides to exploit the resource, and both agents compete for the CPR in the second period. In this setting, the tragedy of the commons emerges, since incumbent and entrant do not internalize the negative effect of its appropriation on each other's profits. Besides this second-period inefficiency, we identify an additional form of inefficiency arising in the first period. In particular, the incumbent ignores the effect that its first-period appropriation imposes on the entrant's future profits, thereby exploiting the resource above its socially optimal level. Therefore, when the stock is high, inefficiencies emerge in both periods and the CPR is over-exploited.

We then discuss a setting of asymmetric information in which only the incumbent is informed. We identify two types of equilibrium outcomes: one in which information is fully transmitted to the potential entrant – referred to as the "informative equilibrium" – and another in which information about the CPR's stock is concealed, denoted as the "uninformative equilibrium." In the informative equilibrium, the low- and high-stock incumbents select different first-period appropriation levels, thus allowing the potential entrant to infer the CPR's stock. Specifically, the high-stock incumbent exploitation coincides with that under complete information, and thus the CPR is over-exploited along both periods. The low-stock incumbent, in contrast, reduces its first-period appropriation below its complete information level as a signal to the potential entrant that the resource is scarce and that entry is unprofitable. Importantly, since the low-stock incumbent's appropriation under complete information was socially optimal, the informative equilibrium predicts that the incumbent under-exploits the resource during the first period in order to deter entry. Hence, the incumbent's strategic incentives help protect the CPR.

Unlike the informative equilibrium, in which the incumbent's first-period appropriation conveys information about the CPR's stock to the potential entrant, in the uninformative equilibrium, both types of incumbent choose the same exploitation level. Hence, the potential entrant cannot infer additional information from the incumbent's actions and chooses to stay out when the CPR is likely to be scarce. Specifically, this equilibrium prescribes that the low-stock incumbent's exploitation coincides with that under complete information, which is socially optimal. The high-stock incumbent, however, mimics the low-stock firm, reducing its first-period appropriation, in order to mislead the potential entrant and deter entry. Such under-exploitation of the resource is hence inefficient, and emerges from the presence of incomplete information. This result suggests that the incumbent operating a high-stock commons can deter entry as if it owned a property right for the use of the resource. Therefore, the informational asymmetry among players acts in this case as an "implicit protection right" for the incumbent.

The strategy profile described in the informative equilibrium explains the appropriation decisions of the Hudson's Bay Company. As discussed in Mason and Polasky (1994), in the eighteenth century, the company faced the threat of entry from French fur traders, and at that moment the company increased beaver harvests. Rather than dissuading them from entering, French fur traders built an outpost in the area in 1741. Hence, the over-exploitation of the resource by the Hudson's Bay Company could be interpreted by the French fur traders as a signal that the resource was abundant. If, in contrast, the CPR is scarce, our equilibrium results suggest that the incumbent strategically under-exploits the resource in order to convey the scarcity of the CPR to the potential entrant and deter entry. Silver hake fishing provides an interesting example of this type of informative signaling. After two decades of intense exploitation by mechanized United States and Canadian fishing boats in the North Atlantic from 1960 to 1980, the available stock of silver hake became significantly depleted. This low stock led to a reduction in the number of vessels and annual catches. More importantly, the incumbent fleet had consistently under-exploited the resource below its annual sustainable catch since the late 1990s, despite experiencing a mild recovery (United Nations Food and Agriculture Organization 2005). This strategy can be rationalized as a signal to potential entrants, informing them that the stock has not yet become sufficiently abundant to support the entry of additional vessels. Under-exploitation is not only applicable to the silver hake, but it also has been reported in several other fishing grounds. For instance, Haughton (2002) highlights the underuse of blackfin tuna, dolphinfish, and diamondback squids, among others, in the Caribbean region. Similarly, a comprehensive study by the United Nations Food and Agriculture Organization (2005) indicates the under-exploitation of the Argentine anchovy in the Southern Atlantic and the yellowfin sole in the Pacific Northwest. One could argue that the under-exploitation observed in these examples might be partially explained by the difficulty of access to the resource or the fishing technology. Our study suggests that, while these technological reasons can lead to under-exploitation of a CPR, the presence of incomplete information exacerbates such under-exploitation under certain conditions.

We also compare the efficiency properties of informative and uninformative equilibria. When the CPR's stock is abundant, we show that the informative equilibrium supports an over-exploitation of the commons, while the uninformative equilibrium predicts an under-exploitation of the resource. A precise policy recommendation would hence depend on which type of inefficiency (under- or over-exploitation) society prefers to avoid the most. If social preferences assign a larger welfare loss to the over-exploitation than to the under-exploitation of the commons, then our results imply that environmental regulators can increase social welfare by promoting the uninformative equilibrium. In particular, this equilibrium can be supported by setting a first-period quota that specifies strong penalties for those incumbents exceeding the first-period appropriation that both types of incumbent select under the uninformative equilibrium. Intuitively, these penalties make the informative equilibrium appropriation less attractive for the high-stock incumbent, inducing it toward uninformative equilibrium appropriation levels. Our findings hence provide an additional role for quotas – a policy tool often used to deal with CPRs.

Related literature. Many authors have analyzed how to avoid the tragedy of the commons in a CPR. We can group them into two different areas, in which studies either (1) modify individual payoffs so that agents' strategic incentives become different from those in a CPR game (Ostrom 1990; Ostrom *et al.* 1994); or (2) insert the unmodified CPR game into an enlarged structure – for example, allowing the game to be repeated over time (Baland and Platteau 1996). This chapter contributes to the second approach by analyzing a CPR game in a context of incomplete information. Similar to this study, theoretical and experimental papers have analyzed the role of uncertainty in the profitability of the CPR (Suleiman and Rapoport 1988; Suleiman *et al.* 1996; Apesteguia 2006). This literature, however, assumes that all players have access to the same information about the resource, thus not allowing for information asymmetries among firms. Our study hence contributes to this literature by, first, examining information settings in which an incumbent holds more accurate information about a resource than potential entrants, which might apply to many CPRs such as fisheries; and second, showing under which conditions the incumbent might choose to actually overprotect the commons.

The research also relates to the literature on entry deterrence in the commons (Mason and Polasky 1994) assuming complete information among players. By allowing for incomplete information and signaling, we compare equilibrium behavior under complete and incomplete information. Therefore, this chapter relates to the literature on entry deterrence in signaling games. Usual entry deterrence models assume that the incumbent's first-period action (e.g., price setting by a monopolist) does not affect the incumbent and entrant's future profits (Milgrom and Roberts 1982; Matthews and Mirman 1983; Bagwell and Ramey 1990). In our setting, in contrast, the incumbent's first-period exploitation depletes the CPR, thus affecting its second-period profits. More importantly, it also affects the entrant's second-period profits, thus imposing a negative external effect on the entrant, unlike Polasky and Bin (2001), who assume that agents do not compete for the same stock in the commons. Our study hence provides an explicit analysis of signaling games in which agents' actions cause intertemporal externalities, and compares it with signaling models in which such externalities are absent. Finally, this research provides an intuitive discussion of the theoretical results developed in Espinola-Arredondo and Munoz-Garcia (2011).

The following section describes the model. Section 3.3 examines equilibrium behavior under complete information. Section 3.4 introduces the signaling game and compares exploitation levels and efficiency under both information contexts. Finally, section 3.5 concludes.

3.2 Model

We study a context in which an incumbent firm exploits a CPR, whose initial stock is either high or low, and a potential entrant who considers whether to exploit the CPR. For simplicity, we assume that there are no entry barriers, but entry is only profitable if the commons' initial stock is high. In addition, we consider that the CPR's stock regenerates over time and the biological regeneration can fully or partially offset the incumbent's first-period appropriation activities. Let us more specifically describe the time structure of this complete information game.

In the first stage, the incumbent incurs an appropriation cost from exploiting the CPR and sells its appropriation in the international market at a given price.[2] If entry does not occur and the resource completely regenerates across time (i.e., the biological regeneration of the commons fully offsets first-period appropriation), the available stock at the beginning of the second period coincides with that in the first period. In this case, the incumbent's first-period actions do not impose intertemporal effects, leading the incumbent to increase first-period appropriation until the point at which its associated marginal cost coincides with the market price. If, however, the resource does not completely regenerate across time – the biological regeneration of the commons does not compensate first-period appropriation – the available stock at the beginning of the second period is lower than that in the first, and the incumbent's first-period actions affect the incumbent's second-period profits. In particular, first-period appropriation produces an increase in all agents' second-period marginal costs. Such an increase, however, is larger when the CPR's initial stock was low than when it was high. Intuitively, the exploitation of the resource is more task-intensive when the stock is low. The appropriation activities, hence, require spending more time or using a more advanced technology, which ultimately increases firms' marginal costs. Similar to the first period, second-period costs are increasing and convex in second-period captures.[3]

If entry occurs, incumbent and entrant compete for the common resource. Second-period costs satisfy similar properties to those in the first-period game but, in addition, every agent's marginal cost of appropriation increases in the other agent's second-period appropriation level, reflecting that the resource became more depleted, and thus firms must incur a larger cost in order to exploit a given level of appropriation. This furthermore illustrates that, for a given level of appropriation, the incumbent prefers to remain the only agent exploiting the CPR than sharing the resource with the entrant.

3.3 Complete information

In this section, we analyze the case in which all agents are accurately informed about the commons' initial stock. We discuss this setting using the solution concept of backwards induction. Hence, let us first study agents' profit-maximizing actions in the second-period game.

Second period, no entry. When entry does not occur, the incumbent selects an action that maximizes its second-period profits, for a given level of first-period appropriation. That is, the incumbent increases second-period appropriation until the point at which the marginal cost of appropriating one more unit coincides with the price that the unit is sold. Importantly, second-period equilibrium profits – those emerging from the incumbent selecting the profit-maximizing appropriation level – are decreasing in first-period appropriation. Intuitively, a larger first-period appropriation reduces the available stock at the beginning of the second period, increasing as a result its marginal costs, and thus reducing profits. In addition, the incumbent's second-period profit-maximizing appropriation is also decreasing in first-period appropriation. Specifically, the CPR is more depleted, making second-period appropriation more costly, which reduces the incumbent's incentives to exploit the resource.

Second period, entry. If entry occurs, firms compete for the resource as in a duopoly setting. Hence, every agent independently selects the exploitation level that maximizes its second-period duopoly profits. The effect of first-period appropriation on the incumbent's equilibrium profits in this case is more involved than under no entry, since a positive and a negative effect coexist. First, an increase in first-period appropriation increases the second-period marginal costs, similarly as under no entry, imposing a negative effect on the incumbent's profits. Nonetheless, first-period appropriation also affects the entrant's second-period costs, inducing this agent to reduce its exploitation level. This reduction ultimately facilitates the incumbent's exploitation of the resource in the second-period game, thus increasing its profits. For simplicity, we assume that the negative effect on profits dominates the positive effect, and therefore an increase in first-period appropriation produces an overall decrease of the incumbent's equilibrium second-period profits upon entry. Intuitively, this occurs when the regeneration rate is sufficiently low, implying that a given increase in first-period appropriation causes a substantial reduction in the available stock during the second-period game.[4] Note that if the CPR totally regenerates across periods, then second-period costs are unaffected by first-period actions, both with and without entry.

First period. We now focus our analysis on first-period actions. In particular, the incumbent chooses first-period appropriation to maximize its stream of discounted profits across both periods. On one hand, when the initial stock is low – and hence entry does not ensue – a given increase in first-period appropriation raises revenue. On the other hand, however, such increase in first-period appropriation entails not only additional costs during that period, but also a subsequent increase in second-period marginal costs, since the CPR will be more depleted, thereby making exploitation more difficult for the incumbent. Therefore, when the incumbent chooses the level of first-period appropriation that maximizes its discounted profits, it increases exploitation until the point at which the additional revenues from more captures offset the increase in first- and second-period marginal costs. A similar argument applies when the initial stock is high, and hence entry occurs. Specifically, the incumbent increases first-period appropriation until its marginal benefit (revenues from selling the additional appropriation) coincides with the increase in first- and second-period costs that such appropriation entails.[5]

Figures 3.1a and 3.1b represent first- and second-period appropriation levels for both types of incumbent, considering the parametric example described in Appendix 1.[6] The appropriation level for the low-stock incumbent lies below that of the high-stock incumbent in both periods. In addition, as the regeneration rate increases, the exploitation level of both types of firms rises.

Discussion. When no entry occurs, the incumbent is the only agent exploiting the resource during both periods, and hence it fully internalizes the effect that its first-period appropriation causes on its future profits. Therefore, the resource is exploited at the socially optimal level. Figure 3.2 describes our findings for the low and high-stock incumbent.

In contrast, when the stock is high and entry occurs, the CPR is over-exploited relative to the socially optimal level during both periods, i.e., FPA_H^{SO} and SPA_H^{SO}.

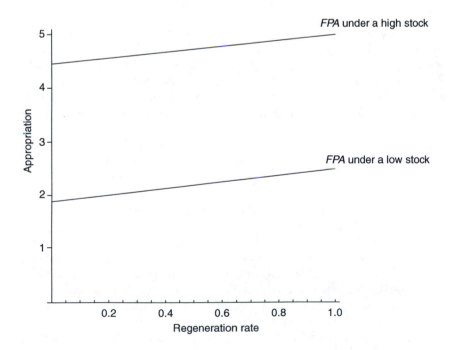

Figure 3.1a First-period appropriation (*FPA*).

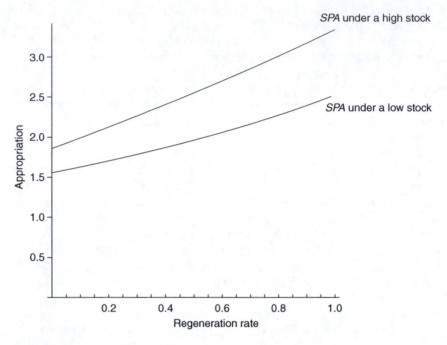

Figure 3.1b Second-period appropriation (*SPA*).

In the second period, both agents select an appropriation level that maximizes their individual benefits, but these appropriation levels impose a negative externality on the other agents' profits, since the resource becomes more difficult to exploit (i.e., second-period marginal costs increase). In short, the tragedy of the commons emerges in the second-period game. In addition, in the first period, the incumbent only takes into account the reduction in future exploitation that its first-period appropriation produces on its own future profits, but ignores the effect it imposes on the entrant's profits (i.e., the incumbent does not consider the "intertemporal externality" of its first-period appropriation). A benevolent planner, by contrast, would select a lower first-period exploitation that internalizes the effect that such appropriation imposes on the future profits of both incumbent and entrant. Therefore, the CPR is over-exploited in both periods.

Finally, note that the above first-period over-exploitation does not emerge when the CPR fully regenerates across time. In particular, full regeneration implies that first-period actions do not impose second-period effects, since biological reproduction entails that the stock becomes completely available again at the beginning of the second period. Therefore, the resource is exploited at its socially optimal level in the first-period game. Nonetheless, the CPR is still over-exploited during the second period, since every agent's actions still impose a negative effect on each other's profits.

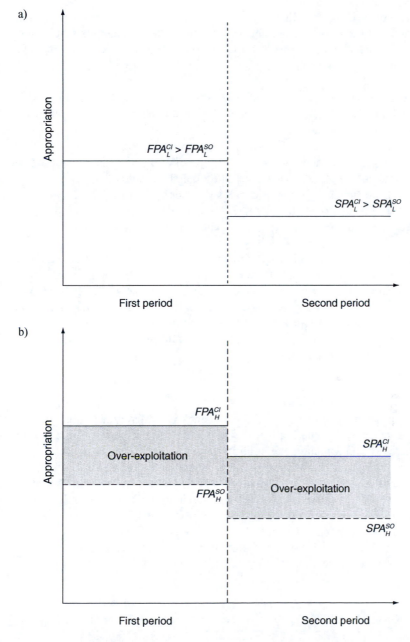

Figure 3.2 Efficiency properties under complete information (CI) for low stock (a) and high stock (b).

3.4 Signaling the commons' stock

In this section, we consider that the incumbent is privately informed about the CPR's initial stock, while the entrant only observes the incumbent's first-period appropriation level, and uses this information to infer the stock's level. The time structure of the signaling game is as follows, and also described in Figure 3.3:

*   Nature decides the realization of the initial stock, either high or low, with probabilities p and $1-p$, respectively. The incumbent is the only agent who observes the initial stock.
*   The incumbent chooses its first-period appropriation level.
*   Observing the incumbent's first-period appropriation level, the entrant forms beliefs about the initial stock of the CPR being high or low.
*   Given these beliefs, the entrant decides whether or not to enter the CPR.
*   If entry does not occur, the incumbent remains the only agent exploiting the CPR; whereas, if entry occurs, both agents compete for the CPR.

We next identify an informative equilibrium whereby the incumbent operating in a low-stock commons selects a different first-period appropriation than one operating in a high-stock commons, and thus the entrant can perfectly infer the CPR's initial stock from the incumbent's actions. Then we describe an uninformative equilibrium in which both types of incumbent choose the same first-period appropriation level, thereby concealing information about the CPR's stock from the potential entrant.

3.4.1 Informative equilibrium

When the probability of facing an abundant stock is relatively large, an equilibrium emerges in which the high-stock incumbent selects the same first-period appropriation as under complete information, while the low-stock incumbent chooses a first-period exploitation that lies below its appropriation level in the complete information context. Intuitively, the low-stock incumbent underexploits the commons in order to reveal the scarcity of the resource to the potential entrant, thus deterring entry. Hence, the entrant's lack of information about the available stock induces the incumbent to give up first-period profits in order to deter entry. The presence of incomplete information therefore serves as a tool to promote the incumbent's own conservation of the CPR when the initial stock

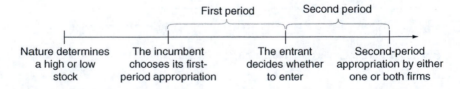

Figure 3.3 Time structure of the signaling game.

is low. In particular, this incumbent chooses a first-period action that, while being as close as possible to its exploitation level under complete information, is too costly for the high-stock incumbent to imitate.

Let us next evaluate the efficiency properties of our equilibrium results. When the initial stock is high, entry occurs and agents' actions coincide with those under complete information, therefore, yielding the same inefficient results, as Figure 3.4 shows. As discussed in the previous section, the resource is

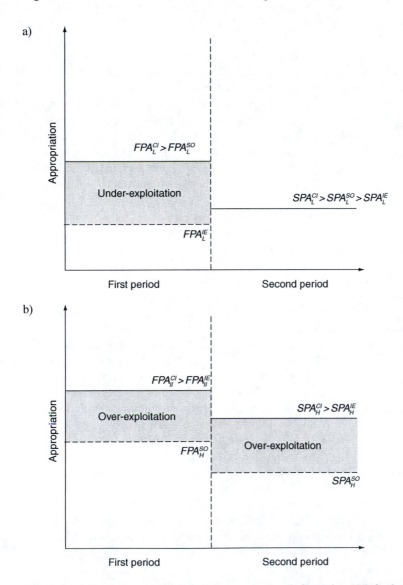

Figure 3.4 Informative equilibrium (IE) vs. complete information (CI) for low stock (a) and high stock (b).

over-exploited both in the second- and in the first-period game, since the incumbent does not take into account the effects of first-period appropriation on the entrant's future profits.

When the initial stock is low (Figure 3.4a), the informative equilibrium predicts that entry is deterred, and therefore the incumbent is the only agent exploiting the commons in the second-period game, thus entailing socially optimal outcomes. However, the incumbent exploits the resource below its complete information level (where appropriation is socially optimal) in order to convey its type to the potential entrant. Therefore, the CPR is under-exploited relative to the social optimum. Importantly, this form of inefficiency is novel in the literature on the commons and arises in this context due to the presence of incomplete information among the players, providing the low-stock incumbent incentives to overprotect the resource in order to deter entry.

Our results therefore identify two forms of inefficiency: the high-stock incumbent's over-exploitation of the CPR (which arises in both information contexts) and the under-exploitation of the resource by the low-stock incumbent. When the stock partially regenerates across time, both inefficiencies emerge; whereas, when the stock fully regenerates, the first type of inefficiency is absent. Similar to our findings under complete information, the first-period appropriation of the high-stock incumbent does not affect future profits when the stock fully regenerates, and thus becomes socially optimal.[7] The second type of inefficiency, however, is still present since the low-stock incumbent seeks to deter entry regardless of the CPR's regeneration rate.[8]

Figure 3.5 represents the effort that the low-stock incumbent exerts in order to convey the scarcity of the stock to potential entrants. (The figure uses the same parametric example as Figure 3.1 in the complete information setting; see Appendix 2 for details). Specifically, the incumbent reduces its first-period appropriation relative to complete information, and such reduction is increasing in the regeneration rate, as depicted in the horizontal axis. Intuitively, when the CPR fully regenerates (in the right-hand side of the figure), the high-stock incumbent has more incentives to mimic the low-type's appropriation in order to deter entry, since second-period profits increase in the regeneration rate. Hence, the low-stock firm needs to substantially reduce its first-period exploitation, which guarantees that the high-type incumbent does not mimic it, and hence its signal remains informative.

Policy implications. Our results suggest that government intervention is unnecessary when asymmetric information is present, since the low-stock incumbent already has incentives to conserve the CPR. Hence, this incumbent would favor a regulation that prescribes socially optimal appropriation levels across periods. Specifically, socially optimal levels for the low-stock incumbent coincide with equilibrium appropriation under complete information, which are higher than those in the informative equilibrium and yield higher profits. Hence, under such regulation, the low-stock incumbent would not need to reduce first-period appropriation in order to deter entry, yielding higher profits than under the threat of entry.

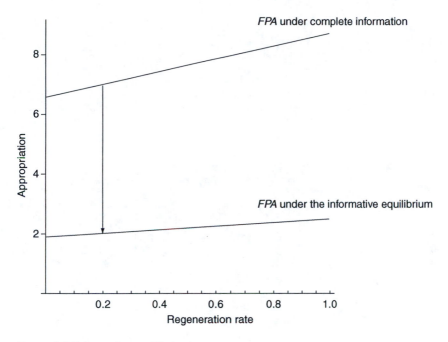

Figure 3.5 Informative equilibrium.

3.4.2 Uninformative equilibrium

When the prior probability of facing an abundant CPR is relatively low, a unique equilibrium outcome arises where, in contrast to our previous discussion, both types of incumbent choose the same first-period appropriation level, specifically that selected by the low-stock incumbent in the complete information setting. As a consequence, the entrant cannot infer the incumbent's type after observing such appropriation level, and decides to stay out, given its low priors. Therefore, the low-stock incumbent does not deviate from its complete information strategy profile. The high-stock incumbent, however, exploits the resource below its complete information appropriation level (i.e., mimicking the actions of the low-stock incumbent, thus deterring entry). Figure 3.6 depicts the effort that the high-stock incumbent exerts in order to mimic the low-stock firm's appropriation decision.

Similar to the informative equilibrium, let us evaluate the efficiency properties of this equilibrium result. First, note that the low-stock incumbent does not deviate from its complete information actions and, since these appropriation levels are socially efficient, the presence of incomplete information does not entail inefficiencies. The actions of the high-stock incumbent, however, introduce inefficiencies in the first-period game, since the resource is exploited below its socially optimal level.[9] This under-exploitation by the high-stock incumbent in the uninformative equilibrium is a form of inefficiency that was not previously

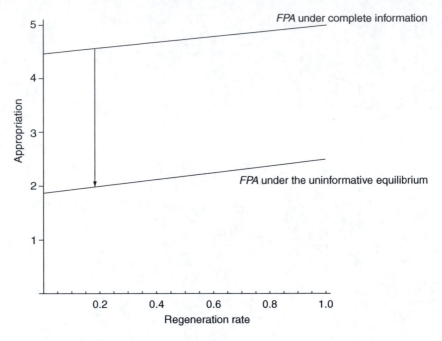

Figure 3.6 Uninformative equilibrium.

examined in the literature on CPRs, which arises in this context due to the presence of asymmetric information among the agents exploiting the resource.

Figure 3.7 summarizes the efficiency properties of the uninformative equilibrium and compares them with those of the complete information game. Since the low-stock incumbent's actions coincide with those under complete information, let us focus on the high-stock incumbent. First, note that the high-stock incumbent deters entry, which implies that second-period appropriation is socially optimal, unlike under complete information in which the incumbent's and entrant's competition for the resource lead to its over-exploitation. Second, the incumbent under-exploits the CPR during the first period under the uninformative equilibrium but over-exploits it in the complete information setting. Importantly, inefficiencies emerge in both cases, since first-period appropriation differs from its socially optimal level. Nonetheless, if society assigns a larger welfare loss to the over-exploitation than to the under-exploitation of common resources, the uninformative equilibrium predicts a larger overall efficiency than that arising in complete information contexts.

3.4.3 Efficiency comparison

Let us finally compare the efficiency properties of the informative and uninformative equilibria. As described in the previous section, the uninformative

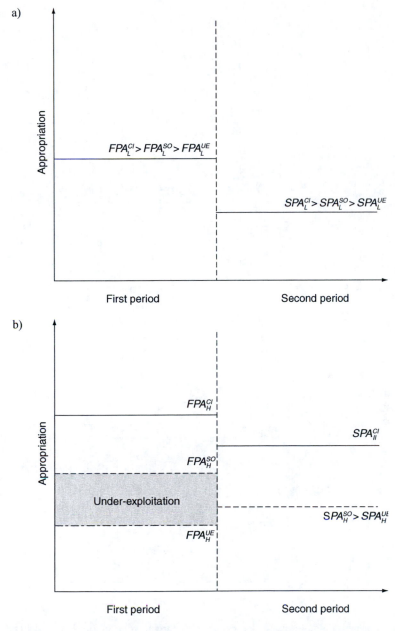

Figure 3.7 Uninformative equilibrium (UE) vs. complete information (CI) for low stock (a) and high stock (b).

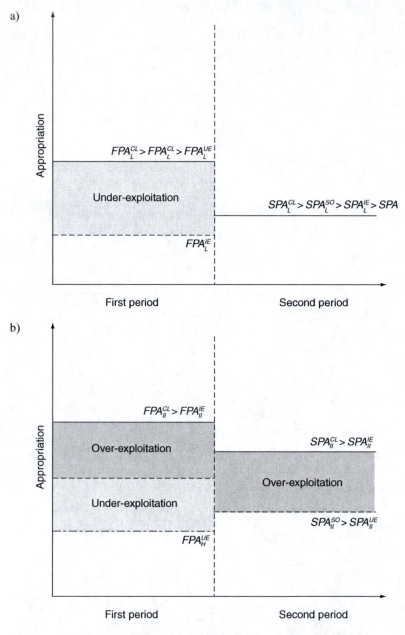

Figure 3.8 Informative equilibrium (IE) vs. uninformative equilibrium (UE) for low stock (a) and high stock (b).

equilibrium leads the high-stock incumbent to under-exploit the resource in the first-period game, while the informative equilibrium prescribes that the CPR is over-exploited during both periods. Therefore, when the CPR's stock is high, our results do not prescribe a precise policy recommendation, as Figure 3.8 summarizes. If, however, social preferences assign a greater welfare loss to over-exploitation than to under-exploitation, then environmental agencies holding private information about the commons' stock being high should promote the uninformative equilibrium. When the initial stock is low, our results predict the presence of inefficiencies in the informative equilibrium, due to the first-period under-exploitation, but socially optimal appropriation levels in the uninformative equilibrium (Figure 3.8).

3.4.4 Policy implications

Quotas. The regulator can support the uninformative equilibrium by setting a first-period quota that specifies significant penalties for those incumbents exceeding the first-period appropriation that both types of incumbent select under the uninformative equilibrium. Intuitively, these penalties make the informative equilibrium appropriation less attractive for the high-stock incumbent.

Strategic information dissemination. Finally, note that our results also provide insights about the regulator's incentives to strategically distribute information to potential entrants (i.e., his interest to modify the information structure from one in which agents are asymmetrically informed to one in which they are all perfectly informed). Specifically, when the prior probability of the CPR being abundant is relatively large, only the informative equilibrium can be sustained. In this context, our analysis in section 3.4.1 illustrates that the equilibrium welfare arising under complete information is larger than that under the informative equilibrium (Figure 3.4), implying that the regulator, if privately informed about the stock, has incentives to strategically distribute information about the abundance of the resource to potential entrants. In contrast, when such prior probability is relatively low, only the uninformative equilibrium is supported. In this case, our findings from section 3.4.2 suggest that overall welfare under the uninformative equilibrium exceeds that under complete information settings[10] and, therefore, the regulator does not have incentives to disseminate information about the commons' stock to potential entrants.

3.5 Conclusions

This study analyzes the tragedy of the commons under incomplete information settings, whereby one agent has access to more accurate information about the available stock than other agents – an information setting mostly overlooked by the existing literature on CPRs. Under complete information, we identify the presence of inefficiencies. Specifically, when the initial stock is high, the incumbent over-exploits the resource in the first period of the game, since it does not internalize the effect that its first-period appropriation causes on the entrant's future profits. Both agents over-exploit the CPR in the second period, given that they ignore the effect that an increase in their appropriation imposes on other agents' contemporaneous profits. Under incomplete information, we describe a novel form of inefficiency. When the initial stock is abundant, the incumbent under-exploits the resource relative to its socially optimal level, as prescribed by the uninformative equilibrium, in order to conceal its type from potential entrants and thus deter entry. Similarly, if the stock is scarce, the incumbent under-exploits the commons, in order to convey its type to the potential entrant, who is deterred from the CPR. Therefore, the presence of incomplete information can facilitate the conservation of the CPR by the incumbent without the need of regulatory measures. In addition, our findings suggest that, under certain contexts, social welfare under incomplete information is larger than under complete information.

The chapter considers a single entrant in a two-period model. If, instead, multiple entrants sequentially choose whether or not to enter the commons, our informative equilibrium still applies. In particular, the low-stock incumbent deters entry in the first period, and selects its monopoly appropriation level in the second period, which reveals the state of the stock to potential entrants, further deterring entry. The high-stock incumbent attracts entry, and chooses its duopoly appropriation in the second period, which also conveys information to future entrants, further attracting more entry. In the uninformative equilibrium, however, our model predicts that the high-stock incumbent selects its second-period monopoly appropriation level, which might not be sensible if entry is still possible in future periods. Indeed, this incumbent chooses a monopoly exploitation level when no future entry exists, but could choose a different appropriation level in order to keep potential entrants uninformed about the stock.

3.6 Appendices

Appendix 1 – Complete information game

Low stock. When the stock is low, θ_L, entry does not occur. Operating by backward induction in this setting, let us first analyze the second-period game. For a given first-period appropriation x, the incumbent's second-period cost function

is $\dfrac{q_i^2}{\theta_L - (1-\beta)x}$, which is increasing and convex in second-period appropriation,

q_i, and decreasing in the regeneration rate, $\beta \in [0, 1]$, and increases in the first-period appropriation, x. In addition, when the stock fully regenerates, $\beta = 1$, the same amount of stock is available in the first and second-period game. Hence, the low-stock incumbent chooses the level of second-period appropriation, q_i, that solves

$$\max_{q_i \geq 0} \quad q_i - \frac{q_i^2}{\theta_L - (1-\beta)x}$$

Taking first-order conditions and solving for q_i the appropriation function is

$$q_i^{L,NE}(x) = \frac{\theta_L - (1-\beta)x}{2},$$ which decreases in first-period appropriation, x, and

where superscript *NE* denotes no entry. Given this profit-maximizing second-period appropriation function, $q_i^{L,NE}(x)$, the incumbent selects the level of x that solves the discounted sum of first- and second-period profits, as follows

$$\max_{x \geq 0} \left[x - \frac{x^2}{\theta_L} \right] + \delta \left[q_i^{L,NE}(x) - \frac{q_i^{L,NE}(x)^2}{\theta_L - (1-\beta)x} \right]$$

where the incumbent's cost function from appropriating x units in the first period

is $\dfrac{x^2}{\theta_L}$ which, similarly to that in the second-period game, is increasing and

convex in first-period appropriation, x, and decreasing in the available stock, θ_L.
Taking first-order conditions and solving for x, we have

$$x^{L,NE} = \frac{\theta_L \left(4 - (1-\beta)\delta \right)}{8}.$$ Therefore, the equilibrium level of second-period

appropriation becomes $q_i^{L,NE}(x^{L,NE}) = \dfrac{\theta_L \left[4 + \delta + \beta(4 - (2-\beta)\delta) \right]}{16}$. For instance,

for parameter values $\theta_L = 5$ and $\delta = 1$, equilibrium first-period appropriation

becomes $x^{L,NE} = \dfrac{5(3+\beta)}{8}$ (depicted in Figure 3.1a), whereas, second-period

appropriation is $q^{L,NE}(x^{L,NE}) = \dfrac{5 \left[5 + \beta(2+\beta) \right]}{16}$ (depicted in Figure 3.1b).

High stock. When the initial stock is high, θ_H, entry occurs. In this setting, the incumbent's second-period profit-maximizing problem becomes

$$\max_{q_i \geq 0} \quad q_i - \frac{(q_i + q_j)q_i}{\theta_H - (1-\beta)x}$$

where q_i (q_j) denotes the second-period appropriation level for the incumbent (entrant, respectively). Taking first-order conditions and solving for q_i, we obtain the incumbent's best response function

$$q_i(q_j; x) = \frac{\theta_H - (1-\beta)x}{2} - \frac{1}{2} q_j$$

Assuming that both firm's cost functions coincide, the entrant's best response function $q_j(q_i; x)$ is symmetric to $q_i(q_j; x)$. Simultaneously solving for q_i and q_j we have

$$q_i^{H,E}(x) = q_j^{H,E}(x) = \frac{\theta_H - (1-\beta)x}{3},$$

which are both decreasing in first-period appropriation, x. Given these profit-maximizing second-period appropriation functions, the incumbent selects x in order to maximize the discounted sum of profits

$$\max_{x \geq 0} \left[x - \frac{x^2}{\theta_H} \right] + \delta \left[q_i^{H,E}(x) - \frac{\left[q_i^{H,E}(x) + q_j^{H,E}(x) \right] q_i^{H,E}(x)}{\theta_H - (1-\beta)x} \right]$$

Taking first-order conditions and solving for x, yields an equilibrium first-period appropriation $x^{H,E} = \dfrac{\theta_H \left[9 - (1-\beta)\delta \right]}{18}$, which implies that the equilibrium

second-period appropriation level becomes

$$q_i^{H,E}(x^{H,E}) = q_j^{H,E}(x^{H,E}) = \frac{\theta_H \left[9 + \delta + \beta(9 - (2-\beta)\delta) \right]}{54}$$ for the incumbent and

the entrant. For the parametric example where $\theta_H = 10$ and $\delta = 1$, first-period

exploitation is $x^{H,E} = \dfrac{5(8+\beta)}{9}$ (as depicted in Figure 3.1a), while second-period

appropriation becomes $q_i^{H,E} = q_j^{H,E} = \dfrac{5(2+\beta)(5+\beta)}{27}$ (as represented in Figure 3.1b).

Appendix 2 – Incomplete information

Informative equilibrium. In the informative equilibrium, the low-stock incumbent selects a level of first-period appropriation x^L that cannot be profitably mimicked by the high-stock incumbent. In particular, this equilibrium is sustained when the following incentive compatibility conditions hold. First, if the low-stock incumbent selects x^L, it deters entry, yielding profits of

$$\left[x^L - \frac{\left(x^L \right)^2}{\theta_L} \right] + \delta \left[q_i^{L,NE}(x^L) - \frac{q_i^{L,NE}(x^L)^2}{\theta_L - (1-\beta)x^L} \right] \tag{1}$$

If, instead, the low-stock incumbent deviates toward the high-stock incumbent's appropriation level, $x^{H,E}$ (found in Appendix 1), it attracts entry, obtaining profits of

$$\left[x^{H,E} - \frac{\left(x^{H,E} \right)^2}{\theta_L} \right] + \delta \left[q_i^{L,E}(x^{H,E}) - \frac{\left[q_i^{L,E}(x^{H,E}) + q_j^{L,E}(x^{H,E}) \right] q_i^{L,E}(x^{H,E})}{\theta_L - (1-\beta)x^{H,E}} \right] \tag{2}$$

Therefore, the first-period exploitation x^L is profitable for the low-stock incumbent when the profits in expression (1) exceed those in (2). For our above parametric examples, where $\theta_H = 10$, $\theta_L = 5$ and $\delta = 1$, this implies that

$$x^L \geq \frac{5\left[9 + 3\beta + \left(9\beta^2 + 54\beta + 161\right)\right]}{25}$$

Similarly, if the high-stock incumbent selects the first-period appropriation level $x^{H,E}$, it attracts entry, obtaining profits of

$$\left[x^{H,E} - \frac{\left(x^{H,E}\right)^2}{\theta_H}\right] + \delta\left[q_i^{H,E}(x^{H,E}) - \frac{\left[q_i^{H,E}(x^{H,E}) + q_j^{H,E}(x^{H,E})\right]q_i^{H,E}(x^{H,E})}{\theta_H - (1-\beta)x^{H,E}}\right]$$

(3)

If, instead, the high-stock incumbent deviates and chooses the same first-period exploitation as the low-type incumbent, x^L, it deters entry, yielding profits of

$$\left[x^L - \frac{\left(x^L\right)^2}{\theta_H}\right] + \delta\left[q_i^{H,NE}(x^L) - \frac{q_i^{H,NE}(x^L)^2}{\theta_H - (1-\beta)x^L}\right]$$

(4)

Therefore, the first-period exploitation x^L must be unprofitable to mimic by the high-stock incumbent – that is, profits in expression (4) are lower than those in (3). For the above parametric example, where $\theta_H = 10$, $\theta_L = 5$ and $\delta = 1$, x^L must satisfy

$$\frac{5\left[27 + 9\beta + \sqrt{5}\left(85 + \beta(46 + 13\beta)\right)\right]}{36} \geq x^L$$

Therefore, the first-period appropriation x^L must simultaneously satisfy

$$\frac{5\left[27 + 9\beta + \sqrt{5}\left(85 + \beta(46 + 13\beta)\right)\right]}{36} \geq x^L \geq \frac{5\left[9 + 3\beta + \left(9\beta^2 + 54\beta + 161\right)\right]}{25}$$

The low-stock incumbent hence selects the highest first-period appropriation that conveys its type to the potential entrant, thus deterring entry. Technically, this level of appropriation survives the Cho and Kreps' (1987) Intuitive Criterion. Hence, this incumbent selects

$$x^L = \frac{5\left[27 + 9\beta + \sqrt{5}\left(85 + \beta(46 + 13\beta)\right)\right]}{36}$$

Therefore, the difference between the first-period appropriation that the low-stock incumbent selects under complete information, $x^{L,NE}$, and that chosen in the informative equilibrium, x^L, represents the under-exploitation effort that the incumbent must exert in order to convey its type to the entrant (as depicted in Figure 3.5). That is,

$$x^{L,NE} - x^L = \frac{5\left[27 + 9\beta + 2\sqrt{5}\left(85 + \beta(46 + 13\beta)\right)^{1/2}\right]}{27}$$

which is positive for all $\beta \in [0, 1]$, and increases in the regeneration rate β since

$$\frac{\partial\left(x^{L,NE}-x^{L}\right)}{\partial\beta}=\frac{5}{72}\left(9+\frac{\sqrt{5}(46+26\beta)}{\left(85+\beta(46+13\beta)\right)^{1/2}}\right)$$

Uninformative equilibrium. In the uninformative equilibrium, both types of incumbent select $x^{L,NE}$ and entry is deterred. This is convenient for the high-stock incumbent if the profits from selecting $x^{L,NE}$ and deterring entry

$$\left[x^{L,NE}-\frac{\left(x^{L,NE}\right)^{2}}{\theta_{H}}\right]+\delta\left[q_{i}^{H,NE}(x^{L,NE})-\frac{q_{i}^{H,NE}(x^{L,NE})^{2}}{\theta_{H}-(1-\beta)x^{L,NE}}\right] \qquad (5)$$

exceed those from selecting $x^{H,E}$ and attracting entry, as described in expression (3). This profit ranking holds, since the difference between (5) and (3) yields

$$\frac{5\left[971+\beta(434+179\beta)\right]}{10,368}, \text{ which is positive for all.}$$

Therefore, for the high-stock incumbent, the difference between its first-period appropriation under complete information, $x^{H,E}$, and that under the uninformative equilibrium, $x^{L,NE}$ (where $x^{H,E}>x^{L,NE}$) measures the under-exploitation effort that this incumbent exerts in order to conceal its type from the potential entrant and thus deter entry. In particular, for the above parametric example, where $\theta_{H}=10$, $\theta_{L}=5$ and $\delta=1$, this difference becomes $x^{H,E}-x^{L,NE}=\dfrac{5(37-\beta)}{72}$, which is positive for all $\beta\in[0,1]$.

Notes

1 We would like to especially thank Stephen Salant, Gene Gruver, Jill McCluskey, and Hayley Chouinard for their insightful comments and suggestions. We are also grateful to all participants of the Fourth World Congress of Environmental and Resource Economists at Montreal, Canada, the seminar participants at the Pontificia Universidad Catolica de Chile, the Summer Meeting of the Association of Environmental and Resource Economists (AERE) at Seattle, and the 8th Meeting on Game Theory and Practice Dedicated to Global and International Issues at the University of California, Riverside.

2 Note that the incumbent's first-period costs are increasing and convex in appropriation. This property can be intuitively understood with the example of a fisherman exploiting a fishing ground. Every additional ton of fish appropriated entails a cost for the fisherman, and such a cost is itself increasing in the amount of appropriation (i.e., the additional cost from the second ton of fish is lower than that associated with the hundredth ton).

3 In addition, to induce positive appropriation levels, we consider that the revenue that firms obtain from selling their first unit is larger than its associated marginal costs. Otherwise, firms would not appropriate positive amounts.

4 Otherwise the incumbent, when deciding its first-period appropriation, would not experience a trade-off between first- and second-period profits.

5 Note that the incumbent's second-period costs are affected by the entrant's exploitation of the resource in the second-period game. In addition, we consider that a given

increase in first-period appropriation produces a larger increase in second-period costs in the case of no entry, in which the incumbent bears all the negative effects of first-period appropriation, than in the case of entry, in which such appropriation affects both agents.

6 The entrant's second-period appropriation coincides with the high-stock incumbent's exploitation since, for simplicity, our parametric example considers that firms are symmetric in their cost functions.

7 Nonetheless, second-period appropriation lies above its socially optimal level, both when the stock fully and when it partially regenerates across time; as described in the section on complete information.

8 Under certain conditions, this incumbent might actually deviate more from its first-period appropriation level under complete information when the resource fully regenerates across time than when it partially regenerates. For more details, see Espinola-Arredondo and Munoz-Garcia (2011).

9 A similar intuition applies to the case in which the resource fully regenerates across periods: Both types of incumbent select the first-period appropriation level that the low-stock incumbent chooses under complete information.

10 Recall that this welfare ranking holds if society assigns a larger welfare loss to the over-exploitation of the resource, as predicted in the complete information setting, than to the under-exploitation of the commons that the uninformative equilibrium prescribes.

References

Apesteguia, J. (2006) "Does information matter in the commons? Experimental evidence," *Journal of Economic Behavior & Organization*, 60: 55–69.

Bagwell, K. and Ramey, G. (1990) "Advertising and pricing to deter or accommodate entry when demand is unknown," *International Journal of Industrial Organization*, 8: 93–113.

Baland, J. and Platteau, J. (1996) *Halting Degradation of Natural Resources: Is there a Role for Rural Communities?* Oxford: FAO and Clarendon Press.

Cho, I. and Kreps, D. (1987) "Signaling games and stable equilibria," *Quarterly Journal of Economics*, 102: 179–221.

Espinola-Arredondo, A. and Munoz-Garcia, F. (2011) "Can incomplete information lead to underexploitation in the commons?" *Journal of Environmental Economics and Management*, 62(3): 402–413.

Food and Agriculture Organization (FAO). (2005) "Review of the state of the world marine fisheries resources," FAO Fisheries Technical Paper No. 457, Rome.

Haughton, M. (2002) "Fisheries subsidy and the role of regional fisheries management organizations: The Caribbean experience," paper presented at the UNEP Workshop on Fisheries Subsidies and Sustainable Fisheries Management, 26–27 April 2001, UNEP, Geneva.

Mason, C. and Polasky, S. (1994) "Entry deterrence in the commons," *International Economic Review*, 35(2): 507–525.

Matthews, S. and Mirman, L. (1983) "Equilibrium limit pricing: The effects of private information and stochastic demand," *Econometrica*, 51: 981–996.

Milgrom, P. and Roberts, J. (1982) "Limit pricing and entry under incomplete information," *Econometrica*, 50: 443–466.

Ostrom, E. (1990) *Governing the Commons*. Cambridge: Cambridge University Press.

Ostrom, E., Gardner, R., and Walker, J. (1994) *Rules, Games and Common Pool Resources*. Michigan: University of Michigan Press.

Polasky, S. and Bin, O. (2001) "Entry deterrence and signaling in a nonrenewable resource model," *Journal of Environmental Economics and Management*, 42(3): 235–256.

Suleiman, R. and Rapoport, A. (1988) "Environmental and social uncertainty in single-trial resource dilemmas," *Acta Psychologica*, 68: 99–112.

Suleiman, R., Rapoport, A., and Budescu, D. (1996) "Fixed position and property rights in sequential resource dilemmas under uncertainty," *Acta Psychologica*, 93: 229–245.

4 Environmental negotiations under uncertainty

Can they improve welfare?[1]

Ana Espinola-Arredondo and Felix Munoz-Garcia

4.1 Introduction

The negotiation of environmental agreements generally involves a certain degree of uncertainty, since countries' representatives cannot accurately predict whether or not other countries have the technical ability to fully comply with the terms of the treaty. Specifically, international environmental agreements (IEAs) usually establish reductions in pollutant emissions that imply the use of or the investment in clean technologies, which not all signatories have access to. In the Montreal protocol, for instance, countries committed to eliminate the use of CFC gases by using a new technology that was available to most of them, which explains the success of this treaty. On the contrary, the Kyoto protocol requires the reduction of several pollutants affecting global warming.[2] This objective can be achieved by using new technologies that may be available to only some countries. Parties that lack this technology could alternatively acquire it by investing substantial amounts. However, some of them might face a severe economic crisis that affects their ability to acquire the new technology. Hence, while the parties involved in the negotiations acknowledge the urgency of curbing climate change, they are also uncertain about the precise implementation of the treaty, since they cannot perfectly observe whether the new technology is available or affordable to other co-signatories.

Importantly, countries' different technological progress can potentially affect the uncertainty they face during the negotiations, and thus their willingness to participate in environmental agreements. Consider, for instance, a bilateral negotiation between Germany and Brazil to reduce a certain pollutant. While most observers agree that Germany has the technical ability to use advanced clean technologies, and thus easily implement the content of the agreement, Brazil just recently started to invest and promote clean technologies, in the last few years, which raises doubts about its ability to fully comply with the terms of the treaty.[3] The presence of this type of uncertainty in international negotiations could entail, at first glance, less successful treaties. In contrast, our chapter demonstrates that such uncertainty can actually promote the signature of the agreement under certain conditions.

This chapter considers a signaling game in which a leader decides whether to sign the agreement and a follower who, after observing the leader's signature, chooses whether or not to join the treaty. We investigate how incomplete information about other countries' technological ability to comply with the IEA can favor or hinder the success of an environmental agreement. Our analysis identifies two types of countries: one in which clean technologies are widely spread, "high-type" country, and another where such technologies are almost inexistent, "low-type" country. In particular, we examine two layers of uncertainty: one in which only the follower is uninformed about the technological dissemination within the leading country, which we refer to as *unilateral* uncertainty; and another where both leader and follower are uninformed about each other's technological dissemination, denoted as *bilateral* uncertainty. Unilateral uncertainty explains strategic settings in which the country acting as the follower has a well-known history of fulfilling the content of IEAs due to a widespread use of clean technologies, while the leader's technological dissemination is more difficult to assess. Bilateral uncertainty instead describes cases in which, for instance, both leader and follower have recently developed their green industries, and thus countries cannot precisely evaluate the extension of clean technologies in each other's economy.

Our results provide different equilibrium outcomes under alternative information contexts. In the case of unilateral uncertainty, a unique equilibrium exists whereby both types of leader sign the treaty and the follower responds by joining if the probability of facing a high-type leader is sufficiently large. Otherwise, a unique equilibrium can be sustained in which both the leader and the follower randomize their participation decision, thus reducing the probability that the treaty becomes successful. Importantly, our results suggest that both countries can participate in the agreement, not only when the leader's type is high – as under complete information settings – but also when it is low. Under bilateral uncertainty, a new equilibrium outcome emerges in which only the high-type leader signs and the follower responds by joining the treaty after observing a signature. This allows the leader to convey its high type to the follower, thus attracting it to the treaty. Such information transmission, however, does not necessarily entail a larger welfare than that arising in equilibrium outcomes when both types of leader sign the treaty.

We also provide a social welfare comparison of our equilibrium results. Specifically, we find that when the type of at least one of the countries is high, social welfare in the equilibrium in which both types of leader sign is weakly larger than in any of the other equilibrium outcomes, and exceeds that under complete information contexts. However, if both countries' type is low, a setting of complete information yields a larger social welfare. Finally, we analyze IEAs negotiated between one leader and multiple followers. In particular, we demonstrate that, as more countries participate in the negotiations, equilibria in which all followers participate in the agreement can be sustained under more restrictive conditions. Intuitively, free-riding willingness become stronger, thus reducing the willingness of a given country to respond by joining the agreement after it has been signed by a larger number of countries.

Related literature. The literature on IEAs has extensively analyzed negotiations under complete information (Barrett 1994a, 1994b, 1999; Cesar 1994).

These studies show that more countries decide to participate in international agreements when the difference between the net global benefit in the non-cooperative and the full-cooperative outcomes is small (i.e., free-riding incentives are small).[4] International negotiations, nonetheless, usually operate under uncertainty, a setting often ignored by the existing literature.

This chapter contributes to the literature by analyzing incomplete information in international negotiations. For instance, Iida (1993) examines international agreements using a repeated bargaining game. Specifically, he assumes that a country is uninformed about other countries' status quo, and therefore it cannot perfectly anticipate whether or not its offers will be accepted in the negotiation. In contrast, we consider that countries are uninformed about each other's technological dissemination, and hence cannot accurately infer whether other signatories will fully comply with the terms of the agreement. In addition, we allow for both unilateral and bilateral uncertainty. Martin (2005) also analyzes the signaling role of the signature of a treaty. Her paper considers two types of agreements – executive treaties and international agreements – which imply different degrees of compliance. Unlike her study, we investigate a case in which not only the follower but also the leader is uninformed, we allow for a more general payoff structure, and compare the welfare properties of different information contexts.[5]

Furthermore, our conclusions are also related to those of Kreps *et al.* (1982), who consider the role of informational asymmetries about players' types in the Prisoner's Dilemma game. Specifically, in their model, players assign some probability to their opponent playing a conditionally cooperative, tit-for-tat strategy. They show that there is a sequential equilibrium in which players choose to cooperate with positive probability. Similarly, we demonstrate that the presence of incomplete information about countries' types may lead to cooperation in situations in which such equilibrium outcome would not exist among perfectly informed countries. Finally, this chapter provides an intuitive discussion of the theoretical results developed in Espinola-Arredondo and Munoz-Garcia (2010, 2011), henceforth EM.

The next section describes the model under incomplete information. Section 4.3 examines the set of equilibria in the case of unilateral uncertainty, whereas section 4.4 analyzes equilibrium predictions under bilateral uncertainty. In section 4.5, we evaluate the welfare properties of our results, section 4.6 extends our analysis to N followers, and section 4.7 concludes.

4.2 Model

Let us analyze the signature and posterior implementation of the IEA as a two-stage game. In the first stage, the negotiation stage of the environmental treaty, the leader announces its participation decision, accepting a given set of non-binding commitment levels. These commitments, specifying countries' reduction of pollutants, can be set by international agencies. Once this announcement is made, the follower chooses whether to participate in the IEA. In the second stage, the implementation of the treaty, countries independently determine their reduction of emissions, as a function of both countries' commitment levels in the treaty. In order to clarify the structure of the game, we next provide a detailed description of each step under a setting of unilateral uncertainty, in which only the follower is uninformed about the leader's type. (Section 4.4 below describes bilateral uncertainty.)

Nature selects the leader's technology, which is *privately* observed by the leader but *unobserved* by the follower. The leader's technology is either high or low, with associated probabilities p and $1-p$, respectively.[6]

1   After observing its technology level, the leading country announces its participation in the treaty. If the leader does not sign, the negotiation game ends.
2   If the leader signs the agreement, the follower chooses to sign or not sign, given its posterior beliefs about the leader's type. If the follower responds by not participating, the negotiation game ends. In the unilateral context, we assume that the follower's technology is high. (The bilateral setting, however, does not require this assumption.)
3   After the negotiation game ends, the follower observes the leader's type. If the treaty is signed, the high-technology leader fully implements the agreement, while the low-technology leader independently selects its reduction in emissions.
4   When the agreement is not signed, both types of leader independently choose a reduction in pollutants that maximizes second-period utility. The high-technology follower behaves as its counterpart leader.[7]

We next describe the payoffs of the leader and follower for each strategic setting.

Payoffs when the treaty is unsuccessful. The treaty can become unsuccessful in two situations. First, if the leader does not sign the treaty, the negotiation game ends. In this case, both leader and follower independently choose the reduction in emission levels (e, in Figure 4.1) that solves the Nash equilibrium (NE) of the second-period game. Second, if the leader signs but the follower responds by not joining the agreement, the treaty is similarly unsuccessful, and both countries' benefits from reducing their emissions coincide with those under no treaty. However, the leader incurs a negotiation cost (NC) from signing the treaty. Therefore, conditional on the follower not joining the agreement, both types of leader prefer not to sign the treaty.

Payoffs when the treaty is successful. This case is described by the participation of both countries in the IEA. Unlike the setting where the treaty is unsuccessful, we consider that, conditional on the follower's participation, both types of leader prefer to sign the agreement. Regarding the follower, we assume that its benefits from joining the IEA are positive when the leader's type is high, and hence fully complies with the terms of the treaty, but are negative when the leader's type is low, since in this case the leader does not fulfill its commitment levels. Hence, the follower prefers to join (not join) the treaty when the leader's

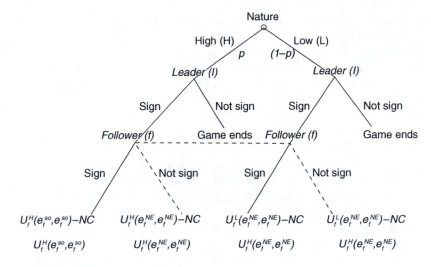

Figure 4.1 Structure of the game.

type is high (low, respectively). Figure 4.1 summarizes the time structure of the game and payoffs for each country.

Complete information. According to the above specification, in a complete information setting, both countries perfectly observe each other's type: The follower chooses to respond joining the IEA after observing a signature originating from a high-type leader, but to not sign when the leader's type is low. Since the leader anticipates such a response, the treaty is successful only in the case when both leader's and follower's type is high, but becomes unsuccessful otherwise. In the following section, we investigate if the introduction of incomplete information about the countries' types allows for emergence of equilibrium outcomes in which countries sign under conditions for which the treaty would not be successful under complete information – namely, when the leader's type is low.

4.3 Unilateral uncertainty

In this section, we examine under which cases the treaty is signed when only the follower is uncertain about the leader's type. We next describe the equilibrium outcomes that can and cannot arise in this context.

Type-dependent strategies. This information setting does not support equilibria in which only the high-type leader participates in the agreement, and thus the leader's signature decision conveys information about the leader's type to the uninformed follower. If the leader chose this type-dependent strategy, the follower would be able to infer its type by observing its action, therefore responding as in the complete information setting, whereby the follower joins an agreement signed by a high-type leader. Such a follower's response, however, would induce the low-type leader to sign the agreement as well – pretending to be a high-type country – violating this strategy profile.

Type-independent strategies. Strategy profiles where, in contrast, both types of leader sign the IEA can be sustained as equilibrium of the signaling game. In particular, the follower cannot infer the leader's type after observing its signature decision (since both types participate in the agreement), and hence responds by joining the treaty if its expected benefit from signing exceeds that from not signing, which occurs when the probability of facing a high-type leader, p, is sufficiently large.[8] (For a numerical example of the parameter values under which this type of strategy can be sustained, see Appendix.) If, instead, probability p is relatively low, then the follower does not sign, and the leader does not necessarily have incentives to sign the treaty regardless of its type. Specifically, this setting only sustains strategy profiles in which countries randomize their participation decision, as we describe next. Figure 4.2 illustrates our equilibrium results for a relatively high and low prior probability p.

Randomized signatures. When the probability of facing a high-type leader, p, is relatively low, a unique strategy profile can be supported in equilibrium in which countries randomize their participation decision. In particular, the low-type leader signs using mixed strategies, whereas the high-type leader participates in the treaty with probability one. Since in this setting a signature can originate from either type of leader, the follower cannot accurately infer the leader's type and responds by joining the IEA also using mixed strategies.

Therefore, the introduction of incomplete information about the leader's type allows for the treaty to become successful under conditions for which complete information environments do not support it. Specifically, while the treaty is unsuccessful under complete information if the leader's type is low, it is signed by all countries with probability one (when priors are relatively high) or at least with a positive probability (when priors are low) under unilateral uncertainty.

Before investigating how our results are affected by the introduction of an additional layer of uncertainty, in which not only the follower but also the leader is uninformed about each other's types, we next discuss the comparative statics of our equilibrium outcome about randomized signatures. First, an increase in the probability that the leader is a high-type country makes the treaty more attractive for the follower, who increases its probability of joining the IEA. Ultimately, this induces the low-type leader to raise the probability with which it signs the agreement, since a signature is likely to be positively responded to by the follower. Second, an increase in the (negative) benefit from signing a treaty

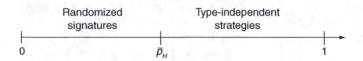

Figure 4.2 Unilateral uncertainty.

with a low-type leader makes the IEA less inviting for the follower. In order to entice the follower into the treaty, the low-type leader needs to be perceived as a high-type country, which it achieves by raising the probability with which it signs. Third, an increase in the leader's negotiation costs makes it more hesitant to sign, reducing the likelihood that a signature originates from a low-type country, since its free-riding benefits decrease. As a consequence, the follower anticipates that it is more likely to face a high-technology leader, raising the probability with which the follower joins the IEA. A converse argument applies when the benefit that the low-type leader obtains from the follower's signature increases.

4.4 Bilateral uncertainty

Let us next investigate countries' signature decisions under information contexts in which both leader and follower are uncertain about each other's types. This setting captures strategic incentives in negotiations between countries that have recently developed their green industries, and thus every country cannot accurately assess the widespread use of clean technologies in another country's economy. Unlike the unilateral uncertainty case, we now allow the follower to have a high or low technology, with probabilities q and $1-q$, respectively.[9] Similarly to the previous section, we consider that the high-type leader prefers to sign a treaty, regardless of the follower's type[10]; whereas, when the leader's technology is low, it prefers to sign (not sign) an agreement with a high-type (low-type, respectively) follower.[11] Likewise, the high-type follower prefers to sign (not sign) an agreement with a high-type (low-type) leader, while a low-type follower obtains a positive (zero) benefit from joining an IEA with a high-type (low-type) leader.[12] Bilateral uncertainty allows for the emergence of a strategy profile that could not be sustained under unilateral uncertainty – namely, a type-dependent strategy profile.

Type-dependent strategies. In this information context, a strategy profile in which the leader signs (does not sign) when its technology is high (low, respectively) can be supported. In this setting, information about the leader's type is hence perfectly transmitted to the follower, who responds by joining the treaty, irrespective of its own type. This result, hence, resembles that under complete information, in which agreements are only successful when the leader is a high-type country. Intuitively, the low-type leader is not attracted to participate in the treaty when q, the probability of facing a high-type follower (who will respond joining the agreement in this equilibrium), is sufficiently low. Hence, only the high-type leader signs the treaty, and such signature conveys its type to the follower, thus inducing it to join.

Type-independent strategies. Similar to unilateral uncertainty, a strategy profile in which both types of leaders sign the agreement, and as a consequence no information is revealed to the follower, can also be sustained under bilateral uncertainty. In particular, the follower must decide whether or not to join the IEA when the probability of facing a high-type leader, p, is sufficiently large. Anticipating the follower's signature in this context, both types of leader participate if the follower's type is likely to be high (i.e., q is large) and there-fore the treaty becomes successful.

Figure 4.3 illustrates these two equilibrium outcomes. When the follower's type is likely to be low (low q) only a type-dependent strategy profile can be sustained. By contrast, when both leader and follower's types are likely to be high (large p and q), a type-independent strategy profile can be supported. (The region where p is low but q is high does not sustain strategy profiles in which countries sign the agreement in pure strategies, but rather, randomize their participation decision, as we describe below.)

In addition, the set of parameter values under which the above type-dependent strategies can be sustained depends upon free-riding incentives. In particular, the low-type leader benefits from signing an agreement with a high-type follower, since it free-rides the follower's compliance of the terms of the IEA. Such free-riding incentives, however, dissuade the high-type follower from joining the agreement. Therefore, when these free-riding incentives decrease, the follower is more attracted to participate, expanding the set of priors, q, under which type-dependent strategies can be sustained.[13] A similar argument can be extended to the region of priors supporting the type-independent strategies, in which an increase in the benefits from signing an agreement with a high-type leader makes the treaty more attractive for the follower, thus inducing it to sign under larger parameter conditions.[14]

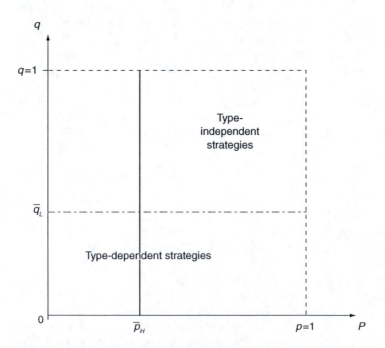

Figure 4.3 Type-dependent and independent strategies.

Our previous results describe the set of equilibria under different conditions on the prior probabilities. However, no equilibrium involving pure strategies exists in the region where $p < \bar{p}_H$ and $q \geq \bar{q}_L$. Similar to unilateral uncertainty, a strategy profile can be sustained in which the low-type leader randomizes its participation decision and the high-type leader signs in pure strategies; whereas, the high-type (low-type) follower responds joining the agreement in mixed (pure) strategies. Figure 4.4 summarizes our equilibrium predictions. Our results, therefore, suggest that the presence of unilateral or bilateral uncertainty allows for the treaty to become successful not only when the leader's type is high ($p=1$), as in complete information settings, but also when its type is low ($p=0$).

In addition, note that Figure 4.4 embodies equilibrium outcomes under unilateral uncertainty as a special case (i.e., when $q=1$ and hence the follower's type is high with certainty) as well as equilibrium outcomes under complete information in its four corners. Indeed, Figure 4.4 describes the following cases: (1) both leader and follower are high type (i.e., $p=q=1$) and the treaty is successful; (2) the leader (follower) is a high-type (low-type) country (i.e., $p=1$ and $q=0$) and the leader's signature is responded to by the follower joining the treaty; (3) the follower (leader) is a high-type (low-type) country (i.e., $q=1$ and $p=0$) and the

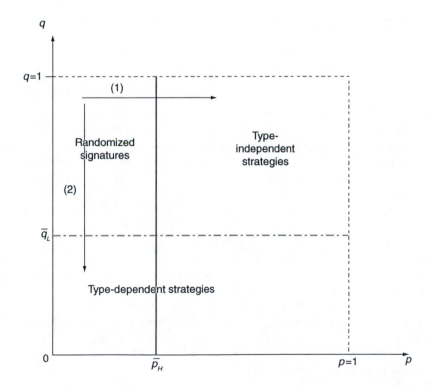

Figure 4.4 Equilibrium outcomes.

treaty is unsuccessful since the follower would not participate; and (4) both leader's and follower's types are low (i.e., $p=q=0$) and the treaty is not signed.

Information transmission. We now analyze how probabilities p and q affect the degree of informativeness of the strategy profile in which countries randomize their participation decision. Specifically, informativeness can be measured as the difference between the probabilities with which the high- and low-type leader sign the treaty. A larger discrepancy in these probabilities implies that when a signature is observed it is more likely to originate from a high-type leader. First, an increase in p makes the IEA more attractive for the uninformed follower, which induces the low-type leader to participate as well. Therefore, both types of leader are likely to sign, ultimately reducing the degree of informativeness. Graphically, an increase in p moves our equilibrium predictions, from the randomized signature to the type-independent strategy profile in which both types of leader sign, as illustrated by arrow (1) in Figure 4.4. Second, a decrease in q makes the treaty less attractive to the low-type leader, which implies that a signature must likely originate from a high-type leader alone inducing both types of follower to sign, converging to their behavior in type-dependent strategy profiles. Hence, the degree of informativeness increases, as depicted by arrow (2) in Figure 4.4.

4.5 Welfare comparisons

Let us now examine the welfare properties of our equilibrium results. Specifically, we investigate how the introduction of incomplete information, graphically represented as a movement from the boundaries to the interior points of Figure 4.4 (bilateral uncertainty), affects social welfare.

Under complete information, the treaty is successful only when the leader's type is high, similar to the type-dependent strategy profile. Hence, social welfare levels coincide in these two settings. In contrast, when the leader's type is low and the follower's is high, the treaty is unsuccessful under complete information. However, under incomplete information, the treaty can become successful with probability one (in the type-independent strategy) or with positive probability (when countries randomize their signature). Since the follower fully complies with the terms of the agreement, social welfare is larger under incomplete than complete information. Finally, when both countries' types are low, the type-dependent strategy prescribes no signature on the agreement, as under complete information, which yields a larger social welfare than that arising in the type-independent strategy. In particular, in this equilibrium outcome, both countries sign the treaty, but none of them comply, while the leader incurs a negotiation cost, which reduces social welfare. Therefore, when the type of at least one of the countries involved in the negotiations is high, social welfare in the type-independent strategy is weakly larger than in any of the other equilibrium outcomes. Table 4.1 summarizes our welfare comparisons in which, for compactness, we use SW_{TI}, SW_{TD} and SW_{RS} to denote, respectively, the equilibrium social welfare arising in the type-independent, type-dependent strategy

Table 4.1 Welfare comparisons

Leader's type	Follower's type	Social welfare ranking
High	High	$SW_{TI}=SW_{TD}\geq SW_{RS}$
High	Low	$SW_{TI}=SW_{TD}\geq SW_{RS}$
Low	High	$SW_{TI}>SW_{RS}>SW_{TD}$[1]
Low	Low	$SW_{TD}>SW_{RS}>SW_{TI}$

Note
1   This welfare ranking result holds as long as the sum of the benefits that leader and follower obtain from participating in the treaty is sufficiently high. Otherwise, $SW_{TI}>SW_{TD}>SW_{RS}$, where the type-independent strategy profile still yields a larger social welfare than any other equilibrium outcome. For more details, see EM (2011).

profiles, and in the equilibrium outcome, when countries randomize their signature decision.

Relative to unilateral uncertainty, our results suggest that the introduction of an additional layer of uncertainty can entail welfare gains or losses. In particular, under unilateral uncertainty only the type-independent strategy profile and the randomized signatures can be sustained, as depicted in Figure 4.4 in the region where $q=1$. Under bilateral uncertainty, however, a type-dependent strategy might emerge if q is sufficiently low, which generates a larger social welfare than that in the other equilibrium outcomes if both leader's and follower's types are low. Otherwise, the type-dependent strategy profile produces a lower welfare. As a consequence, additional layers of uncertainty can be welfare improving when both countries' types are low, but becomes welfare reducing otherwise.

Policy implications. From a policy perspective, our results suggest that international environmental agencies, such as the Intergovernmental Panel on Climate Change (IPCC), have incentives to organize the negotiation of treaties between countries whose technological ability is relatively uncertain for other parties (e.g., countries that recently developed their green industries). In this setting, our results suggest that the treaty can become successful in conditions for which it will not be under complete information contexts. In addition, if this agency holds information about the leader's economy widely using clean technologies, it might choose to distribute this information to all countries involved in the negotiations. In the context of our model, this ensures that the follower responds by joining the agreement. Finally, we show that if the leader's use of clean technologies is low but that of the follower is high, international agencies can achieve successful treaties by "planting seeds of doubt" about the leader's type. In terms of our model, this modifies equilibrium predictions from one in which the follower does not join the leader to one in which the follower responds by randomizing its participation decision, and thus the agreement is successful with positive probability.

4.6 Extension to *N*-followers

Let us next investigate how our equilibrium results are affected by an increase in the number of followers. For simplicity, we focus on a signaling game with unilateral uncertainty in which, first, the leader decides to participate in the IEA and afterwards each high-type follower, uninformed about the leader's type, sequentially chooses to respond joining the treaty. Similar to the previous analysis, a treaty is successful when at least two countries sign it.

Intuitively, the introduction of additional followers increases the free-riding incentives of any given country. In particular, a follower that observes the signature of the leader and all previous countries obtains lower benefits from participating in the treaty, since all followers before his turn are already participating (so the treaty will be successful) and followers will fully comply the content of the agreement in the unilateral uncertainty setting. In terms of our previous equilibrium outcomes, this implies that the type-independent strategy profile in which all countries (i.e., the leader and all *N* followers) sign the treaty can only be sustained if *p* (the probability that the leader's type is high) is sufficiently large. If such probability is moderately high, all but the last follower sign the treaty, and a similar result follows for lower prior probabilities, in which fewer followers join the IEA. These type-independent strategy profiles in which both types of leaders and all followers participate, all but one follower signs, etc. are graphically represented in Figure 4.5, which, in order to facilitate comparison, also includes the case with only one follower, examined in section 4.2.

Additionally, note that when priors are sufficiently low, a strategy profile can be sustained in which countries randomize their participation decision.[15] Therefore, the introduction of several followers shrinks the set of parameter values for

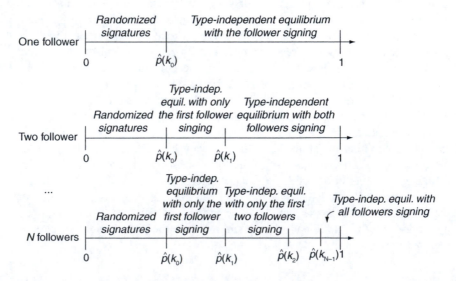

Figure 4.5 Equilibrium predictions for *N* followers.

which type-independent strategy profiles can be sustained in which all followers participate. Nonetheless, as the number of followers increases, the set of priors supporting this "fully cooperative" equilibrium sustains now "partially coopera- tive" equilibria in which a subset of followers participates in the agreement.

4.7 Conclusions

Our chapter examines how uncertainty can promote or hinder the signature of inter- national agreements. First, we demonstrate that, relative to complete information, the introduction of one layer of uncertainty can facilitate the emergence of successful treaties that cannot be sustained under complete information. The introduction of bilateral uncertainty can, however, entail equilibrium outcomes in which countries sign the IEA under the same conditions they would have participated in the treaty under complete information. In addition, when the type of at least one of the countries involved in the negotiations is high, we demonstrate that the presence of incomplete information produces welfare improvements. If, however, both countries participat- ing in the treaty have a low type, incomplete information entails welfare losses.

The model describes a context in which countries interact only once. However, an enlarged setting could consider a repeated game structure in which signatory countries renegotiate the terms of the agreement or interact in the negotiation of new treaties. In this environment, countries' beliefs not only depend on the signature decisions but also on the compliance history of their co- signatories. Hence, a country's current fulfillment of the agreement would be determined by its technological ability to comply, as in our model, and by the future reputational consequences that such compliance entails. In addition, the model considers that the domestic political situation is unaffected by the signa- ture and posterior implementation of the agreement. However, a different setting could capture the effect of these decisions into a country's political situation (e.g., affecting the likelihood that the incumbent party is re-elected), thus modi- fying the parameter conditions under which our equilibrium outcomes can be supported. Finally, we extend our model of unilateral uncertainty to the case of N followers, showing that equilibrium outcomes are not substantially affected. A further extension can investigate how the results under bilateral uncertainty are modified when N followers participate in the negotiations.

4.8 Appendix

Let us assume that the leader has a negotiation cost equal to $NC \in \mathbb{R}^+$ and that its payoffs are $U_l^K\left(e_l, e_f\right) = Benefit_l^K\left(e_l, e_f\right) - Cost\left(\theta_K\right) = \ln\left(m\left(e_l + e_f\right)\right) - \dfrac{e_l}{\theta_K}$ where K denotes leader's type $K = \{H, L\}$. Similarly, the payoff that the high-type leader obtains when facing a K-type leader is

$$U_f^K\left(e_l, e_f\right) = Benefit_f^K\left(e_l, e_f\right) - Cost\left(\theta_H\right) = \ln\left(m\left(e_l + e_f\right)\right) - \dfrac{e_f}{\theta_H}.$$

Hence, if both high-technology countries sign a treaty, the socially optimal

emission level, obtained from maximizing $\max\limits_{e_l,e_f} U_l^H\left(e_l,e_f\right)+U_f^H\left(e_l,e_f\right)$, is

$e_i^{so}=\theta_H$ for every country and countries' payoffs from signing an IEA are thus U_l^H $(e_l^{so},\ e_f^{so})=\ln(2m\theta_H)-1-NC$ and $U_f^H\ (e_l^{so},\ e_f^{so})=\ln(2m\theta_H)-1$ for the leader and follower, respectively. If the treaty is successful but the leader has a low-

technology, then the social planner maximizes $\max\limits_{e_l,e_f} U_l^L\left(e_l,e_f\right)+U_f^L\left(e_l,e_f\right)$,

yielding the socially optimal emission levels $e_l^{SO}=0$ and $e_f^{SO}=2\theta_H$, and therefore socially optimal payoffs are $U_l^L\ (e_l^{so},\ e_f^{so})=\ln(2m\theta_H)-NC$ for the leader and U_f^L $(e_l^{so},\ e_f^{so})=\ln(2m\theta_H)-2$ for the follower.

However, if only the K-type leader signs the treaty but the high-type follower does not, the treaty is unsuccessful and each country independently solves $\max\limits_{e_i} U_i^K\left(e_l,e_f\right)$,

where $i=\{l,\ f\}$, yielding the Nash equilibrium emission level $e_i^{NE}=\dfrac{\theta_K}{2}$ and

countries' equilibrium payoffs are $U_l^K\left(e_l^{NE},e_f^{NE}\right)=\ln\left(m\left(\dfrac{\theta_K+\theta_H}{2}\right)\right)-\dfrac{1}{2}-NC$

and $U_f^K\left(e_l^{NE},e_f^{NE}\right)=\ln\left(m\left(\dfrac{\theta_K+\theta_H}{2}\right)\right)-\dfrac{1}{2}$ for the leader and follower,

respectively. Finally, if the leader does not sign the treaty, the negotiation game

ends, and countries also independently choose their emission levels, $e_i^{NE}=\dfrac{\theta_K}{2}$.

Nonetheless, the leader's payoff does not include the negotiation cost – that is,

$$U_l^K\left(e_l^{NE},e_f^{NE}\right)=\ln\left(m\theta_K\right)-\dfrac{1}{2}.$$

Given the above equilibrium payoffs, we next find the cutoff value of probability $p(\bar{p}_H)$ for which the equilibrium in which both types of leader sign (type-independent strategies) is supported – that is, $p\geq\bar{p}_H$. In particular, from Lemma 1 in EM (2010), cutoff $\bar{p}_H$ is

$$\bar{p}_H=\frac{-\left[U_f^L\left(e_l^{so},e_f^{so}\right)-U_f^L\left(e_l^{NE},e_f^{NE}\right)\right]}{\left[U_f^H\left(e_l^{so},e_f^{so}\right)-U_f^H\left(e_l^{NE},e_f^{NE}\right)\right]-\left[U_f^L\left(e_l^{so},e_f^{so}\right)-U_f^L\left(e_l^{NE},e_f^{NE}\right)\right]}$$

$$=\frac{-\left[\ln\left(2m\theta_H\right)-\ln\left(m\left(\dfrac{\theta_L+\theta_H}{2}\right)\right)-\dfrac{3}{2}\right]}{\left[\ln\left(2m\theta_H\right)-\ln\left(m\theta_H\right)-\dfrac{1}{2}\right]-\left[\ln\left(2m\theta_H\right)-\ln\left(m\left(\dfrac{\theta_L+\theta_H}{2}\right)\right)-\dfrac{3}{2}\right]}$$

which for the numerical case where $\theta_H = 1/2$, $\theta_L = 1/4$, and $m = 1$, implies that $\bar{p}_H = 0.73$.

Notes

1 We would like to especially thank Gene Gruber, Bouwe Dijkstra, and Robert Rosenman for their insightful comments and suggestions. We are also grateful to all participants of the 8th Meeting on Game Theory and Practice Dedicated to Global and International Issues at the University of California, Riverside.

2 Countries committed to reduce four greenhouse gases (carbon dioxide, methane, nitrous oxide, sulphur hexafluoride) and two groups of gases (hydrofluorocarbons and perfluorocarbons) produced by them.

3 For example, there are more wind power stations installed in Germany nowadays than in any other country. In addition, three of the ten largest wind power manufacturers are located in Germany, as reported in McKinsey & Company (2008).

4 This literature was extended by models allowing countries to impose "sanctions" on defecting countries, Barrett (1992 and 1994a) and by models linking the negotiations of transboundary pollution with other issues, such as free-trade agreements; see Whalley (1991), Carraro and Siniscalco (2001), and Ederington (2002).

5 In a different setting, the literature on international trade has recently examined tariff agreements where countries are privately informed, for instance, about the extent to which the import-competing sector of another country is affected by an efficiency shock; see Lee (2007), Martin and Vergote (2008) and Bagwell (2009).

6 The leader observes its technology, while the follower is informed about the probability distribution over the leader's type. For instance, the follower could observe the type of products that the leader's economy mainly produces (e.g., raw materials, semiconductors, etc.) and use this information in order to assess the probability that the leader's technology is high.

7 The second-period investment game hence shares the incentive structure of standard public good games, where every country reduces pollutants, and the total reduction in emissions from the leader and follower produces an improvement in the global environmental quality. The only dimension of asymmetry in the model is therefore the leader's type.

8 In addition, as the benefit from joining an agreement with a high-type leader increases, relative to those of participating in a treaty with a low-type leader, the IEA becomes more attractive for the follower, who responds by joining under larger parameter conditions.

9 Similar to the unilateral uncertainty case, the leader, despite not observing the follower's technology, knows the probability distribution over the follower's types – that is, observes q.

10 The high-type leader, however, obtains a larger benefit from signing an agreement with a follower who is also a high-type country.

11 This indicates that the negotiation cost that the low-technology leader must incur outweighs the small environmental benefit of participating in an IEA with a follower whose type is also low, ultimately yielding a negative benefit from signing the agreement.

12 Recall that two low-technology countries choose the same set of second-period actions (e.g., reduction of pollutant emissions) when the treaty is signed and not signed. Hence, the follower's benefits from joining such an agreement are null, whereas the leader's benefits are negative since it must incur the negotiation costs.

13 Specifically, a decrease in these free-riding incentives produces an upward shift in cutoff $\bar{q}_L$ in Figure 4.3, thereby expanding the set of priors under which type-dependent strategy profiles can be sustained. For more details about cutoff $\bar{q}_L$, see EM (2010).

14 In particular, an increase in the benefits from signing an agreement with a high-type leader entails a leftward shift in cutoff $<pbar>_H$.
15 Similar to the randomizations described with only one follower, the low-type leader signs using mixed strategies, whereas the high-type leader participates with probability one; and at least one follower responds by joining the agreement with a probability between 0 and 1.

References

Bagwell, K. (2009) "Self-enforcing trade agreements and private information," *NBER Working Paper*, No. 14812.

Barrett, S. (1992) *Convention on Climate Change: Economic aspects of negotiations.* Paris: OECD.

Barrett, S. (1994a) "Strategic environmental policy and international trade," *Journal of Public Economics*, 54: 325–38.

Barrett, S. (1994b) "Self-enforcing international environmental agreements," *Oxford Economic Papers*, 46: 878–94.

Barrett, S. (1999) "A theory of full international cooperation," *Journal of Theoretical Politics*, 11: 519–41.

Carraro, C. and Siniscalco, D. (2001) "Transfers, commitments and issue linkage in international environmental negotiations," in A. Ulph (ed.), *Environmental Policy, International Agreements and International Trade*, Oxford: Oxford University Press.

Cesar, H. (1994) *Control and Game Models of the Greenhouse Effect*. Berlin: Springer-Verlag.

Ederington, J. (2002) "Trade and domestic policy linkage in international agreements," *International Economic Review*, 43(4): 1347–68.

Espinola-Arredondo, A. and Munoz-Garcia, F. (2010) "Keeping negotiations in the dark: Environmental agreements under incomplete information," School of Economic Sciences Working Paper series, 2010–20, Washington State University.

Espinola-Arredondo, A. and Munoz-Garcia, F. (2011) "When does disinformation promote successful treaties?" School of Economic Sciences Working Paper series, 2011–11, Washington State University.

Iida, K. (1993) "When and how do domestic constraints matter? Two-level games with uncertainty," *Journal of Conflict Resolution*, 37: 403–26.

Kreps, D., Milgrom, P., Roberts, J., and Wilson, R. (1982) "Rational cooperation in the finitely repeated prisoner's dilemma," *Journal of Economic Theory*, 27: 245–52.

Lee, G. M. (2007) "Trade agreements with domestic policies as disguised protection," *Journal of International Economics*, 71(1): 241–59.

Martin, L. (2005) "The president and international commitments: Treaties as signaling devices," *Presidential Studies Quarterly*, 35(3): 440–65.

Martin, A. and Vergote, W. (2008) "On the role of retaliation in trade agreements," *Journal of International Economics*, 76(1): 61–77.

McKinsey & Company (2008) "Germany 20|20: Future perspectives for the German economy," Frankfurt, Germany: McKinsey & Company.

Whalley, J. (1991) "The interface between environmental and trade policies," *The Economic Journal*, 101: 180–9.

5 Enforced geographic separation as a factor in avoiding the tragedy of the commons

Dmytro Zhosan and Roy Gardner

This chapter examines the potential effects of dividing a commons into smaller areas on appropriation efficiency. Most of the successful cases of collective action in common-pool resources (CPR) management involve some kind of geographic separation of the commons and subsequent assignment of de jure or de facto property rights. A simple model that incorporates separation and cooperation rules and norms into a standard game of the commons setup is presented, and conditions under which this game results in an efficient equilibrium are analyzed. We tested the conclusions of this model using a laboratory experiment utilizing both undergraduate students and professional fishermen, and our abbreviated results of this experiment appear below. This chapter shows that, under some simple assumptions, enforcing the geographic separation of a commons may become a valuable and effective tool in a successful co-management system.

5.1 Introduction

A lot of scholarly attention has been given to the "Tragedy of the Commons" since it was so named by Garrett Hardin in 1968. Economists, environmentalists and biologists have devoted countless studies to the phenomenon and have essentially had all the same findings; people are self-serving and will use a commonly owned resource to their personal advantage without giving much thought to group cooperation or sustaining the resource for later use. This has been commonly modeled as a Prisoner's Dilemma game, with each player's selfish interests leading to the downfall of the group and the depletion of a resource. Recognizing people's inability to make the best decisions for the society, in many instances, the government has stepped in to help the appropriators of the resource manage its use. This intervention has been met with much success in some circumstances and has proved no more successful than having left it alone in others. Having the government swoop in to rescue the resource is not the only option for conquering the tragedy of the commons. In this chapter, we present a simple intuition underlying a model that can be used to justify enforcing geographic separation as a policy tool in managing a commons, using fishery as an example. It is inspired by an example of a successful commons management by

Maine lobstermen, in which territoriality (first traditional and more recently formal) seems to be an important aspect in the industry's success. Our laboratory experiment, conducted using undergraduate students and industry professionals as subjects, provides results that support the claim that enforcing geographic separation may be a valuable co-management tool.

For the purpose of this chapter, the CPR will be defined following the guidelines outlined by Gardner *et al.* (1990) as "natural or man-made resources where exclusion is difficult, and yield is subtractable," focusing on the fact that one person's use of a resource diminishes the potential for other people's use of this resource, rather than particular ownership of the resource. With this type of a resource, the appropriation game easily becomes one of a Prisoner's Dilemma (PD) type. While it is in the best interest of all the users as a group to limit their effort, and thus preserve the resource for future use (or if destruction is not an issue here, to maximize the possible group rents extracted from the resource), the dominant strategy for every individual appropriator is to "defect" and increase their individual level of effort to maximize their rents. Since all the users will behave in this way, the tragedy of the commons will occur whenever the number of users is large enough (or, whenever all of the users combined have the capability to exert a total level of effort in excess of that, which maximizes group rents). For a more detailed discussion of Prisoner's Dilemma's application to CPR and its limitations, see Wade (1987).

If there is a unique equilibrium in this game, what can then explain the fact that we do observe a nontrivial number of examples in which commons are preserved and more or less successfully managed? From the theoretical standpoint, there are two possible explanations to the tragedy of the commons not showing in certain situations – i) in some cases, games other than Prisoners' Dilemma can be used to model the situations; ii) in the other cases, a simple Prisoners' Dilemma can be extended to include the repetitions, existence of social norms, other factors. Even without any other factors, Folk Theorem suggests cooperation as a possible subgame–perfect equilibrium in an infinitely repeated PD.

However, since people do not live infinitely long, modifying a utility function to include the effects of group affiliation seems like a reasonable way to go in explaining efficient examples of CPR appropriation. When repeated (even finitely repeated) game environment is combined with the existence of social norms, etc., one can easily imagine a situation in which appropriators will be interested in coming up with a set of rules governing the use of a CPR and then following these rules to maximize group rents.

5.2 Commons in theory and real life

Although Garrett Hardin is most frequently cited as the first to describe the "Tragedy of the Commons" in his 1968 article of the same title, the problem was recognized in society and discussed much earlier. Ostrom gives credit to Aristotle for recognizing that "what is common to the greatest number has the least care bestowed upon it. Everyone thinks chiefly of his own, hardly at all of the common interest" (Politics, Book II, Ch. 3, as quoted in Ostrom 1986, p. 2). It is obvious that the inefficiency in the use of a commons is derived from the "self-ishness" of the individuals; however, this "selfishness" is not at all malicious, but simply a result of a rational person's trying to maximize their own best utility in a complicated system.

Gordon (1954) demonstrated that an economically efficient level of fishing effort is generally lower than the level of effort that achieves "maximum sustained physical yield" (a typical target in government policies primarily relying on biological factors), and yet rational fishermen would end up exerting an even higher level of effort, thus completely dissipating any possible rents from the fishery.[1] The incentives of the fishermen to harvest as many fish as possible as quickly as possible are explained by the fact that a fish in the sea has no value to the fisherman because there is no guarantee that, if not caught immediately, it will be there to catch the next day (Gordon 1954).

Hardin's theory translated very easily and cleanly into a PD game, with its unique destructive Nash Equilibrium. However, multiple examples of relatively successful CPR management around the world suggested that other models may be more appropriate in some situations. Ostrom *et al.* (2002) suggested that not all problems related to CPR fit the PD framework so nicely. Other problems may more accurately be modeled by assurance games or games of chicken, depending on the exact details of each situation. Dawes (1980, pp. 182–3) argues that two-person repeated PD games are not representative of social dilemmas in general, since the key characteristics of a two-person repeated PD game generally do not apply with the large number of agents involved in a typical social dilemma situation.

Since the "tragic" outcome seems to be present in most of the theoretic models, a question arises of what can be done (or how the nature of a resource or appropriation process can be affected) so that the outcome will be more efficient. While there is no unique policy approach that can be applied to any and all commons in the world, several directions exist that can be loosely combined into privatization, complete government control and self-management categories. Zhosan (2009) provides a more detailed insight into these approaches.

Privatizing the resource is primarily intended to solve the non-excludability issue triggering the tragedy of the commons by making the appropriators bear the entire cost of their decisions and correspondingly increasing the efficiency. However, simple assignment of property rights may not be enough. Gibson *et al.* (2002) claim that institutions and users' incentives are more important than de jure property rights, and they use them to explain the observations of some communal forest plots being used more efficiently than privately owned ones.

Complete government control over the resource use is another policy that may help avoid the tragedy of the commons. Under this regime, government controls all (or most) of the aspects of the resource use and implements and enforces policies that are supposed to lead to an efficient outcome. In a typical fishery case, this kind of policy would involve licensing, catch quotas, regulation on gear and days at sea, etc. However, implementation lags and errors in data collection and reporting, combined with appropriators' resistance, often significantly decrease the efficiency of government control (see Zhosan 2009; Mason 2002), suggesting that while complete government control has the potential to solve the tragedy of the commons, it should be used as a last resort only if other means fail.

Collective action (either as complete self-management by appropriators or as some form of co-management of appropriators and the government) seems to be an appealing option for solving the tragedy of the commons problem. In both cases, should a correct set of incentives and institutions develop in the commons, an efficient outcome becomes more likely than the tragedy of the commons.

Self-management of the commons implies that the local community manages the common pool without any intervention from outside international authority, public agencies or governments (Ostrom 1986). If this policy can run successfully, its cost effectiveness to the government would be in the government's best interest. Faysse (2005) presents a thorough survey of different factors that may be affecting the efficiency of CPR appropriation under self-management. Based on these factors, and following evidence from the field and experimental laboratories, the appropriation of a commons has higher chances of being more efficient as more of the following conditions are met: a commons is a small, well-defined resource, and there is a small, well-defined group of appropriators of the resource who determine and modify the rules for access and use; members of the group are relatively homogeneous in their endowment, ability, goals and (limited) outside options; the appropriators have a shared goal of use and sustainment of the resource; the game is repeated infinitely or finitely but with an uncertain ending point; appropriators have close to perfect information about behavior/compliance of others; punishment for defectors must be predetermined and carried out.

Group size is quite reasonably put on top of this list. The argument that smaller groups will have a better chance of acting in a collectively efficient manner dates back to Olson (1965). One can easily see that most of the other conditions have a larger probability to hold in a smaller group than in a larger one.

Clearly, enforced geographic separation (as one of the tools of co-management discussed below) addresses some of the aspects, by decreasing the group size, limiting the outside options and, what may prove to be more important, creating stable groups of appropriators that can design rules, monitor the group members' behavior and, if necessary, punish the defectors. Another important contribution of enforced separation is that others cannot encroach on the group's conservation effort or (as in the case of the Maine lobster industry) the effects of the others' activities on the group's commons are quite limited. Based on the results of the experiment reported in this chapter, enforcing the geographic separation does not necessarily have to be accompanied by a priori assignment of formal property rights, which can make this an attractive policy choice, especially on the commons in which such assignment has a high probability of generating conflict (e.g., Chesapeake Bay crabbing industry).

All of the above characteristics can be found in the "lobster gangs" of Maine, which with their relatively unique structure provide a very interesting field for studying the efficient use of CPR. In Maine, a large population of lobster fishermen is organized into small communities on a geographic basis (official larger zones and semi-official smaller exclusive fishing areas – harbors). These communities are relatively homogeneous in most ways. Each community has its exclusive fishing areas that it can protect and also shares some fishing areas with the neighboring communities (for a more detailed description of territoriality, see Acheson and Gardner 2004). These exclusive territories developed historically and only relatively recently have been put into a legal framework. Each community sets its fishing rules within the general framework defined by state legislation and monitors how the members follow those rules. The game is played through generations, with sons replacing fathers, and everyone knows what everyone else is doing, so violators can be punished either informally (reputation, ostracism, etc.) or formally (fines, molested gear, etc.). For a more detailed summary of the Maine lobster industry, regulation and organization, see Acheson (1988, 2003).

If community self-management of the commons fails, due to a large population's lack of social control and/or inability to enforce the rules, the government can intervene to counter certain inefficiencies while still granting managerial power to the community, thus creating a co-management system. Co-management dictates a sharing of power between the government and the community, in which both parties play important roles in creating efficient and sustainable policies. The government contributes administrative assistance and/ or scientific expertise and enabling legislation, while the local resource users provide knowledge of the traditional management systems and practices developed from years of experience in the local environment. In a co-management scenario, the power of the government and the wisdom of the local community are jointly incorporated. In this scenario, government sets strategic goals that affect individuals' incentives and then individuals develop strategies to achieve those goals.

Co-management is a provocative alternative to the old Leviathan models and is becoming popular in the development of fishery models. Co-management theories share the idea that the resource users must become more involved in the management process. They must be allowed to participate in regulatory decision making, implementation and enforcement (Jentoft *et al.* 1998). Jentoft *et al.* offer two key arguments that support co-management. For one, the resource users possess knowledge, based on their experience, that may fruitfully add to fisheries science and, hence, produce more enlightened, effective and equitable remedies and solutions to the management challenge. They also claim that participation of users enhances the legitimacy of the regulatory regime and, hence, compliance.

In a number of fishery examples, including those provided by Ostrom (1986), Jentoft and Kristoffersen (1989) and Zhosan (2009), appropriators were able to manage the commons efficiently via either a self-management or a co-management system that involved some sort of territorial division and consequent use access restriction with a significant regulatory power granted to fishermen.

By incorporating community in management, new conditions arise that do not exist in the central government control. First and foremost, the government must be able to trust the community to follow set rules and there must not exist any incentive for the community to deviate from these rules. The government must be confident that the community will make beneficial decisions that promote biological and economic sustainability. Second, there must be an effective way of transferring management responsibilities between the government and the community. Community organizations must remain updated on their responsibilities to the fishing industry, and in doing so incur transaction costs. Both community and government must be willing to incur these costs accrued from sharing information.

Many fisheries are not part of a tight-knit community. For example, in offshore fisheries where the population of competitors is large, there is a "lack of social control" over the resource. A lack of social control means there will be huge incentives for individuals to cheat anonymously (i.e., overfishing or using illegal gear). In a situation like this, the conditions required for successful self-management do not hold. The population is too large, negating all local community trust, and there is no obvious way for local individuals to enforce the rules. Since these conditions are broken, fishermen will have the incentive to cheat the system by over-exploiting the stock. A government control may be necessary in a situation like this (which itself is problematic outside the exclusive economic zones), but as the example of New England groundfish industry shows (Zhosan 2009), even a long period of government control may not guarantee that the resource will be used efficiently. In private conversations with the authors (during the experimental sessions in 2009), a number of Maine groundfishermen cited the lack of access restrictions as one of the key reasons for the industry's decline and expressed their willingness to work cooperatively with the government and the other fishermen to restore the fisheries. Many of them perceived an introduction of territoriality (zoning system) similar to the one used in the lobster industry as a tool that would essentially force the fishermen to work cooperatively with each other to achieve an efficient outcome.

From the theoretical standpoint, several models can be used to analyze appropriators' behavior on a fishery that can be separated geographically into smaller areas. Even in a traditional PD-type game, changing the players' utility functions to include the effects of such factors as altruism, conscience, norms and, potentially, coercion can make agents' behavior more cooperative (Dawes 1980, pp. 175–8). The model described below presents a similar extension of a standard PD-type game and modifies players' utility functions to include the utility from being part of a cooperative group, following the rules of a group as well as punishment for not following those rules. While this model assumes that agents choose fishing areas at their own will (complete self-management), it can be easily modified to incorporate government policy by making the area choice decision carry an explicit cost.

This simple repeated game assumes a population of agents choosing their actions in a CPR-type setting. The commons is divided into two separate resources (areas), and each agent can only appropriate from one area in a given round. The production of each of the areas is described by the function $f_j(X_j)$, where X_j is the total level of effort exerted by all the agents in the area and the production functions are common knowledge. While putting a specific functional form on the production functions is not critical at the moment, the following requirements need to hold:

$$f'_j(X_j) > 0, \forall \ X_j < X^*_j,$$

$$f'_j(X_j) < 0, \forall \ X_j > X^*_j, \tag{1}$$

$$f'_j(X_j) = 0, \text{ when } X_j = X^*_j$$

and

$$f''_j(X_j) < 0.$$

Each agent is endowed with X_i perfectly divisible units of effort in every round that can be allocated between appropriation activity and leisure. Assume that the total effort endowment (individual effort endowment times the number of agents) is large enough to generate the tragedy of the commons result in each area in equilibrium. A unit of effort allocated to leisure pays zero to the agent,[2] and a unit of effort allocated to the appropriation activity brings the agent the payoff calculated as follows:

$$\pi_{ij} = \frac{f_j(X_j)}{X_j} x_{ij}. \tag{2}$$

Here, π_{ij} is the payoff of agent i in area j and x_{ij} is the effort level of agent i in area j. Under the standard tragedy of the commons assumptions, each agent is maximizing their utility $u_i(\pi_i)$ such that

$$\frac{du_i}{d\pi_i} > 0.$$

As long as the average product from the commons area is positive, the agent's payoff increases as their level of effort increases and thus individual's utility increases in their level of effort as well over this interval. If this setup is left the way it is, and in every round of the game an agent first chooses the area to appropriate in and then the level of appropriation effort, then the standard tragedy of the commons result will be achieved in both areas, assuming the game is finitely repeated. Over a number of rounds, assuming that moving between the areas does not cost anything to the agent, agents will be re-locating between the areas following the higher average product signal until they arrive at a stable equilibrium in which the average product in both areas will be equal to zero.

What if this standard setup is modified to allow the agents in the areas to come up with some rules that may potentially increase the appropriation efficiency? Unless changes to the game setup and the utility function are made, this will not change the tragedy of the commons result, since each agent will have an incentive to break the rules in the last round and thus any possible cooperation will break down from the very beginning.

Let us modify the game setup in the following manner. A game lasts for a finite number of rounds. In each round, agents first simultaneously and independently choose the area in which to exert the appropriation effort. Depending on their area choice, each agent receives payoff described by equation (2) and the corresponding level of utility. While there is no explicit cost to change the appropriation area between rounds,[3] in all but the first round of the game changing the areas means joining an already established group of appropriators. Since newcomers are rarely welcome in situations like this, some resistance from the established group members can be anticipated. While assuming that the new member will be directly punished for joining the group may be unrealistic, this group resistance can be modeled by depriving the newcomer of the "cooperation" utilities described in steps two and three for one round.

Next, the agents simultaneously and independently decide on whether or not to participate in the process of rule formation in the area. Since the production function in the area is common knowledge, so is the level of total effort that maximizes production. If a group is able to come up with the rule, this rule is aimed at maximizing the efficiency and under this rule each agent agrees to put in $x_{cij} = X^*_j/n_j$ units of effort, where n_j is the number of agents in area j. If a group is able to reach the agreement, each participating agent receives an additional utility $v_i(g_j)$, where g_j is the proportion of group members in the area that participated in the agreement. This utility function is increasing in g and is equal to zero if g_j is zero – the agreement was not reached.

After the "rule-making" stage, the agents simultaneously and independently make their decisions on effort levels. If an agent did not participate in the process of making rules, the agent is assumed to follow their dominant profit-maximizing strategy of maximizing the effort level at this stage. Those agents who participated in the rule-making process have the option of choosing the cooperative level of effort described above or defecting on the group agreement and following the individual profit-maximizing strategy by putting in $x_{dij} > X^*_j/n_j$ units of effort and thus behaving in the same manner as the agents who did not participate in the rule-making process. The round ends at this stage for the defecting agents. The round also ends at this stage if there were no defections and all of the agents in the area participated in the rule-making process and followed the group agreement. Agents receive additional utility from being part of the cooperative group represented by $\mu_i(c'_j)$, where c'_j is the proportion of group members that followed up on the agreement. This utility is equal to zero if nobody cooperates and follows "the more the merrier" rule as the proportion of cooperating agents increases. If not all of the agents cooperated or defected in this stage, the game proceeds to the fourth stage, otherwise the next round begins with the first stage.

At this stage, after observing all agents' effort levels, cooperating agents can choose whether or not to punish the defectors. While one can make punishing the defectors costly, for simplicity of this analysis the cost of punishing the defectors is assumed to be zero. In fact, the punisher receives a constant positive utility z_i from enforcing the rules, but only if the punishment is targeted at a defecting agent. This utility from punishment is set at a low positive value in order to make the agent not indifferent between punishing and not punishing the defectors. This "sweet revenge" essentially guarantees that any deviation from the established appropriation rules will be punished by the cooperating individuals and may even be enough to overcome the positive cost of punishment should one be introduced in the model. The defector then receives the (dis)utility $w_{ij}(n_j^c/n_j^d)$, where n_j^c is the number of cooperating agents in the area and n_j^d is the number of defecting agents in the area. This disutility function is equal to zero if there were no cooperating agents (thus nobody punished) and is strictly decreasing in n_j^c/n_j^d.

Since in a finitely repeated PD setup it is the incentive to cheat in the last round that destroys any chance of cooperation, let us consider the utilities in the last round to see if cooperation can be supported as equilibrium in this modified game. The utility of a cooperating agent who did not change the appropriation area in the last round of this game, assuming some of the agents defect on the agreement, is as follows

$$U_{ij}^c = u_i\left(\frac{f_j(X_j)*X_j^*}{X_j*n_j}\right) + v_i(g_j) + \mu_i(c_j') + z_i \ . \tag{3}$$

If, on the other hand, no other agents defected, the utility of the same cooperating agent is described by the following function:

$$U_{ij}^c = u_i\left(\frac{f_j(X_j^*)}{n_j}\right) + v_i(g_j) + \mu_i(c_j'). \tag{4}$$

Considering that the value of z is very low, a cooperating individual will strictly prefer the all-cooperate outcome to an outcome in which even one individual defects as each component of his utility function (except for the very low z) will be strictly higher in the cooperation outcome than in the defection one.

Now consider defecting agents. The utility of a defecting agent who participated in the rule-making process is described by equation (5), and the utility of a defecting agent who did not participate in the rule-making process is described by equation (6), assuming these agents did not change the appropriation area in the last round.

$$U_{ij}^d = u_i\left(\frac{f_j(X_j)}{X_j}*x_{ij}\right) + v_i(g_j) + w_i\left(\frac{n_j^c}{n_j^d}\right) \tag{5}$$

$$U_{ij}^d = u_i\left(\frac{f_j(X_j)}{X_j}*x_{ij}\right) + w_i\left(\frac{n_j^c}{n_j^d}\right) \tag{6}$$

Other things being equal, the agent who has an intention to defect and follow individual profit-maximizing strategy would strictly prefer participating in the rule-making process and then defecting on the agreement, since the second component of the utility function (5) is non-negative and thus (5) > (6). The question then becomes under what circumstances defecting on the group agreement becomes not an optimal strategy for an agent. In other words, under what circumstances is the utility in equation (3) greater than the utility in equation (5), assuming the same level of total effort in the area? While the exact answer depends on the specific forms of the utility and production function components, one can claim that in a group where a sufficiently large number of agents cooperates in creating the rules and then follows those rules, it will be optimal for other agents to also cooperate, since the high positive value of the third component of equation (3) combined with high negative value of the third component of equation (5) may well exceed the effect of increased appropriation effort payoff. In fact, one may claim in this model that, if all agents defect after the rule-making round, an agent may benefit by starting to follow the group optimal policy and then punishing the defectors in exchange for z.

What about the area choice? Since switching the area involves the loss of all the cooperation components of the utility function, an agent will have an incentive to switch the area only if the average payoff from fishing in his new area significantly exceeds the average payoff from fishing in his prior area. While this may be the case in early rounds of the game, this payoff differential will be eliminated quickly by rational agents moving into the area with a higher payoff. Once the utility from payoff differential becomes lower than the cooperation utility sacrificed, all the area changing activities will seize and the appropriator group will reach a stable equilibrium with all the agents cooperating on the efficient outcome. While one may argue that area choice is not by itself an efficiency-improving factor, a situation similar to the zoning regulation of the lobster industry described above illustrates the area option importance quite well. In a real-life environment, agents may be more likely to cooperate with the group if they need to limit their effort by 25 percent, rather than by 50 percent. Creating smaller areas within the commons achieves just that. As the number of appropriators in an area decreases, each appropriator can exert a higher level of effort and thus needs to "sacrifice" less.

Thus, addition of rules and norms to the standard utility function in the PD-type commons game affects the equilibrium and suggests that the tragedy of the commons result is not unavoidable. Zhosan and Gardner (2011) report the detailed results of an experiment conducted using a model similar to the one described above. A brief description of this experiment and the summary of this experiment's results are provided in the next section.

Analyzing the results of this experiment helps in answering the following questions in a repeated-game environment. First, since most commons can be separated into smaller areas, what will the appropriator's behavior be like if the separation is not enforced in any manner and they are free to choose any area without restriction or cost? Second, will enforcing the separation be enough by itself to increase appropriation efficiency and, more importantly, generate some sort of cooperative behavior among subjects? Since enforced separation essentially creates smaller appropriator groups with limited exit opportunities, is it possible that the agents, especially when they know the collectively efficient outcome, will start behaving in the efficient manner at their own will, without additional institutions? Or do Olson's predictions about small-group efficiency need a stronger sense of group identity, potentially one introduced by communication?

Very few people would argue that pre-decision communication has a significant effect on individual behavior in experiments involving social dilemmas by increasing the proportion of cooperative decisions made by the subjects. Dawes (1980) reports the results of a number of experiments (e.g., Rapoport *et al.* 1962; Bixenstine *et al.* 1966; Edney and Harper 1978a, 1978b) in which the authors find that communicating groups cooperated more. In their own study, Dawes *et al.* (1977) observed that communication about the dilemma increased the proportion of cooperative decisions to 72 percent, compared to 31 percent in the no-communication setting. In fact, in this study, Dawes *et al.* (1977) utilized a framework that allowed them to go beyond the simple communication/no-communication analysis and to study the effects of different potential aspects of communication on individual behavior. They separated the effects of humanization (getting acquainted with the other group members through an unrelated communication), discussion (discussing the dilemma with the other group members) and commitment (discussion followed by group members making commitments about their behavior and trying to elicit commitments from the others). Their experiment allowed them to conclude that humanization had no effect on the behavior, compared to the no-communication setting, and that commitment (at least one required by the experimenters) had no effect compared to the discussion setting.

In a more recent study, Ostrom *et al.* (1992) studied the effects of communication, punishment and communication combined with punishment in an experimental CPR environment. They found that repeated communication increased efficiency levels to 99 percent in low-endowment treatments and 73 percent in high-endowment treatments, with defection rates of 5 and 13 percent, respectively. This leads to the third question addressed in the experiment below: since separation allows for smaller groups to be created, and also allows the appropriators to compare their results to those of other group(s), will allowing communication within the areas increase efficiency more significantly than what was reported previously in the literature? The existence of another group operating on the neighboring commons may either provide an example of more efficient cooperative behavior that can be followed or provide an example of inefficient uncooperative behavior and its consequences. In either case, this may have an additional efficiency-improving effect. The fourth question addressed in this experiment is whether or not the smaller group size will increase the effectiveness of informal punishment of defectors (see Masclet *et al.* 2003 for rationale and analysis of informal punishment in public goods experiments).

5.3 Experimental design, results and discussion

Readers interested in detailed descriptions of experimental procedures, production and payoff functions, derivation of the efficient outcome and Nash equilibria, as well as numerical results, should refer to Zhosan and Gardner (2011). The experiment involved subjects recruited from undergraduate student populations at Bates College and Ripon College, as well as two groups of professionals recruited among Maine lobstermen and groundfishermen (a total of 120 subjects in 15 trials). Trials were conducted in three protocols: baseline, enforcement and treatment.

In the baseline protocol, each trial consisted of two sets of ten identical settings to account for the potential influence of the restart effect in the enforcement and treatment protocols. In the enforcement protocol, each trial consisted of four sets of ten identical settings to create conditions similar to the treatment protocol and provide a baseline learning pattern. In the treatment protocol, each trial consisted of four settings: enforcement, enforcement after information provision, communication and punishment.

In all protocols, each setting consisted of ten rounds. In each round, subjects were endowed with 15 hours to allocate between fishing in two defined commons (fishing areas Alpha and Beta) and/or taking advantage of an outside opportunity. Each fishing area had a quadratic production function with decreasing returns to scale, according to the rules described above. One of the areas was made more productive than the other. Based on their decisions in each round (a total of 20 rounds in baseline protocol and 40 rounds in other protocols), subjects earned points. Subjects were paid in cash, in private, at the end of a trial, at a defined exchange rate from points to dollars (students – 240 points per dollar, fishermen – 48 points per dollar). The exchange rate was provided in the experimental instructions.

Eight subjects participated in each trial. According to the design, the efficient outcome occurred with three subjects choosing area Alpha and five subjects choosing area Beta. In addition to this, to achieve 100 percent efficiency, each subject had to limit the number of hours allocated to fishing to ten hours – two-thirds of the subject's total time endowment. At the same time, the symmetric Subgame Perfect Nash Equilibrium (SPNE) of this repeated game had the same allocation of subjects across all areas, with each subject spending the entire time endowment on fishing. This SPNE resulted in 75 percent efficiency.

Baseline protocol (three trials) was implemented to address the first question above. In this protocol, in each round subjects were first asked to identify the fishing area of their choice and, then, after being informed of the total number of subjects in their area (but not the identities of those subjects), were asked to decide on the number of hours they wanted to spend fishing. After the round ended, all subjects were informed of the total effort level in each area, average return to fishing in each area and (privately) the number of points they earned. Then the next round began with the fishing area choice for that round. In this protocol, the separation was not enforced, meaning that if a subject wanted to move to a different fishing area in the next round, this decision carried no cost to the subject. This protocol consisted of two identical ten-round settings with a ten-minute break between the settings.

The results of this baseline protocol highlighted some of the problems facing policy makers in the commons situation. In the absence of enforcement, even the smallest differences in return to fishing (as low as 0.04 of a point per hour) between the areas immediately triggered the reallocation of a large number of subjects into the more productive area. Even though 15/60 rounds ended with an efficient number of subjects in each area (three–five split described above), only three of those rounds were consecutive with the same group composition, suggesting a need for a factor that can increase the stability of this allocation to allow the subjects to start considering the effects of their fishing effort decisions rather in addition to location choices. Additionally, the fact that 12/60 rounds ended with seven subjects in an area that was significantly more productive in the previous round suggests that the grim picture of appropriators destroying the commons by "wiping out" one area after another, based on their relative productivity, is, in fact, quite realistic.

The two major policy problems outlined by the baseline protocol are the unpredictability of the number of appropriators in an area at any given moment, which has the potential to complicate the design and implementation of many policy decisions based on biological targets (e.g., days at sea regulation, trap limits, etc.); and the instability of group composition, which essentially eliminates any chance for potential group cooperation on conservation efforts, especially considering the fact that any effort limitation resulting in a higher payoff in an area would result in "outsiders" coming in in the next time period. In fact, there was no evidence of group behavior aimed at effort limitation in the baseline protocol.

Enforcing the geographic separation has the potential to alleviate these two problems, and the enforcement protocol (four trials) was implemented to test the effects of such enforcement on individual and group behavior as well as efficiency. This protocol primarily addressed the second question identified at the end of the previous section. The decision-making process in the enforcement protocol trials was identical to that of the baseline protocol trials with one exception. In this protocol, changing the fishing area from the previous round carried a cost of 24 points. One can view this cost as either the utility loss due to reallocation as described above or purely a policy variable that a government can control.

The introduction of an enforced separation clearly addressed one of the policy maker's problems described above – the stability of the number of users in an area. Not only did the introduction of a movement cost decrease the number of moves and the number of subjects relocating in response to payoff differences, but also the minimum difference in payoffs needed to trigger reallocation of subjects went up compared to the baseline protocol trials, even after accounting for the movement cost. The occurrence of an extremely large number of subjects fishing in one area became extremely rare – 3/160 rounds – and the SPNE allocation of users clearly was the modal allocation of subjects, occurring in 94/160 rounds. Since communication was not allowed in this protocol, and every setting (a total of 16) started with no area assignment (other than the knowledge of the prior history in settings two through four of each trial), most of the settings did not start with an efficient number of users in each area, but as the setting progressed, the subjects were able to solve the coordination problem, arriving at the three–five user split across areas, with this allocation becoming quite stable. Most of the settings (10/16) ended up with five or more consecutive rounds resulting in the SPNE number of users in each area, three of these settings having nine such rounds, and in one of the settings all ten rounds exhibited this user allocation.

This shows that creating clearly defined areas within the commons has the potential of establishing the stable groups of appropriators even without the formal assignment of property rights. This result is quite important, considering the fact that any assignment of property rights over the commons by the policy maker is likely to be met with some degree of resistance, unless it merely formalizes a traditional arrangement (akin to the zoning system in the Maine lobster industry). After the smaller areas are created on the commons, over time the appropriators can solve the coordination problem with each area being used by an efficient number of users. Stable groups will be formed and the potential for a successful co-management system will be created. The analysis of efficiencies in the enforcement protocol supports this expectation. The test for difference in means of per-round net efficiencies between the rounds in which the coordination problem was successfully solved (mean=0.839) and the ones in which the coordination problem was not solved (mean=0.772) produced a significant result (t=2.771, p-value=0.007), indicating the efficiency-improving potential of enforced geographic separation.

At the same time, it does not look like this creation of the stable groups was by itself sufficient to encourage subjects to limit their fishing effort in the experiment. Data show that, as subjects become more experienced and learn more about the resource's capacity and the behavior of the others, their fishing behavior approaches that of the SPNE prediction (i.e., fishing for the entire 15 hours in each round) rather than that of the efficient group payoff-maximizing effort limitation. Even though in every group some subjects tried to signal their willingness to limit the fishing effort, the suit was not followed and, as trials progressed, all subjects increased their fishing effort, leading to the situation in which efficiencies of above 90 percent were quite common in the first settings of all trials, but nearly disappeared in the last two. One should notice that in this protocol subjects could not formally identify with the members of their groups, thus behavior in one's own best interest seems quite logical. The communication setting introduced in the treatment protocol aimed at addressing this issue.

This protocol involved both student subjects (six trials) and professional lobstermen and groundfishermen (one trial each). The first two settings of the treatment protocol were exactly the same as the settings in the enforcement protocol and, not surprisingly, demonstrated similar behavioral patterns. The information session between those treatments essentially sped up the learning process described above. In the third setting of this protocol, subjects were allowed to communicate with others in their fishing area for up to three minutes before making their fishing effort decisions. The individual effort decisions and payoffs were kept private and not disclosed to the groups. Even though the communication was completely voluntary, only 1/64 subjects openly refused to participate in the communication sessions.[4] While based on the earlier experimental results (i.e., Ostrom *et al.* 1992) it was expected that communication would increase the efficiency, the effect of communication observed in this protocol exceeded all expectations.

With communication, all groups but one (the groundfishermen group) reached the efficient number of users in each area by the second round of the setting, the groups became stable and communication boiled down to discussing the optimal strategies and trying to convince the occasional defectors to behave in accordance with the group agreements. While not all of the subjects followed the agreements reached by the groups, with 24/64 subjects defecting at least once, the appropriation efficiency still increased drastically. In all groups, the introduction of communication produced a significant increase in efficiencies compared to the last non-communication setting. Even though lobstermen demonstrated the lowest average efficiency of all groups (the group was "experimenting," trying to beat the system), their average efficiency was still more than 95 percent, much higher than that observed in earlier experiments involving communication on the commons.

The results of this setting support earlier observations that communication significantly increases the appropriation efficiency on the commons. Moreover, they provide a compelling case in favor of a co-management system, in which the government creates institutions that involve appropriators in the decision-making process. Separating the commons in this case allows for smaller groups to be created, and with a smaller group the appropriators are less willing to defect on group agreements, even if the identity of a defector is unknown. When some of the participants were asked why they never defected on the group agreement, they answered "It was not worth it," suggesting that in a small(er) community the utility from being part of a cooperating group can outweigh the potential monetary gains from defecting. In addition, knowing that outsiders cannot easily capitalize on conservation efforts of a group (whether these efforts are caused by the desire to maximize the group payoff or the intent to preserve the resource for future use) provides an additional stimulus for the group members to cooperate on establishing the rules aimed at achieving the efficient outcome.

As mentioned earlier, another important factor in maintaining the cooperation is the group's ability to identify and punish the defectors. The fourth setting of the treatment protocol allowed the subjects to do so by informing them of the individual effort levels of other subjects in their area and providing them with the ability to express their dissatisfaction with the others' behavior. In this setting, if a subject received a warning (informal punishment) in more than two rounds, this subject lost 50 points for every third warning received. The sanctioning mechanism turned out to be quite effective, increasing the efficiency in seven out of eight groups. In one group, the efficiency decreased due to a punishment war that started after one of the subjects was punished without committing an offense. On the individual level, of the 24 subjects who defected on group agreements in the communication treatment, only eight defected when punishment was an option. They seemingly disregarded the informal punishment, but made sure not to defect often enough to trigger the point loss. Even the non-cooperative subject mentioned above decided to start cooperating after having received two warnings from the other group members.

The results of this punishment setting are consistent with those reported by Masclet *et al.* (2003) and suggest two important conclusions. First, small groups of appropriators can, by themselves, be quite efficient at monitoring the behavior of group members and maintaining cooperation within groups by punishing the defectors. Second, in small groups, informal punishment (bad reputation, ostracism, etc.) has the potential to increase cooperation without the negative efficiency effects of formal sanctions (fines, etc.). In this aspect, enforced geographic separation can aid the groups significantly by decreasing the monitoring costs and increasing the efficiency of a sanctioning mechanism. The mechanism, however, has to be used with caution to avoid the punishment wars similar to the one mentioned above.

5.4 Conclusions and policy implications

The tragedy of the commons is certainly not unavoidable. Group size, group homogeneity and the type of games that appropriators play all contribute to the efficiency of CPR appropriation and may explain the multiple success stories observed in the real world. Smaller, well-defined homogeneous groups with common goals tend to be more efficient than larger and less homogeneous groups in which common goals are not easily defined. Government intervention in the commons may help solve the problem, but is not guaranteed to work unless it is conducted in a timely manner and is successful in creating the incentives to cooperate among the appropriators. Co-management may be a viable alternative to self-management or complete government control if certain conditions are met. Appropriators' ability to separate the commons into smaller areas based on geographic principle also has a potential to create efficiency-contributing group arrangements.

As shown above, enforced geographic separation may be a useful tool in solving the problems of the efficient commons appropriation. One should understand that this separation is not a panacea by itself but rather one of the steps in implementing a successful co-management system. In this kind of system, a government does its part by first dividing a larger commons into smaller areas and creating rules that complicate free movement of appropriators between areas. As discussed above, the government does not need to go further and establish property rights or assign specific appropriators to a certain area, thus avoiding a potential conflict over an "unfair" assignment. Based on the experimental results, appropriators will create an efficient allocation of users over all areas over time.

The one thing that needs to be taken into consideration is that most of the experimental and theoretical results above apply in a situation in which the group of appropriators is sufficiently small, as the efficiency of communication, enforcement cost and the effectiveness of informal punishment rely significantly on small-group dynamics and values. This suggests that, in creating the smaller areas, a policy maker should always analyze the equilibrium number of appropriators in each area to allow for small manageable groups. At the same time, creating too many areas may result in higher management costs, thus negating potential benefits of co-management. There is no rule of thumb as to the optimal group size, as it would depend on the specific population of appropriators, their traditions, institutions and cultural norms.

The results discussed in this chapter can be generalized to cases in which the appropriator groups are not homogeneous. While in most real-world situations the appropriators differ in their endowments, ability, utility and other characteristics, these differences per se do not automatically preclude the groups from designing and implementing efficient rules. The existence of such differences also does not necessarily suggest that certain appropriators will be more likely to defect on group agreements or take actions that go against the logic of collective efficiency. The case of the Maine lobster industry, among others, provides an example of groups in which internal heterogeneity does not impair efficiency.

Fishermen in these groups differ in their wealth, quality of equipment, ability, experience and knowledge of the fishery. At the same time, they all work together devising rules, which are often more restrictive than the one imposed by state legislation, and defections from these rules are uncommon. Generally in these communities, the wealthier and more experienced fishermen serve as leaders when it comes to rule creation and enforcement, keeping group benefit in mind, consistent with the idea first expressed by Olson (1965). One may argue that it is the existence of heterogeneity that allows the leadership to form in this situation, and thus it is an example of a situation in which heterogeneity improves efficiency. In fact, quite often new group members (fishermen just entering the industry) are allowed by the groups to utilize more traps than the other group members (i.e., exert a higher effort level) and receive other advantages so that they can faster recover the significant entry capital costs. This tradition seems to pursue two goals. The first goal is an expectation of reciprocity – an appreciative person will be less likely to disobey the group decisions later. The second goal is more materialistic – a person who is in a financial hardship will be more likely to try and increase their profit by free-riding on the conservation efforts of the others.

The theoretical analysis in section 5.2 does not rely on an assumption that all agents are identical or that all users participate in rule creation or follow the socially efficient rules. It merely suggests that, if the number of cooperating agents in the group is large enough, the others would follow suit. The case of the uncooperative fisherman observed in the experiment confirms this expectation. One can anticipate that the critical proportion of cooperating agents necessary to make following the rules a dominant strategy for everyone would be directly related to the degree of heterogeneity in the group. Faysse (2005, pp. 242–7) surveys multiple studies addressing the theoretical aspects and evidence pertaining to the effects of heterogeneity on the appropriation efficiency on the commons. He concludes that the effects of most types of heterogeneity on the efficiency are at best ambiguous. The one type of heterogeneity that can hinder efficiency is heterogeneity in exit options (Faysse 2005, p. 247). This result is not surprising, as agents with more attractive outside options will be less concerned about preserving the resource for future use. However, as long as the number of such agents is relatively small compared to the group size, the others can adjust their behavior to accommodate the non-cooperators, giving up equality in favor of group efficiency.

While the introduction of enforced separation is likely to be originally met with opposition by some of the current appropriators, it is highly likely that this opposition will eventually give way to cooperation under the influence of the other group members. In the Maine groundfish industry, mentioned above, fishermen admitted that they viewed the potential introduction of territoriality and co-management as a way for the group to bring everyone into cooperation with the others for the greater good of the resource, much like the uncooperative subject that was forced to follow the group's optimal behavior.

Once smaller areas are created, the government should pass most of the managing powers over these areas onto the appropriators, allowing them to utilize their expertise in devising the appropriation rules, monitoring the group members' behavior and penalizing the defectors. Additionally, this can make the rule-creation process more efficient by eliminating the significant bureaucratic lags often present in policy making. The importance of appropriators' experience should not be underestimated. In the experiment reported above, professionals were able to achieve higher appropriation efficiency than the students in the settings where the institutions were minimal (no communication or punishment). This suggests that appropriators do have enough knowledge and experience to implement the institutions needed to manage the resource efficiently on their own. Enforcing the geographic separation in this situation would increase the effectiveness of these institutions by minimizing the potential free-riding by the outsiders.

Notes

1 One can logically follow Gordon's path all the way to Hardin's "Tragedy of the Commons" as exceeding the "maximum sustainable yield" has the potential to completely destruct the resource.
2 Setting payoff from leisure equal to zero is simply a normalization of payoffs. One can set it at a level above zero and change the payoffs from the commons accordingly.
3 As mentioned above, this can be changed to incorporate government policy. Introduction of a positive movement cost will only strengthen the result.
4 This subject, a groundfisherman, claimed that in real life fishermen keep their intentions secret and do not discuss anything with the others, and that he intended to keep his behavior as close to real life as possible. Other members of his cohort were willing to work with each other to accommodate the non-cooperative subject, and the group

was still able to reach very high efficiency levels. At the same time, the unwillingness to communicate and cooperate was not observed among the lobstermen, probably because they have a tradition of working cooperatively on devising and implementing the conservation rules in the industry on multiple levels, from small harbor "gangs" to larger zones.

References

Acheson, J. (1988) *The Lobster Gangs of Maine*. Hanover, NH: University Press of New England.

Acheson, J. (2003) *Capturing the Commons: Devising Institutions to Manage the Maine Lobster Industry*. Hanover, NH: University Press of New England.

Acheson, J. and Gardner, R. (2004) "Strategies, conflict and the emergence of territoriality: The case of the Maine lobster industry," *American Anthropologist*, 106(2): 296–307.

Bixenstine, V.E., Levitt, C.A. and Wilson, K.V. (1966) "Collaboration among six persons in a Prisoner's Dilemma game," *Journal of Conflict Resolution,* 10: 488–96.

Dawes, R.M. (1980) "Social dilemmas," *Annual Review of Psychology*, 31: 169–93.

Dawes, R.M., McTavish, J. and Shaklee, H. (1977) "Behavior, communication, and assumptions about other people's behavior in a commons dilemma situation," *Journal of Personality and Social Psychology*, 35(1): 1–11.

Edney, J.J. and Harper, C.S. (1978a) "Heroism in a resource crisis: A simulation study," *Environmental Management*, 2(6) 523–7.

Edney, J.J. and Harper, C.S. (1978b) "The effects of information in a resource management problem: A social trap analog," *Human Ecology*, 6(4): 387–95.

Faysse, N. (2005) "Coping with the Tragedy of the Commons: Game structure and design of rules," *Journal of Economic Surveys*, 19(2): 239–61.

Gardner, R., Ostrom, E. and Walker, J. (1990) "The nature of common pool resource problems," *Rationality and Society*, 2: 335–58.

Gibson, C.C., Lehoucq, F.E. and Williams, J.T. (2002) "Does privatization protect natural resources? Property rights and forests in Guatemala," *Social Science Quarterly*, 83(1): 206–25.

Gordon, H. (1954) "The economic theory of a common property resource: The fishery," *Journal of Political Economy*, 62: 124–42.

Hardin, G. (1968) "The Tragedy of the Commons," *Science*, 162: 1243–8.

Jentoft, S. and Kristoffersen, T. (1989) "Fishermen's co-management: The case of the Lofoten fishery," *Human Organization*, 48(4): 355–65.

Jentoft, S., McCay, B.J. and Wilson, D.C. (1998) "Social theory and fisheries co-management," *Marine Policy*, 22: 423–36.

Masclet, D., Noussair, C., Tucker, S. and Villeval, M.-C. (2003) "Monetary and nonmonetary punishment in the voluntary contributions mechanism," *The American Economic Review*, 93(1): 366–80.

Mason, F. (2002) "The Newfoundland cod stock collapse: A review and analysis of social factors," *Electronic Green Journal*, 1(17), available at: http://escholarship.org/uc/item/19p7z78s.

Olson, M. (1965) *The Logic of Collective Action: Public Goods and the Theory of Groups*. Cambridge, MA: Harvard University Press.

Ostrom, E. (1986) "How inexorable is the Tragedy of the Commons? Institutional arrangements for changing the structure of social dilemmas," Distinguished Faculty Research Lecture, Indiana University.

Ostrom, E., Dietz, T., Dolsak, N., Stonich, S. and Weber, C. (eds) (2002) *The Drama of the Commons*. Washington, DC: National Academy Press.

Ostrom, E., Walker, J. and Gardner, R. (1992) "Covenants with and without a sword: Self-governance is possible," *The American Political Science Review*, 86(2): 404–17.

Rapoport, A., Chammah, A., Dwyer, J. and Gyr, J. (1962) "Three-person non-zero-sum nonnegotiable games," *Behavioral Science*, 7: 38–58.

Wade, R. (1987) "The management of common property resources: Collective action as an alternative to privatization or state regulation," *Cambridge Journal of Economics*, 11(2): 95–106.

Zhosan, D. (2009) "Nash Equilibria on a spatial commons: Theory and experimental evidence," Ph.D. thesis, Indiana University.

Zhosan, D. and Gardner, R. (2011) "Problems of the commons: Group behavior, cooperation and punishment in a two-harbor experiment," paper presented at the 8th Meeting on Game Theory and Practice Dedicated to Global and International Issues University of California, Riverside, July 2011.

6 Experimental studies of games with a dynamic public bad

Svetlana Pevnitskaya and Dmitry Ryvkin

We employ a laboratory experiment to investigate the effects of environmental context and termination uncertainty on decisions in a dynamic game with a public bad. Every period, subjects decide on their own production level that generates private revenue and "emissions." Emissions accumulate over time and act as a public bad. We characterize and use as benchmarks the Markov perfect equilibrium and social optimum, and find that observed decisions are between the two predictions. We find no significant effect of termination uncertainty on decisions in all except the last few rounds where, in a fixed-end setting, subjects allocate their entire endowment to production. We find a strong effect of environmental context that partially substitutes for experience. The effect of experience is most pronounced in the fixed-end treatment, in which production allocations and the level of the public bad become lower after the restart.

6.1 Introduction

In the last two to three decades, considerable attention has been given to global environmental problems created by the byproducts of industrial progress, such as greenhouse gas emissions and other types of pollution. Most economies face costs of climate change, pollution, disappearing species, and resources. International efforts to curb the cost of pollution and climate change aim at creating efficient institutions promoting joint efforts at emission reductions, such as the Kyoto Protocol. At the United Nations Climate Change Conference in 2011, COP17 in Durban, the 194 parties to the UNFCCC agreed on a package of decisions known as the Durban Platform, which include the launch of a protocol or legal instrument that would apply to all members, a second commitment period for the existing Kyoto Protocol, and the launch of the Green Climate Fund.[1] An advanced framework for the reporting of emission reductions for both developed and developing countries was also agreed upon, taking into consideration the common but differentiated responsibilities of different countries. These initiatives address one of the main problems of the failure of the current Kyoto Protocol; namely, heterogeneity in emissions and industrial development among countries. One of the latest setbacks since the COP17 agreement is Canada's withdrawal from the Kyoto Protocol. This apparent lack of success in achieving efficient solutions calls for more thorough economic analysis of incentives of participating countries, including the effects of heterogeneity.

Most economic models of successful coordination and cooperation of players have been defined in the domain of gains. One of the common models is a setting of a "public good" which, if provided, benefits all the participants regardless of the level of their contribution. The problems of pollution and climate change open a new direction in economic analysis, as they impose costs (rather than benefits) on all participants, regardless of who generated them. Such an environment leads to a new class of problems involving a "public bad." Further, unlike the typical static public good game, the effects of pollution accumulate over time. A study led by the National Oceanic and Atmospheric Administration (Solomon *et al.* 2010) indicated that it would take more than 1,000 years to reverse changes in temperatures and sea levels, even if all carbon dioxide emissions were to stop immediately. Therefore, the effect of emissions on climate change (and associated costs) requires a dynamic approach to analysis. There is a relatively new but already established literature on theoretical models of games with a dynamic public bad.[2] While these models propose self-enforcing mechanisms leading to curbed emissions, low rates of success of existing environmental agreements, as well as findings of deviations of actual human behavior from theoretical predictions in other settings, suggest the experimental investigation of decision making in games with a dynamic public bad as a promising alternative approach.

Economic experiments have become an established methodology for exploring the robustness and applicability of theoretical predictions to the success of real policies and institutions. Human decisions are almost always affected by behavioral considerations that are not part of classical "rationality" assumptions about economic agents. The economic experiments allow the identification of which (if any) parts of the mechanism or institution may trigger such deviations and therefore reduce or eliminate the desired objectives. In this chapter, we provide an overview of experimental results of behavior in games with a dynamic public bad, based on Pevnitskaya and Ryvkin (2011, 2013), and discuss their policy implications.

The research questions addressed in these studies range from testing theoretical assumptions of dynamic public bad models to exploring behavioral regularities. Slow reduction of pollution and weak response to existing incentives may be due to the fact that decision makers have difficulty in anticipating the dynamic and accumulating costs of pollution and climate change, and care only about their current profits from production. Another factor affecting behavior is the degree to which other-regarding considerations play a role in agents' decisions in this type of game; specifically, are agents concerned with overall costs and benefits to the society or only with their own profits? Both of these theoretical questions are crucial for the design of successful policies. Agents' heterogeneity has been identified as one of the obstacles in the efficiency of international agreements. Developing countries, many of which operating obsolete and highly polluting technologies, are not willing to sacrifice their economic growth by setting targets for low emissions. Using an experimental setting, we can evaluate the extent (if any) to which social welfare matters in decisions of high-pollution agents. At the same time, we can explore the decisions of low-pollution agents in the heterogeneous setting. New policies such as transfers of benefits may alleviate some of the barriers in the design of future agreements.

We also discuss policy implications of behavioral phenomena that can be tested in the experimental laboratory. Considerable resources are devoted worldwide for educating the public about the dangers and costs of climate change and pollution. We are also beginning to observe efforts to promote pro-environmental values. If such values and preferences matter in deciding the trade-off between production and pollution reduction, it is important to evaluate them. The presence of such phenomena in the laboratory would indicate strong evidence of the effect of pro-environmental preferences on behavior.

The rest of the chapter is organized as follows: The next section describes a theoretical framework and experimental design used to test the policy-relevant questions outlined above. Section 6.3 reports on the main findings. Section 6.4 provides policy implications, and section 6.5 concludes.

6.2 Methodology

6.2.1 Model environment

The experiments were conducted in the controlled environment of the laboratory that mimics key features of economic decision making in the presence of anthropogenic climate change.[3] All the experiments have been conducted in the same basic setting of a multi-period game in which subjects, representing firms or countries, make production decisions that generate private revenue, but have an environmental byproduct in the form of accumulating "emissions." Emissions act as a "public bad," imposing a cost on all participants.

In our design, subjects are matched in groups of two that stay fixed over the entire duration of the experiment. In each period, each subject is awarded an endowment of ten experimental tokens. The subjects then decide how many tokens to keep and how many to expend as an input in the production process. The subjects' revenue for the period is the sum of the tokens they keep and the production input tokens multiplied by five. Naively, it makes sense to expend all tokens for production in order to maximize revenue. However, production generates emissions. Each subject's production tokens are multiplied by an emission factor and added to the common stock of emissions. In the baseline environment, the emission factors are equal to 1 for all subjects, but they are different in the treatments with heterogeneity. The evolution of the common stock of emissions follows slow reversibility dynamics, with 75 percent of common stock carried over from one period to the next. The presence of common stock imposes costs on both players in the group. Specifically, the size of the common stock, in tokens, is subtracted from each player's revenue in each period.[4]

6.2.2 Treatments

The basic model environment described above was used to address three main research questions:

1   How is behavior affected by formulating the instructions in a meaningful environmental context, as opposed to neutral context?
2   How is behavior affected by uncertainty about the number of periods in the game as opposed to a game of fixed and commonly known duration?
3   How is behavior affected by heterogeneity in the subjects' emission factors?

To address these questions, we designed five experimental treatments. The first three treatments, discussed in detail in Pevnitskaya and Ryvkin (2013), concern questions (1) and (2). In the fixed-end treatment with neutral context (FE-N), subjects played the game for 20 periods. In the fixed-end treatment with context (FE-C), subjects played the same game but the instructions were formulated using terms like "pollution," "environmental damage," etc. In the uncertain-end treatment (UE), the subjects were informed that the game might be terminated at the end of each period with probability 0.05.

The uncertain-end setting without context (UE) was used as a baseline for studying question (3) with the remaining two treatments, discussed in detail in Pevnitskaya and Ryvkin (2011b), that differ by the configuration of emission factors of subjects: heterogeneous with high-pollution propensity (HH) and heterogeneous with low-pollution propensity (HL). In both treatments, one subject in each pair had the emission factor equal to 1 and the other subject had it fixed at 1.25 in treatment HH and 0.75 in treatment HL.

In all treatments, subjects participated in two dynamic games in order to assess the effects of experience.

6.2.3 Theoretical predictions

Two solution concepts were used to generate theoretical predictions. Treating the environment as a non-cooperative game, the first solution concept is the Nash equilibrium and its refinements for dynamic games. This solution can be regarded as a "rational actor" benchmark, as it assumes that subjects are selfish, only caring about their own monetary payoff. The second solution concept is the one maximizing social welfare. In social dilemmas, the problem of anthropogenic climate change being one of them, these two solution concepts typically yield drastically different predictions, with the Nash equilibrium resulting in Pareto deficient behavior. In experimental studies of social dilemmas, observed behavior typically falls between these two extremes, indicating that subjects act as individualistic payoff maximizers only to a degree.

In all the five treatments of our experiments, the Nash equilibrium solution predicts that in each period selfish subjects expend all of their tokens for production. Thus, in equilibrium, players completely disregard the presence of emissions and their impact on members of the group. As expected, the socially optimal solution is very different. In the treatments with certain end (FE-N and FE-C), it is socially optimal for both players to expend zero tokens for production in the first 16 periods, and then switch to expending ten tokens in periods 17 through 20. In the treatments with uncertain termination and intermediate or high-pollution propensities (UE and HH), it is socially optimal for both players to expend zero tokens for production in all 20 periods. Finally, in the heterogeneous treatment with low-pollution propensity (HL), it is socially optimal for the player with emission factor of 0.75 to expend ten tokens for production, and for the other player with emission factor of 1 to expend zero tokens for production.

Similar to other social dilemmas, our experimental environment provides a stark contrast between individual payoff maximization and socially optimal behavior. The important difference between the two solutions is that the social optimum is "sustainable" while the equilibrium solution is not. Sustainability here is defined as the ability of players to have long-run economic growth in the form of nondecreasing payoffs. The equilibrium pollution levels are too high to have long-run sustainability.[5]

6.2.4 Implementation of the experiment

A total of ten sessions with 208 subjects were conducted in the XS/FS laboratory at Florida State University (for a summary of treatments and theoretical predictions, see Table 6.1).[6] The experiment was computerized using the experimental software z-Tree (Fischbacher 2007). Subjects were seated at separated computer terminals and worked independently of one another. They were volunteers recruited from the population of undergraduate students through the online announcement system ORSEE (Greiner 2004). Each subject participated only in one session of the experiment.

Upon arrival to the laboratory, subjects were randomly assigned to computer terminals. After the standard formal consent procedure, experimental instructions were distributed in paper form and read out loud by the experimenter. Subjects were allowed to ask clarifying questions. After reading the instructions, the subjects were guided through a sample round of decisions to become familiar with the interface and then filled out a paper-based questionnaire to ensure that they understood the task. The experimenters checked each subject's questionnaire individually and proceeded with the experiment only after all the subjects answered all the questions correctly.

At the beginning of the experiment, the subjects were randomly matched in groups of two for the entire duration of the session. Communication between the subjects was prohibited and the identities of other participants not disclosed.

Subjects completed two decision sequences. The second sequence was only announced after the first sequence was completed. In the treatments with fixed termination, each sequence lasted 20 periods. In the treatments with uncertain termination, subjects were shown the outcome of a random draw of an integer

Table 6.1 Summary of experimental treatments and theoretical predictions

Treatments	FE-N	FE-C	UE	HH	HL
Sessions	2	2	2	2	2
Subjects	34	44	44	44	42
Groups	17	22	22	22	21
Periods	20		Uncertain termination with 5% probability		
Nash equilibrium inputs	(10, 10)	(10, 10)	(10, 10)	(10, 10)	(10, 10)
Socially optimal inputs	(0, 0) in periods 1–16, (10, 10) in periods 17–20		(0, 0)	(0, 0)	(0, 10)

from the set $\{1, 2, \ldots, 20\}$ at the end of each period. Subjects were informed that if any number between two and 20 is drawn, the sequence would continue; otherwise, the sequence would terminate. The minimal number of periods in the four sequences was 18, so for consistency in data analysis we only use the first 18 periods.

Each session lasted about 90 minutes, with subjects earning about $20 on average, including a $10 show-up fee. Subjects were privately informed about their earnings and paid with a check.

6.3 Results

6.3.1 Context

The effect of environmentally loaded context on behavior in the experiment was measured by comparing treatments FE-N and FE-C. The left panel in Figure 6.1 shows the evolution of the mean level of pollution observed in the two treatments. The grey bars show pollution in treatment FE-N, and the black bars in treatment FE-C. Periods one through 20 correspond to the first sequence of decisions (without experience), while periods 21 through 40 correspond to the second sequence (with experience). Figure 6.1 shows that, in the absence of experience, subjects produced significantly less pollution in the treatment with context. However, with experience, the difference between the two treatments is reduced substantially. Subjects do not seem to benefit from their experience in the presence of context.

The details of the statistical comparisons between the two treatments are discussed in Pevnitskaya and Ryvkin (2013). The following findings were reported:

1   Without experience, production expenditures are lower in the presence of context than without it. Pollution levels are lower and long-run payoffs are higher in the treatment with context.

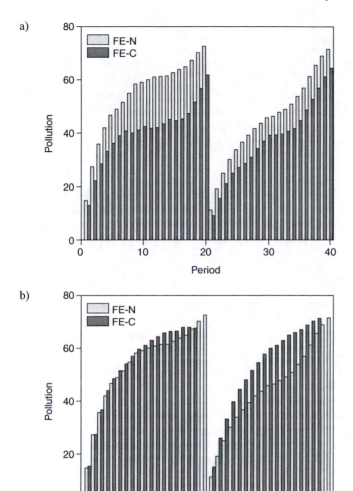

Figure 6.1 Evolution of observed mean level of pollution over time. *(a)*: Comparison of pollution in the treatments with neutral context (FE-N) and environmental context (FE-C). *(b)*: Comparison of pollution in the treatments with fixed (FE-N) and uncertain termination (UE).

2   With experience, the difference between production expenditures without or with context is not statistically significant. There are no significant differences in the pollution levels and payoffs. There is, however, a systematic difference in the end-game effect, and production inputs in the treatment with context are significantly lower in the final periods.

3   Experience substitutes for context, with the exception of decisions in the final periods.

The substitution between environmental context and experience is somewhat similar to the observation of Cooper and Kagel (2003, 2009) that context facilitates learning to play strategically in complex games. The important difference is that in our setting strategic play, understood as individually rational payoff maximization, is not aligned with socially optimal action. Environmental context can play the role of a signal that modifies players' beliefs about each other's behavior and improves cooperation.

Subjects may also experience direct utility from pro-environmental behavior, even if it has no real environmental consequences, if they believe they are doing something "right" or "moral," or want to be perceived as such by others.[7] These preferences are closely related to social norms that evolve over time and can be manipulated to an extent through advertising and education.

6.3.2 Termination uncertainty

The effect of termination uncertainty was explored by comparing treatments FE-N and UE, both under neutral instructions. The right panel in Figure 6.1 shows how the mean level of pollution changed over time. As seen from the figure, there is essentially no difference between the two treatments in the first sequence (periods one through 20, no experience), with the exception of the expected end-game effect in treatment FE-N. However, in the second sequence (periods 21 through 40, with experience), pollution drops substantially in treatment FE-N (again, with the exception of the end-game effect) but stays practically at the same level in the treatments with uncertain termination.

The absence of a significant effect of termination uncertainty without experience in Pevnitskaya and Ryvkin (2013) is in contrast with studies of indefinitely repeated games (e.g., Dal Bo 2005; Camera and Casari 2009). One explanation is that the probability of termination in those studies was relatively high, whereas the 5 percent termination probability in our experiment is so low that subjects view it as a game with an indefinite but large number of periods. After the first sequence, however, subjects realize that the game does terminate unexpectedly; therefore, they do not curb their emissions in the second sequence as much as they do in the fixed-end treatment where they know the duration of the sequence with certainty.

6.3.3 Technological heterogeneity

Treatments HH and HL varied the subjects' pollution propensities to study the effect of technological heterogeneity. Treatment UE in which both group members have the emission factors equal to 1 serves as the baseline for comparison. Treatment HH is the high-pollution propensity heterogeneous treatment with emission factors 1 and 1.25, whereas treatment HL is the low-pollution propensity heterogeneous treatment with emission factors 1 and 0.75.

Figure 6.2 shows the difference in the observed per capita production inputs, pollution levels, and payoffs between treatments HH and HL and the baseline treatment UE. The details of the statistical comparisons across the three treatments are reported in Pevnitskaya and Ryvkin (2011). The results are as follows.

1   There are no differences in behavior between player types in the heterogeneous treatments. That is, on average, players with emission factors of 1 and 1.25 behave the same way in treatment HH, and players with emission factors 1 and 0.75 behave the same way in treatment HL. This is an important result, as it shows that players who are less technologically advanced do not curb emissions, as compared to their more technologically advanced partners, even with experience.
2   Production input levels are lower than those predicted by Nash equilibrium but higher than the social optimum in all treatments. In treatment HH, the input levels are lowest starting from period 7 of the first sequence; furthermore, in the second sequence they are approximately halfway between the socially optimal and Nash equilibrium levels.
3   Pollution level is between the Nash equilibrium and socially optimal levels in all treatments. In the first sequence, the levels of pollution are the same for treatments UE and HH, and lower for treatment HL. With experience, in the second sequence, treatment HH has the lowest pollution due to strong adjustment of production behavior.
4   In the second sequence, payoffs in treatment HH reach the same level as in treatment UE.

These results indicate that players facing the accumulating pollution problem are unlikely to adjust their behavior unless they face severe economic losses. This is consistent with slow response of participants to existing institutions, and calls for more attention to the design of mechanisms with stronger incentives.

6.3.4 Summary

Our results show that context matters, whereas termination uncertainty, generally, does not matter if one ignores the end-game effect and cross-game experience. We also explored the basic effect of heterogeneity in pollution propensity. Interestingly, we did not find a difference in behavior between heterogeneous player types facing the same dynamic public bad problem. The players with high impact factors did not reduce the level of output, even if it meant that they contributed more to the public bad than their counterparts. The overall pollution propensity, however, turned out to play a significant role. In the treatment with unfavorably high-pollution propensities, in which subjects faced steeper pollution costs, they significantly adjusted their behavior with experience.

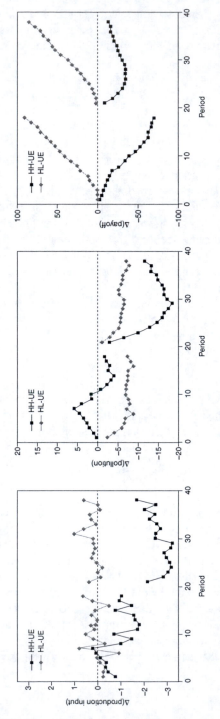

Figure 6.2 The difference in mean per capita production inputs (left), average pollution levels (middle), and average per capita payoffs (right) between treatments HH and UE, and between treatments HL and UE.

6.4 Policy implications

In this section, we discuss policy implications of experimental results. Pollution level was below the Nash equilibrium but above the socially optimal level in all treatments. This finding indicates that pollution-mitigating institutions are necessary to solve the social dilemma between local economic growth and global environmental sustainability. Unless participants face severe costs of pollution and climate change, they are reluctant to sacrifice profits from production to reduce pollution that imposes costs on everyone. While this result is consistent with the state of affairs in the world, it causes concerns since recovering from severe losses in the field is very different from the laboratory and as a society we do not have the clean restart option.

We find that the results of previous studies of public good games with heterogeneity that reported differences in behavior between player types[8] do not carry over to the setting of games with a dynamic public bad. We do not observe any differences in behavior between subject types in the heterogeneous treatments. This confirms concerns that developing countries would likely not curb emissions at the expense of production and suggests that, in the absence of enforcement mechanisms, countries with different pollution abatement technologies would not adjust their production according to the environmental damage they generate, and the more polluting countries may follow with pollution reduction only if the less polluting countries lead. Thus, the overall level of technological development, as reflected by the average emission factor, is more important to curb pollution levels than the development of individual members. Policy implications of these findings are twofold. First, there need to be incentives for developed countries to take major steps in curbing their own pollution. Second, specific arrangements, potentially involving transfers, need to be designed for developing countries to improve their technologies and provide greater incentives to curb emissions.

Under unfavorable conditions, countries are more likely to curb emissions and reach sustainability, and the effect is significant with experience. When decision makers do not face significant costs, they are less likely to take into account the dynamic effects of accumulating pollution and climate change. Thus, paradoxically, environmental regulation may be more necessary in the presence of a moderate damage than in the presence of a more obvious damage. In the latter case, the results of continuing "business as usual" are too obvious to ignore, while in the former case the relatively slow and subtle build-up of pollution may lead to the "boiling frog syndrome."

Decision makers learn faster and adjust their behavior toward lower levels of pollution in a setting with a finite and commonly known horizon. Introducing uncertainty in the game slows the adjustment with experience and results in higher levels of pollution. This result supports policies with a fixed timeline target and raises interest in studying the response to other types of uncertainty, similar to other aspects of the field.

Experimental results on the effect of context support policies and educational efforts aimed at explaining the danger of pollution and climate change and promoting pro-environmental preferences. The results support the effect of "green" advertising on consumer behavior and adoption of clean technologies.[9] Even in a laboratory setting in which pro-environmental actions have no material effects, subjects with such preferences are reluctant to pollute. Our results provide evidence on the significance of "green" framing in the field and support the effectiveness of environmental outreach.

The implications of our results should be taken with caution. One important limitation of our design is the group size of two players. It is well known from the experimental literature on social dilemmas and coordination that the level of cooperation is likely to decrease with group size, and two-player groups typically exhibit relatively high levels of cooperation compared to larger groups. Thus, our results, and their implications, likely provide a "best-case scenario" in terms of possible levels of cooperation in settings with a dynamic public bad. A more detailed exploration of the effect of group size is part of our current research agenda.

6.5 Conclusions

The increasing dangers associated with climate change and costs of pollution motivate the investigation of a new class of dynamic games with a public bad. When agents face a problem of maximizing their own payoff from production that generates a negative externality (e.g., pollution), the typical outcome is overproduction and excessive pollution that imposes costs on the entire society. Historically, various institutional arrangements at the international level have brought insignificant results in curbing emissions and slowing down the global warming. We report the results of experimental studies investigating aspects of human decision making that could explain the sluggish response to incentives in the existing institutions and help design more successful policies.

In our experimental design, subjects have an opportunity to allocate resources to production that yields private payoff but also generates emissions that accumulate and act as a public bad. The observed behavior indicates that subjects take into account the dynamic costs of the public bad but to a lesser extent than prescribed by the social optimum. External institutions are, therefore, necessary to curb emissions and slow down environmental damage. Further, in treatments with heterogeneity in emission propensity, subjects with higher propensity to pollute do not choose to reduce production in order to limit their contributions to the public bad and costs imposed on all group members. This result shows the need for specific arrangements to enable developing countries to curb emissions without substantial setbacks in their economic growth. Such policies may involve direct transfers and sharing of technologies between developed and developing countries.

The experimental evidence shows faster learning and adjustment to lower levels of pollution in games with less uncertainty. In a setting with uncertainty about the number of periods, subjects do not significantly curb pollution even with experience, possibly reflecting a response to increased complexity of the dynamic nature of the game. Uncertainty about the timing and possible costs of climate change is a crucial feature of the decision-making setting in the field and should be investigated in more detail. In the presence of uncertainty, adjustment toward lower emissions was only found when the costs of pollution were severe. This finding suggests that decision makers in the field are unlikely to curb emissions voluntarily until the damage becomes obvious, and calls for bold and immediate coordinated action in the form of enforceable pollution reduction agreements before it is too late.

There is evidence of support of the effect of outreach and educational programs aimed at forming pro-environmental preferences. When faced with environmental context in their economic decisions, subjects reduce their pollution levels, despite the fact that curbing emissions in the lab does not have any direct effect on the environment. The effect of "green" outreach, education, or advertising in the field should be even greater, since it combines the warm glow of choosing an action that is viewed as good with direct utility of having a positive impact on the environment.

Experimental results discussed in this chapter inform policies aimed at promoting cooperation in reducing emissions and fighting climate change. They also suggest further directions for research. The main extensions include varying the group size, introducing other types of uncertainty into the game, and allowing for investment in clean technologies.

Notes

1 The United Nations Climate Change Portal, http://change.nature.org.
2 See, for example, Dutta and Radner (2004), Heal and Tarui (2010), Pindyck (2009), and Harstad (2010).
3 Pevnitskaya and Ryvkin (2011, 2013) provide more details of the experimental design. A similar design was used previously by Saijo *et al.* (2009), whose study focuses on the effects of intergenerational transfers of information and utility in the presence of dynamic negative externalities.
4 Formally, the model can be specified as follows. Let x_{it}, a number between 0 and 10, denote the production input chosen by player $i=1$, 2 in period $t=1, 2, \ldots$. Player i's payoff in period t is given by $\pi_{it}=10-x_{it}+5x_{it}-Y_{t-1}$, where Y_t is the amount of pollution accumulated by the end of period t. Pollution evolves as $Y_t=0.75Y_{t-1}+(q_1x_{1t}+q_2x_{2t})$, where q_1 and q_2 are the emission factors of players 1 and 2. The initial condition for pollution is $Y_0=0$. Player i's total payoff in the game is the sum of her payoffs from all periods until termination.
5 We use the term "sustainability" here not in a game-theoretic but in an economic/environmental sense of nondecreasing payoff. Due to the nature of the social dilemma under consideration, the social optimum cannot be sustained as Nash equilibrium, in the sense that profitable unilateral deviations from it are possible.
6 As in Pevnitskaya and Ryvkin (2011, 2013).
7 Interestingly, this effect may not arise in all contexts. Abbink and Hennig-Schmidt (2006) report no effect of context in a bribery experiment in which subjects can be expected to refrain from an action framed as "corruption" because it is "wrong" or "immoral," though individually optimal.
8 For example, Marks and Croson (1999) report the results of an experiment involving a provision-point public good game with heterogeneous public good valuations and find that, generally, contributions are heterogeneous.
9 See, for example, Cason and Gangadharan (2002), Vermier and Verbeke (2006), and Hartmann and Apaolaza-Ibanez (2010).

References

Abbink, K. and Hennig-Schmidt, H. (2006) "Neutral versus loaded instructions in a bribery experiment," *Experimental Economics*, 9: 103–121.

Camera, G. and Casari, M. (2009). "Cooperation among strangers under the shadow of the future," *American Economic Review*, 99: 979–1005.

Cason, T. and Gangadharan, L. (2002) "Environmental labeling and incomplete consumer information in laboratory markets," *Journal of Environmental Economics and Management*, 43: 113–134.

Cooper, D.J. and Kagel, J. (2003) "The impact of meaningful context on strategic play in signaling games," *Journal of Economic Behavior and Organization*, 50: 311–337.

Cooper, D.J. and Kagel, J. (2009) "The role of context and team play in cross-game learning," *Journal of the European Economic Association*, 7: 1101–1139.

Dal Bo, P. (2005) "Cooperation under the shadow of the future: Experimental evidence from infinitely repeated games," *American Economic Review*, 95: 1591–1604.

Dutta, P. and Radner, R. (2004) "Self-enforcing climate-change treaties," *Proceedings of the National Academy of Sciences*, 101: 5174–5179.

Fischbacher, U. (2007) "z-Tree: Zurich toolbox for ready-made economic experiments," *Experimental Economics*, 10: 171–178.

Greiner, B. (2004) "An online recruitment system for economic experiments," in K. Kremer and V. Macho (eds), *Forschung und wissenschaftliches Rechnen 2003* (pp. 79–93). GWDG Bericht 63, Göttingen: Ges. für Wiss. Datenverarbeitung.

Harstad, B. (2010) *The Dynamics of Climate Agreements*. Kellogg School of Business, mimeo.

Hartmann, P. and Apaolaza-Ibanez, V. (2010) "Beyond Savanna: An evolutionary and environmental psychology approach to behavioral effects of nature scenery in green advertising," *Journal of Environmental Psychology*, 30: 119–128.

Heal, G. and Tarui, N. (2010) "Investment and emission control under technology and pollution externalities," *Resource and Energy Economics*, 32: 1–14.

Marks, M. and Croson, R. (1999) "The effect of incomplete information in a threshold public goods experiment," *Public Choice*, 99: 103–118.

Pevnitskaya, S. and Ryvkin, D. (2011) "Behavior in a dynamic environment with costs of climate change and heterogeneous technologies: An experiment," in M. Isaac and D. Norton (eds), *Research in Experimental Economics*, vol. 14 (pp. 115–150), Bingley, UK: Emerald Press.

Pevnitskaya, S. and Ryvkin, D. (2013) "Environmental context and termination uncertainty in games with a dynamic public bad," *Environment and Development Economics*, 18, in press.

Pindyck, R. (2009) "Uncertain outcomes and climate change policy," *NBER Working Paper*, No. 15259.

Saijo, T., Sherstyuk, K., Tarui, N., and Ravago, M. (2009) "Games with dynamic externalities and climate change experiments," University of Hawaii Working Paper.

Solomon, S., Plattnerb, G.-K., Knutti, R., and Friedlingstein, P. (2010) "Irreversible climate change due to carbon dioxide emissions," *Proceedings of the National Academy of Sciences of the USA*, 106(6): 1704–1709.

Vermier, I. and Verbeke, W. (2006) "Sustainable food consumption: Exploring the consumer\attitude-behavioral intention gap," *Journal of Agricultural and Environmental Ethics*, 19: 169–194.

Part II
Game theory and political economy applications

7 Regional fisheries management organizations and the new member problem

From theory to policy

Gordon R. Munro

7.1 Introduction

This chapter is concerned entirely with the translation of recent developments in game theory analysis of natural resource and environmental issues from the realm of academic books and journals to that of policy decision making. As such, it is an attempt, within the context of one natural resource area, to address the question posed by the editors of the 2008 volume *Game Theory and Policymaking in Natural Resources and the Environment*, namely "...whether or not game theory has developed sufficiently, and the conflicts and problems associated with sharing of natural resources and amenities have worsened enough, that game theory may assist in evaluating various policies designed to improve their management" (Albiac *et al.* 2008, p. 1). While this author answers the question with "yes," I would also maintain that effecting the translation of game theoretic insights into the realm of policy making requires patience and perseverance in abundance, and is itself a game theoretic exercise.

The natural resource area upon which this chapter focuses is the management of internationally shared capture fishery resources, which are estimated to account for as much as one-third of world marine capture fishery harvests. The Food and Agriculture Organization of the UN (FAO) states that "...effective management of shared fish stocks stands as one of the great challenges towards achieving long-term sustainable fisheries."[1]

Most emphasis in this chapter will be given to the management of shared fish stocks through the emerging regime of so-called Regional Fisheries Management Organizations (RFMOs). RFMOs, it will be seen, are concerned with management of fish stocks moving between the waters under the control of coastal states[2] and the "high seas."

The problem of the management of internationally shared fish stocks, and the emergence of RFMOs, did not come about overnight, but were rather the product of the evolution of world capture fisheries management. Some background is in order.

7.2 Background to the internationally shared fish stock problem

We commence with the proposition that marine capture fishery resources are extremely difficult to manage in either biological or economic terms. The resources are not visible until capture, and they are, with few exceptions, mobile. As a consequence, it has, until very recently, been difficult – or more to the point costly – to establish effective property rights to these resources, be the property rights private or public. Marine capture fishery resources were thus historically seen as the quintessential "common pool" resources. It is easy to be persuaded that "common pool" conditions can, and do, lead to resource over-exploitation and economic waste.

Other than in a few isolated cases, however, the "common pool" nature of ocean capture fishery resources was not seen as a significant problem, until the end of World War II. Indeed, the "common pool" nature of these resources was enshrined in international law in the doctrine of the Freedom of the Seas, dating back to the early seventeenth century. Under international law, the oceans were divided into coastal state territorial seas, and the remainder the high seas. The territorial sea is very narrow, today extending out to 12 nautical miles from shore (UN 1982, Article 3).[3] Within the high seas, all resources, including fishery resources, were deemed to be *res communis*, the property of all, open to exploitation by all states (Orrego Vicuña 1999).

The rationale underlying the Freedom of the Seas doctrine, as applied to fishery resources, was that ocean fishery resources are inexhaustible. In economic terms, the natural capital that constitutes marine capture fishery resources was seen as "free" capital. When the Freedom of the Seas doctrine was propounded in the early seventeenth century, the rationale had merit. Given the then state of fishing technology, it was too costly (not to say dangerous) to exploit heavily fishery resources a significant distance from shore. The fishery resources were thus "protected by economics."

Steady advances in fishing technology, leading to falling harvesting costs, stripped away this economic protection. As "free" natural capital became scarce, the consequences of the "common pool" nature of the resources, in terms of over-exploitation, became apparent. The process was gradual, however, such that as late as the last quarter of the nineteenth century reputable scientists were continuing to insist that ocean capture fishery resources were inexhaustible. Not until the late 1930s was recognition given to the fact that steps had to be taken to curb the over-exploitation of world ocean fishery resources.[4]

Since that time, the management of world fishery resources has gone through a process of evolution and development, which remains ongoing. The first attempts at control of fisheries exploitation outside of the very narrow territorial seas consisted of international organizations, such as the International Commission for Northwest Atlantic Fisheries, established in 1949, off Canada and the United States. Increasing coastal state dissatisfaction with the effectiveness of international management of ocean capture fishery resources led ultimately to what was to be a revolutionary change in the management of world fishery resources.

In response to coastal states attempting to extend their jurisdiction over marine resources unilaterally, following the end of the Second World War, the United Nations convened a series of conferences on the Law of the Sea, commencing in 1958, with coastal states, dissatisfied with the international management of ocean capture fishery resources, eagerly joining in the process. The third, and final, such conference (1973–1982) was the one to bring about the revolutionary change to world fisheries management.

The Third UN Conference on the Law of the Sea gave rise to the 1982 UN Convention on the Law of the Sea (UN 1982). Under the convention, coastal states are given the right to establish Exclusive Economic Zones (EEZs) extending out to 200 nautical miles[5] from shore. The EEZ regime, which became all but worldwide, is believed to encompass approximately 90 percent of the commercially exploitable marine capture fishery resources (Alexander and Hodgson 1975). It was, and is, argued that, to all intents and purposes, the coastal state has property rights to the fishery resources within the EEZ (McRae and Munro 1989). Thus, the Freedom of the Seas doctrine, as it pertains to capture fisheries, was sharply reduced. The "common pool" aspects of the ocean capture fishery resources were thus also much diminished, or so it appeared. Granting coastal states extensive property rights to ocean capture fishery resources, however, has proven to be one thing; putting the property rights into effect quite another.

The mobility of capture fishery resources made it apparent, well before the 1982 UN Convention was up for signing,[6] that the EEZ regime would be confronted with the "shared" fish stock problem. It was seen as inevitable that the typical coastal state would find some of its EEZ fishery resources crossing the EEZ boundary. The FAO was to categorize such internationally "shared" capture fishery resources as follows:

A Transboundary fish stocks – fishery resources that are to be found in two or more neighboring EEZs.
B Straddling fish stocks – fish stocks that are to be found both within the EEZ and the adjacent high seas.[7]
C Discrete high seas stocks – fish stocks that are confined to the remaining high seas (see Munro *et al.* 2004).

The initial interest in shared fish stock management was focused on Category A, EEZ to EEZ fish stocks. Given the estimate that only 10 percent of capture fishery harvests were based on fish stocks within the remaining high seas, straddling fish stocks seemed to be of little importance.

This view of the world of fisheries was to prove to be completely unfounded. Be that as it may, the emerging problem of managing transboundary fish stocks gave rise to the first application of game theory to fisheries economics. The development of fisheries economics for the purposes of analyzing the management of these resources was, in turn, to provide the foundation for the economics of management of capture fishery resources through RFMOs. The issue of the management of these resources was also to provide the first opportunity to persuade fisheries policy makers of the usefulness of game theoretic concepts. We can thus look upon the management of transboundary fish stocks as a precursor to the management of straddling stocks through RFMOs.

7.3 The management of transboundary fish stocks: a precursor to RFMO management of fisheries

The inescapable strategic interaction between and among coastal states sharing transboundary fish stocks forced economists to recognize that they would make no significant progress in developing the economics of transboundary fish stock management unless they blended their dynamic economic model of the fishery, used for investigating intra-EEZ fisheries management, with game theory (Bailey *et al.* 2010). Munro (1979), doing just this, explored the problem of establishing cooperative fishery management regimes that were stable through time, given various asymmetries between and among the players. Munro was followed quickly by Clark (1980), and Levhari and Mirman (1980), who examined the consequences of non-cooperative management of such resources. The 1980 trio of authors were in agreement that one could, with confidence, anticipate a classic Prisoner's Dilemma outcome.[8]

The management of transboundary stocks was to give economists their first lesson in the need for patience and perseverance in persuading policy makers of the value of game theoretic concepts. Let the concepts of the Prisoner's Dilemma and side payments serve as examples.

While the concept of the Prisoner's Dilemma is seen as virtually self-evident by those with even limited knowledge of game theory, it is a concept that many policy makers find difficult to accept. The lack of acceptance is, for example, embedded (implicitly) in the 1982 UN Convention itself. The 1982 UN Convention calls upon coastal states sharing a transboundary fish stock to come together and negotiate on establishing a cooperative management regime for the resource (UN 1982, Article 63(1)). What the 1982 UN Convention does not do is require the coastal states to reach an agreement. If the coastal states do not, then each coastal state is to manage its share of the resource in accordance with its other obligations under the Convention (Munro *et al.* 2004). The assumption is that each coastal state, being responsible, will manage its segment of the resource to the best of its ability. While the results may not be optimal, they should be adequate. Cooperation is desirable, but not really essential.[9]

What has happened since 1982 is that there have been examples emerging of transboundary fish stocks managed non-cooperatively, leading to serious depletion of the resources. Economists have been able to take these examples to drive home the Prisoner's Dilemma message, demonstrating that the "players" were neither irrational nor irresponsible, but rather were entirely rational in their behavior. One dramatic example has been provided by Australia and New Zealand involving the South Tasman Rise trawl fishery, based upon an orange roughy resource.

Orange roughy, a groundfish (white fish), is a high-valued, slow-growing resource, and as such is vulnerable to over-exploitation. The South Tasman Rise orange roughy resource is technically a straddling stock, to be found in the Australian Fishing Zone (EEZ) and the adjacent high seas. The Australians discovered the resource in 1997 and assumed that the only other state that would have an interest in exploiting it was New Zealand. Hence, it was a transboundary fish stock de facto.

The Australians acted responsibly and attempted to establish a cooperative management regime with their New Zealand counterparts. This should have been straightforward. The two states have common cultural backgrounds. They both have exemplary records of domestic fisheries management. The cooperative resource management agreement was, however, ill designed and broke down. The cooperative fish game degenerated into a competitive game.

With evidence provided by both Australian and New Zealand government sources, it was a straightforward task for this author to show in the aforementioned FAO publication on shared fish stock management (Munro *et al.* 2004) how the two "players" in the resultant atmosphere of distrust and suspicion rationally adopted strategies that resulted in serious over-exploitation of the resource. While the two players did eventually return to cooperation, it was too late. While there are now some signs of recovery of the resource (Derek Staples, personal communication), there is no indication, at the time of writing, that the recovery has been sufficient to allow a resumption of fishing. Indeed in 2007, Australia and New Zealand agreed that there should be no fishing on the South Tasman Rise in 2007–2008, and *indefinitely thereafter*. No fishing permits for the fishery have been granted since that time (Australian Government 2012).

In the FAO publication, the following is emphasized. The moral to be drawn from the South Tasman Rise orange roughy fishery experience is not that Australia and New Zealand should be held up for censure. It is rather that, if these two coastal states can fall into the Prisoner's Dilemma hole, then all coastal states sharing transboundary fish stocks are vulnerable (see Munro *et al.* 2004, pp. 51–54). The message is getting through that cooperation does matter critically in the management of transboundary fish stocks and is not merely a useful addition. The Norway-FAO Expert Consultation on the Management of Shared Fish Stocks, referred to in the Introduction, states in its final report that:

the Consultation concluded that, with very few exceptions, non-cooperative management of shared fish stocks carries with it the threat of overexploitation ... cooperation in the management of these resources is to be seen as an *essential* [italics added] pre-requisite for effective management...

(FAO 2002, p. iv)

With regards to the second game theoretic concept, side payments, the concept basically refers to transfers between and among the players, which may, or may not, be monetary in form. In a transboundary fishery context, the consequence would be that a given coastal state's economic return from the fishery would not be determined solely by that state's fleets' harvests, within the coastal state EEZ.

Early work on the application of the theory of cooperative games to the economics of the management of transboundary fish stocks put emphasis on the massive simplifications that are forthcoming from the introduction of side payments (Munro 1979).[10] The point was also made that side payments allow the "players" to focus on the economically sensible policy of dividing the net economic benefits from the fishery, as opposed to, say, dividing the harvests.

It has been this author's observation that, within policy circles, the concept of side payments has, in the past, met with considerable resistance. In part, this is due to game theory terminology. To many policy makers, the term "side payments" carries with it the connation of bribes and corruption. Those who do accept the concept often look for euphemisms – for example, "negotiation facilitators" (FAO 2002). Nonetheless, the concept is gradually beginning to take hold. Let one example suffice.

One of the most complex cooperative management regimes for transboundary fish stocks consists of the regime for the management of the several different Pacific salmon species shared by Canada and the United States, from northern California to the Gulf of Alaska. A major source of the complexity lies in the fact that the United States is not a single player in the game, but is rather a five-player coalition, a coalition that is often marked by instability.

The legal foundation for the cooperative fishery management regime rests upon the Canada–United States Pacific Salmon Treaty of 1985 (Treaty 1985). The Treaty-based cooperative arrangement operated successfully from the time of the signing of the Treaty in 1985 until 1993, at which time the Treaty seized up. A climatic regime shift, which had a very positive impact upon Pacific salmon stocks off Alaska, and a very negative impact upon Pacific salmon stocks off Washington and Oregon, and southern British Columbia, had upset the bargaining arrangement. The cooperative fishery game had not met the time consistency test.

The Treaty remained in a state of paralysis for almost six years. The history of the Treaty paralysis period provides powerful testimony to the predictive power of the Clark, and Levhari and Mirman models. "Fish wars"[11] erupted (Munro et al. 1998).

Economists at the time, this author included, pointed to the fact that the Treaty arrangements contained not even a hint of side payments.[12] The argument that the author and others made, basically a common-sense argument, is that side payments serve to broaden the scope for bargaining. The scope for bargaining contained within the 1985 Treaty in its original version, had proven to be too narrow to provide the Treaty with sufficient resilience to withstand the environmental shock in the form of the climate regime shift (see Miller and Munro 2004).

In the late 1990s, the two sides, alarmed at the growing consequences of non-cooperation,[13] came together in an attempt to "patch up" the Treaty. The author and some of his colleagues were invited to meet with the Canadian negotiating team. They reiterated the point that the Treaty arrangements, as the arrangements then stood, provided a too-narrow scope for bargaining. They were able to point to other cooperative fisheries management regimes (e.g., the Norway–Russian Barents Sea cooperative fisheries management regime) in which side payments like provisions were incorporated into the regime.[14]

In mid-1999, Canada and the United States signed the Pacific Salmon Agreement (U.S. Department of State 1999), the "patch up" agreement. Buried within the Agreement was a small implicit side payment arrangement.[15] While the side payments are indeed small, the precedent had been set.

The Treaty was then formally renewed on 1 January 2009 (Canada, Department of Fisheries and Oceans 2009). Contained within the renewed Treaty provisions are explicit side payments from the United States to Canada.[16] While the sizes of the side payments are not exceptionally large, the side payments precedent, within Canada–United States Pacific salmon cooperative management arrangements, has been reinforced and expanded upon.

7.4 Straddling fish stocks and RFMO management of fisheries

We come at last to the question of game theory and fisheries management policy with regards to straddling fish stocks. We first recall that the scope of the straddling fish stock management issue caught the international community by surprise. With it being estimated that no more than 10 percent of world capture fishery harvests are, and would be, based upon fish stocks to be found in the remaining high seas beyond the EEZs, straddling fish stocks were seen as being of little importance. The perceived lack of importance is reflected in the quality of the articles in the 1982 UN Convention covering straddling fish stocks.[17]

The 1982 UN Convention articles pertaining to straddling fish stocks are to be found in Part V, the Exclusive Economic Zone (Articles 63(2) and 64, and Part VII, the High Seas (Article 87, and Articles 116–120) (UN 1982). In Article 87, the Freedom of the Seas, pertaining to fisheries in the high seas, is reiterated. This freedom is of particular interest to so-called Distant Water Fishing States (DWFSs), which can be defined as fishing states, some of whose fleet operate well beyond the home waters (i.e., EEZs) of these states[18] (UN 1982, Article 87).

The Article 87 Freedom of High Seas fishing rights are constrained by Articles 116–120 of the 1982 UN Convention that call upon DWFSs exploiting straddling fish stocks to recognize the interests of relevant coastal states and cooperate with these coastal states for the purposes of conserving the stocks (UN 1982, Articles 116–120). These constraining articles are, however, models of vagueness and opaqueness (Munro *et al.* 2004). As a reflection of this vagueness, the rights and duties of coastal states, and those of DWFSs, pertaining to the high seas portions of straddling stocks are very unclear. This lack of clarity made it very difficult in the early days of the 1982 UN Convention to establish effective cooperative fisheries management arrangements for these stocks. Competitive fishery games became the rule, and the Prisoner's Dilemma played itself out with a vengeance.

An example is provided by the Alaska Pollock resource in the Bering Sea. Historically, Alaska Pollock has been the largest single species in the North

Pacific. In the 1980s, the United States and Russia established EEZs on the western and eastern sides of the Bering Sea, but the EEZs together did not encompass the Bering Sea. There remained a high seas enclave in the middle, known as the Doughnut Hole. Several DWFSs were attracted to the enclave. The resultant Doughnut Hole fishery game was competitive, with no significant attempt to establish cooperative resource management until 1992. In that year, the two Bering Sea coastal states persuaded the four leading DWFSs in the region to sign a convention calling for a temporary moratorium in the Doughnut Hole (Munro *et al.* 2004). The cooperation had come too late. The Doughnut Hole had been reduced to a near marine desert. The "temporary" harvest moratorium continues in place at the time of writing.

Experiences, such as that in the Doughnut Hole, compelled the UN to convene another international conference, popularly referred to as the UN Fish Stocks Conference 1993–1995 to address the fisheries management issues. The Conference brought forth an agreement, popularly referred to as the 1995 UN Fish Stocks Agreement (UN 1995).[19] The Agreement is not meant to supplant any part of the 1982 UN Convention. Rather its purpose is to buttress the 1982 UN Convention, with particular emphasis on Part VII (Munro *et al.* 2004).

Under the terms of the 1995 UN Fish Stocks Agreement, straddling fish stocks are to be managed, on a region-by-region basis, by the Regional Fisheries Management Organizations (RFMOs), referred to briefly in the introduction. A RFMO is to have as members relevant coastal states and DWFSs with a "real" interest in the fishery resources under the jurisdiction of the RFMO.

There are now some 16 RFMOs (Lodge *et al.* 2007), two examples of which are the Northwest Atlantic Fisheries Organization (NAFO), off the coasts of Atlantic Canada, and those of the United States,[20] and the Western and Central Pacific Fisheries Commission (WCPFC), encompassing the world's richest tropical tuna resources to be found in the South Pacific and the neighboring coastal states of Southeast Asia.

The geographical competence of the typical RFMO is open to some confusion. Under Article 3 of the Agreement, it appears that the RFMO management jurisdiction applies only to the high seas portion of these stocks. Article 7, however, makes the necessary provision that the management of the high seas and intra-EEZ portions of the straddling stock must be consistent (UN 1995, Articles 3 and 7). It makes sense, then, to think of the RFMO managing the entire resource.[21]

With respect to game theoretic analysis of RFMO fisheries management, the analysis of non-cooperative management[22] need not detain us. The analysis is virtually identical to that of the non-cooperative management of transboundary stocks. Indeed, we have already referred to the fact that the history of the pre-1995 management of straddling fish stocks provides powerful testimony to the predictive power of the economic theory of non-cooperative management of shared fish stocks. It is the economics of cooperative fisheries management within the RFMO that provides interest, due to the significant differences between the economics of such management and that of the cooperative management of transboundary fish stocks. To begin, there is the question of numbers. The typical transboundary fish stock game has a small number of players. Considerable progress can be made with the two-player cooperative game model. The typical straddling fish stock game, by way of contrast, has a large number of players.[23] Two-player games are of very limited value. Coalition games have now become standard in the development of the economics of RFMO management.

Beyond this there are the clearly related problems of free-riding and new members, neither of which arise, except in the most unusual circumstances, in the economic management of transboundary fish stocks.

In the case of transboundary fish stocks, free-riding (as opposed to outright non-compliance) is a theoretical possibility. It is, however, difficult to find examples of free-riding in practice (Munro *et al.* 2004). This, to a considerable extent, is probably due to the fact that the property rights to the relevant resource(s) are not seriously in doubt.[24] By way of contrast, the property rights to the high seas portions of straddling stocks are at best opaque. Free-riding is a chronic problem in straddling fish stock management.

The constant threat of free-riding (similar to what is found in environmental games) can be attributed in large part to the ambiguity surrounding the RFMO fisheries jurisdiction in the high seas, an ambiguity that is not apparent in the 1995 UN Fish Stocks Agreement. The Agreement is explicit. No state is to fish in the high seas under RFMO jurisdiction, unless it is a member of the RFMO, or unless, while being a non-member, it agrees to abide by the management rules laid down by the RFMO – commonly referred to as cooperating non-members (UN 1995, Article 8). International law, however, now intervenes.

A fundamental principle in international law is that an international treaty confers benefits, and imposes obligations, only upon those parties that have ratified the treaty. Legal experts have argued that this principle, the Pacta Tertiis principle,[25] does indeed apply to the 1995 UN Fish Stocks Agreement (Franckx 2000). What then about DWFSs, which have not ratified the Agreement?

International legal experts go on to say that, if the provisions of a treaty acquire status of customary international law,[26] a non-ratifying state can ignore the treaty provisions, only if it publicly proclaims both its disagreement with the treaty provisions and its intention to disregard those provisions. There is no agreement among legal experts that the 1995 UN Fish Stocks Agreement has acquired the status of customary international law (Munro and Sumaila 2011).

There appears to be greater agreement that Parts V and VII of the 1982 UN Convention have acquired customary international law status. The articles contained therein do call upon DWFS members to cooperate among themselves and with coastal states for the purpose of conserving straddling these stocks. The aforesaid articles have, however, demonstrated their weakness.

Be that as it may, the end result is that legal experts make a distinction between illegal fishing and unregulated fishing (FAO 2001). Illegal fishing is just what it says. Unregulated fishing, on the other hand, is much more nebulous. It may be morally reprehensible, but it is not strictly illegal. It is not entirely clear what can be done about it.

Fishing by a state, in high seas under the jurisdiction of a RFMO, in contravention of RFMO management regulations is, if that state has not ratified the 1995 UN Fish Stocks Agreement, deemed to be *unregulated* fishing. Unregulated fishing is free-riding, pure and simple

The impact of uncontrolled, unregulated fishing upon the stability of the Grand Coalition that is the RFMO has now been analyzed in detail through the use of partition function games in a series of articles, with the first being the 2003 article of Pintassilgo (2003). In essence, the question is whether the would-be free-rider can be bribed into coming into and remaining within the RFMO.

The Pintassilgo 2003 article was followed by the 2008 article by Pintassilgo and Lindroos (2008). The article demonstrates that, if the players are symmetric, the RFMO will be unstable, if the number of players, n, is $n>2$ (Pintassilgo and Lindroos 2008). This analysis was, in turn, followed up in 2010 by Pintassilgo *et al.* in an article that allows for asymmetry among the players (Pintassilgo *et al.* 2010).

The existence of asymmetry among players does have a positive impact upon the stability of the RFMO Grand Coalition. The increase is not great, however. Pintassilgo *et al.* demonstrate that the probability of the RFMO Grand Coalition being stable, in the face of uncontrolled unregulated fishing, is negligible for $n \geq 5$ (Pintassilgo *et al.* 2010).

The conclusion that uncontrolled unregulated fishing (free-riding) poses a serious threat to the stability of RFMOs is now understood and accepted within policy circles. Thus, for example, the 2007 report of the Independent Panel on Recommended Best Practices for RFMOs (Lodge *et al.* 2007) states in its Introduction and Overview that "[a] core conclusion is that the success of international cooperation depends largely on the ability to deter free riding ... success depends upon a careful manipulation of the costs and benefits, punishments and incentives for each participant" (Lodge *et al.* 2007, p. x).

Member states of RFMOs are in fact attempting, with increasing vigor, to curb unregulated fishing. Blacklisting of vessels engaged in unregulated (or illegal) fishing is becoming increasingly common, as is cooperation among RFMOs.[27] The two North Atlantic RFMOs, for example, the Northwest Atlantic Fisheries Organization (NAFO) and the Northeast Atlantic Fisheries Commission (NEAFC), have a mutual agreement to the effect that a vessel blacklisted by one RFMO is automatically blacklisted by the other (Lodge *et al.* 2007).

7.5 New members

The problem of establishing stable RFMOs would be much reduced if the following were true: (i) with the announcement of an attempt to establish a RFMO, all fishing states with a "real" interest in the relevant fisheries are required to declare themselves at once, or forever remain outside; (ii) vigorous measures are put in place to prevent free-riding by those who remain outside. Such, however, is not the nature of the RFMO regime as set out in the 1995 UN Fish Stocks Agreement. The subtle and complex issue of new members remains.

Under the terms of the 1995 UN Fish Stocks Agreement, what we might refer to as the "charter" members of a RFMO must be prepared to accommodate new members (UN 1995, Articles 8, 10, and 11). A prospective new member can be barred outright, only if it refuses to abide by the resource management regime laid down by the charter members.

The typical new member will be a DWFS.[28] Experience to date has taught us that a RFMO may have many new members appearing on its doorstep, and has taught us further that their appearance can be spread out over an indefinite period of time.

An example is provided by the Western Central Pacific Fisheries Commission, to which we referred at an earlier point. When the RFMO was established, the "charter" members were basically the members of the South Pacific Forum Fisheries Agency, a few Southeast Asian states (e.g., The Philippines) and DWFSs, which had a history of operating in the region (e.g., China, Japan, the United States). In the recent past, several Latin American DWFSs have expressed a newfound "real" interest in the fishery resources (e.g., Ecuador, Mexico, Panama).

A trio of legal experts, with particular expertise in Law of the Sea issues, Örbech, Sigurjonsson, and McDorman, argue that prospective new members of an RFMO "must be offered *just and reasonable* [italics added] shares of the TAC available under a [RFMO] management plan" (Örbech *et al.* 1998, p. 123). The question becomes how one interprets *just and reasonable*. Kaitala and Munro (1997)[29] demonstrate, by applying a simple, straightforward game theory model, that a seemingly appropriate interpretation of *just and reasonable* could easily lead to the stability of the RFMO being undermined. The seemingly appropriate interpretation is that the "charter" members and the new members should receive equal shares of the net economic returns from the fishery.

Many, if not most, of the RFMOs that have been and are being established have been and are faced with fish stocks that were over-exploited in the past, and which must now be rebuilt. Kaitala and Munro thus focus on cases in which the "charter" members of the RFMO find themselves required to engage in a fishery resource investment program (Kaitala and Munro 1997).

Basically, the Kaitala and Munro argument runs as follows: If the "charter" members engage in the resource investment, they will have to restrict their harvests for perhaps an extended period of time, to enable the resource to grow. Suppose that, when the resource investment targets are reached, new members appear on the horizon. If the Örbech *et al.* allocation rules, as interpreted, are applied, the new members would be free-riding. Having incurred none of the resource investment costs, they would now be enjoying, without charge, shares of the fruits of the investment.

The "charter" members cannot be expected to be myopic. They could be expected to foresee that the fruits of their resource investment would, in part, be skimmed off by the free-riding new members. Kaitala and Munro demonstrate that, if the number of new members is great enough, each "charter" member will calculate that it would be worse off under cooperation than it would be under competition. The resource investment would not take place; the cooperative resource management regime would be rendered powerless.[30]

The potential threat posed by new members to the stability of RFMOs is now being recognized within the realm of policy making. Turning once again to the report of the Independent Panel on Recommended Best Practices for RFMOs, for example, we find the following among its general recommendations for RFMOs.

"In each RFMO, the members should seek means of accommodating new members that will not undermine the stability of the RFMO" (Lodge *et al.* 2007, p. 117). What then is to be done? There are essentially three proposals that have been set forth in the game theory literature, all three of which are summarized in the 2000 article by Pintassilgo and Costa-Duarte (2000). The first proposal can be termed the Waiting Time solution. New members should be welcomed into the RFMO, but are to be informed that they will have to wait until they begin receiving benefits.

There is, in fact, suggestion of this solution in the current policy of granting prospective new members status of "cooperating non-members." The Western and Central Pacific Fisheries Commission, for example, has associated with it some nine cooperating non-members. It is recognized that the status of cooperating non-members is that of second-class citizenship, and it is recognized further that such status should be transitory in nature (Lodge *et al.* 2007).

The question is whether the waiting period will sufficiently reduce the benefits of new members such that the "charter" members believe that they will be better off under cooperation than they would be under competition.[31] Pintassilgo and Costa-Duarte (2000) insist that the waiting period can do just that. Kaitala and Munro (1997), on the other hand, present a counter example in which the waiting period essentially has no impact.[32] In any event, if game theorists cannot agree upon the impact of the waiting period solution, it will be difficult to convince policy makers of its validity.

The second solution, often referred to as the Transferable Membership solution, owes its origins to Kaitala and Munro (1997), who did, in turn, adopt the concept from a draft agreement prepared by a group of "like minded" coastal states,[33] during the UN Fish Stocks Conference. The significance of adopting the concept from the draft agreement is that, in so doing, one had the assurance that it was not beyond the realm of legal possibility.

The idea is that a new member can join the club if, and only if, a "charter" member is prepared to transfer its membership to the new member. The concept was refined by talking in terms of transferring harvest rights or quotas. A "charter" member would then have the possibility of transferring a part of its harvest quota, rather than its harvest quota in its entirety.

No one seriously expects a "charter" member of a RFMO to transfer part or all of its harvesting rights – quotas – to a new member free of charge. A "charter" member could, however, conceivably be willing to sell, or lease, part, or all of its RFMO harvesting quota. Thus, one can envisage new members being able to buy, or lease, their way into the RFMO. This would be comparable to a domestic fishery with Individual Transferable Quotas (ITQs), in which prospective new entrants to the fishery gain access by buying or leasing quota. Having said this, the basic point is that "charter" members would no longer be faced with the returns from their resource investments being dissipated by new members.

There is one consequence of this solution that must be brought forward. It can be argued that, if this solution is adopted, the "charter" RFMO members would be granted de facto collective property rights to the fishery resources under the jurisdiction of the RFMO.[34]

The third approach, or solution, can be referred to as the Fair Sharing solution (Li 1998; Pintassilgo and Costa-Duarte 2000). The game theoretic analysis underlying this approach is a characteristic function game approach. Rather than players receiving equal shares, players receive shares according to their contributions to the Grand Coalition payoff. Thus, prospective new members would receive shares only if they contribute to the total economic pie. Inefficient new members, for example, would receive little or nothing. The consequence is that the "charter" members would see their net economic returns from the fishery protected,[35] without having to turn to quota sales and leases.

The 1995 UN Fish Stock Agreement does in fact state that, in determining the nature and extent of participatory rights for new members, the "charter" members should *inter alia* take into account "the respective contributions of new and existing members to conservation and management of the stock..." (UN 1995, Article 11(c)). Also, to many, the solution, in comparison with having new members buy/lease their way into the RFMO, may be ethically more appealing.

The drawback to the scheme is that it is very difficult to administer. How does one effectively assess the potential contribution, now and in the future, of a prospective new member, given the absence of complete information? The problem becomes increasingly difficult with a large number of participants, which leads the proponent of the Fair Sharing solution, Li, to state that "...in the end full utilization of the stock might have to be declared, effectively forever barring new entrants, including truly efficient ones" (Li 1998, p. 258). RFMOs, as we have already indicated, are characterized by large numbers. Forever barring new entrants is directly contrary to the spirit of the 1995 UN Fish Stocks Agreement, and all but guarantees the exacerbation of the free-rider problem.

Pintassilgo and Costa-Duarte report on an attempt to assess the three approaches by applying them, through simulation techniques, to a specific straddling stock fishery, namely the North Atlantic Bluefin tuna fishery. Their conclusions are: (i) that new members can indeed create a threat to the stability of cooperative management of the resource; and (ii) that the Transferable Membership approach "...despite possible problems, is generally the most efficient solution" (Pintassilgo and Costa-Duarte 2000, p. 375). One problem that they identify, and upon which we shall comment, is the fact that international quota trade is uncommon.[36]

7.6 From theory to policy

In the discussion of the RFMO new-member problem, we are, by a process of elimination, left with the Transferable Membership solution (selling and leasing of harvest quota to new members). There is now clear evidence that this solution is being discussed by policy makers, and that it may well be on the verge of implementation.

The question now to be raised is how, in this specific case, did we get from game theoretic analysis to policy? The author draws upon his own experience with the FAO, through its Expert Consultation on the Management of Shared Fish Stocks, and the Independent Panel on RFMO governance, to which references have been made many times.

The beginning, and obvious, strategy in this translation from theory to policy game is first to put the basic ideas and conclusions arising from our theoretical analysis in a series of policy articles, and conference papers, with the ideas and concepts being expressed in jargon-free language,[37] and with the intuition underlying these ideas and concepts made absolutely explicit. This leads the way to the second strategy of persuading the non-academic authors of policy documents to incorporate these ideas and concepts as recommendations in the documents. It will come as no surprise to learn that these documents carry far more weight with the makers of policy than do articles by academics.[38]

In discussions on the new-member problem, which the author had in the FAO Expert Consultation and with his fellow members of the Independent Panel, the first step was to gain agreement on the potential threat of new members to the stability of RFMOs. The implicit free-riding argument was persuasive.

Then, particularly within the Independent Panel, the author raised the question of what alternatives to the Transferable Membership (quota trading) solution to the new-member problem are available in the real world. It was agreed that there are essentially two alternatives that are being adopted by the RFMOs of the real world. The first alternative, as exemplified by the two North Atlantic RFMOs, the Northwest Atlantic Fisheries Organization (NAFO) and the Northeast Atlantic Fisheries Commission (NEAFC) (Munro *et al.* 2004), is to declare all fisheries under the jurisdiction of the RFMO to be fully allocated and to advise new members that their allocations will be limited to new fisheries (by and large fisheries that currently have no economic value) and (in the case of NAFO) the "others" categories in the current allocations (i.e., the crumbs from the table). Recall our discussion of the Fair Allocation scheme.

Willock and Lack (2006) describe this approach as "effectively closing the door on new members" (p. 27). Strictly speaking, this approach is not contrary to the 1995 UN Fish Stocks Agreement. Article 11 of the Agreement states that current members of a RFMO in determining accommodation for new members "...shall take into account, *inter alia*, the status of the straddling stocks and highly migratory fish stocks and the existing level of fishing effort in the fishery" (UN 1995, Article 11(a)). As we have already noted in our discussion of the Fair Allocation solution, "closing the door" is, nonetheless, contrary to the spirit of the 1995 UN Fish Stocks Agreement, and is virtually certain to exacerbate the free-riding problem. Prospective new members, feeling themselves to have been unfairly excluded from the club, will cease to regard unregulated fishing as a morally reprehensible activity.

The second alternative, as exemplified by the International Commission for the Conservation of Atlantic Tunas (ICCAT) and the Commission for the Conservation of Southern Bluefin Tuna (CCSBT), is to grant prospective new members harvest allocations, at the expense of current, or "charter," members. Commonly, an attempt is made to mask the pain to "charter" members by adding harvesting allocations to new members to the existing Total Allowable Catch (TAC).[39] Rational "charter" members can be expected to strip the mask away. Thus, for example, South Africa, a "charter" member of ICCAT, referred to this alternative, then being followed by ICATT, as "nothing less than ICCAT-sanctioned overfishing in complete violation of our convention."[40] It is not difficult to persuade policy makers of the risks associated with this second approach.[41]

There still remained the question of whether such international quota trades are in fact acceptable under international law. Fortunately, the question has been addressed explicitly by Australian legal expert Andrew Serdy in a 2007 article.[42] In the article, Serdy argues that international trade of quota is fully compatible with international law (Serdy 2007). Indeed, he goes farther and maintains that such trade would speed the provisions of the 1995 UN Fish Stocks Agreement on their way toward achieving the status of customary international law. The transferability (i.e., sale or lease) of national quota between existing RFMO members and prospective new members, he argues:

> will tend to hasten the parallel crystallization of the customary rule of cooperation in international fisheries law into a requirement that non-members abide by the RFMOs rules in order to fish, as long as these are non-discriminatory. This test should not be hard to satisfy, since a would-be new entrant can, at any time, by becoming a member of the RFMO ... make itself eligible to buy quota from an existing member – and refusal of an offer is non-discriminatory.

(Serdy 2007, p. 281)

Both the report of the FAO Expert Consultation and the report of the Independent Panel refer explicitly to the Transferable Membership (quota trades) as a possible solution to the new member problem. The 2002 FAO report states that "if ... it were possible for prospective New Members to purchase quota from existing members of RFMOs, this would serve to ease the problem of quota allocations to New Members" (FAO 2002, para. 63)

The report of the Independent Panel discusses the solution in greater detail. To begin, we have already cited part of one of the report's general recommendations pertaining to new members. Let us now cite the recommendation in its entirety:

> In each RFMO the members should seek means of accommodating new members that will not undermine the long-term stability of the RFMO, *such as by allowing new members to purchase or lease fishing opportunities from existing RFMO members* [italics added].
>
> (Lodge *et al.* 2007, p. 117)

The report of the Independent Panel has a full chapter on the allocation of (fishing) rights. After noting that one of the major impediments to RFMOs securing stable and effective allocation regimes is the problem of accommodating new members (Lodge *et al.* 2007, p. 35), the chapter devotes a full section to the trading of national allocations. The section commences: "...an approach to new members ... that is receiving increasing attention and is likely to be tested by RFMOs is for fishing opportunities to be traded" (Lodge *et al.* 2007, p. 36). The section goes on to discuss the trading of allocations, both for the purpose of accommodating new members and for enhancing intra-RFMO efficiency. It notes that intra-RFMO trading has already occurred in several RFMOs (Lodge *et al.* 2007, pp. 36–38).

We turn finally to a document that gives clear evidence that the solution is being seriously discussed within RFMOs. The document, which was issued in 2009, comes from the OECD Committee for Fisheries, and is titled *Strengthening Regional Fisheries Management Organizations* (OECD 2009). The OECD document draws heavily upon the report of the Independent Panel (Lodge *et al.* 2007).

The document, as well as providing a general discussion on strengthening RFMOs, presents several case studies, with one being on the RFMO, the Commission for the Conservation of Southern Bluefin Tuna (CCSBT). One of the authors of the chapter, Frank Meere, was a former managing director of the Australian Fisheries Management Authority.[43]

Southern Bluefin tuna is a high-valued, slow-growing species. The fish spawn off northwest Australia and are harvested off Australia, New Zealand, and the Pacific between New Zealand and South Africa (Bjørndal and Martin 2007). The fishery was initially a pure open access one. Given the high value of harvested Bluefin tuna, and the fact that the resource is slow growing, the inevitable result of pure open access was serious over-exploitation of the resource. By the 1980s, the over-exploitation had reached a level sufficient to threaten the future of the resource. In the early 1990s, the three states most heavily involved in exploiting the resource, Australia, Japan, and New Zealand, established the CCSBT (ibid.).

Two aspects of the CCSBT are readily apparent. The first is that it continues to be the case that a large resource investment program is required, if the resources are to provide, through time, anything approaching the maximum economic returns to the CCSBT members (ibid.).

The second is that the CCSBT's inability to deal effectively with prospective new members has been a serious hindrance to effective resource management (Bjørndal and Martin 2003, p. 27). It will be recalled that the CCSBT was cited as an example of a RFMO accommodating new members by giving the new members harvest allocations that are then added to the hitherto agreed upon TAC.

Thus, the CCSBT presents a fine example of the threat of implicit free-riding, with all that it implies. The authors of the CCSBT case study raise as an issue: "...the extent to which these hard fought gains [from resource investment] could be dissipated by new fishing states entering the fishery..." (OECD 2009, p. 36).

What then is to be done? The question of quota trading is raised. The chapter states: "...an issue ... is what role, if any, quota trading might play in ... attracting new members?" After arguing that there are no legal barriers to such trading, the authors of the chapter go on to state:

> given the nature of the fishery ... quota trading may occur in the *not too distant future* [italics added]. In fact ... it makes sense where the stock is severely depleted and being rebuilt, and where there is little or no scope to accommodate an increase in the global TAC for states wishing to enter the fishery....
>
> (OECD 2009, p. 38)

The authors then go on to talk about the administrative processes that would have to be developed for quota trading to occur. There is no reason why this should be an insuperable barrier. What is important is that the Transferable Membership approach (quota trading) has now gone beyond the realm of academic journals and conferences into the realm of serious policy discussion. It needs only to be added that once one RFMO adopts the quota-trading solution to dealing with new members, others are certain to follow.

7.7 Conclusion and policy implications

In a paper arising from his presentation to the Sixth Meeting on Game Theory and Practice in 2006, the author argued that, with reference to the management of international fishery resources, game theory is highly relevant. It is all but impossible to analyze the economics of the management of these resources other than through the lens of game theory, the argument continued (Munro 2008).

The argument also continued, however, that game theory results are poorly understood by policy makers, implying that game theorists have yet to have any significant influence upon policy makers. Since 2006, the author has had to revise his opinion. There is now increasing evidence that the results of our game theoretic analysis has begun to have an impact in the realm of policy.

This chapter attempts to illustrate the growing influence of game theory analysis in the context of the management of fisheries, by giving particular emphasis to a major problem facing the emerging regime of Regional Fisheries Management Organizations (RFMOs). A solution to this problem, arising from game theory analysis, is now being given serious consideration by policy makers. We can say more.

In discussing this problem, reference was made to a 2009 publication forthcoming from the OECD Committee on Fisheries, *Strengthening Regional*

Fisheries Management Organizations (OECD 2009). It is worth looking more closely at this document. In the introductory chapter, the publication sets forth the goals of a successful RFMO in broad general terms. The first such goal is: "...a stable cooperative agreement that is time consistent (i.e., able to withstand exogenous shocks)" (OECD 2009, p. 18). There is, of course, no possible way of analyzing means of realizing this goal, without turning to game theory.

Indeed, the 2009 OECD publication draws heavily upon the report of the Chatham House[44]-based Independent Panel to Develop a Model for Improved Governance by RFMOs (Lodge *et al.* 2007), to which extensive reference has been made in this chapter. The report of the Independent Panel, in discussing the conditions necessary for maintaining the stability of RFMOs through time, states that "...a fundamental feature of the management of [fish stocks under RFMO jurisdiction] is the fact that ... there will be a *strategic interaction* between and among states exploiting these stocks" (Lodge *et al.* 2007, p. 10). The report goes on to state that economists were forced, as a consequence, to recognize that they could make no progress in analyzing the economic management of these fish stocks, without incorporating the theory of strategic interaction, game theory, into their analysis. The report then follows with an extensive and detailed discussion of the relevance to the issue at hand of the theories of both competitive and cooperative games (Lodge *et al.* 2007, Chapter 3).

Signs of the growing influence of game theory analysis upon policy makers are thus encouraging; nonetheless, the point made in the introduction bears repeating. Both patience and perseverance continue to be required. The aforementioned solution to the so-called "new-member" problem was first put forward more than 15 years ago.

7.8 Acknowledgments

The author gratefully acknowledges the support received from the Global Ocean Economics Project at the Fisheries Centre, University of British Columbia, Vancouver, Canada. The Project is funded by the Pew Charitable Trusts Philadelphia, USA.

Notes

1   Cited in Munro *et al.* (2004, p. iv). An internationally shared fish stock can be defined as a fish stock exploited by two or more states (or entities).
2   A coastal state is imprecisely defined as a state having a "significant" amount of marine coastline (e.g., the three North American states), as opposed to landlocked states, such as Austria and Switzerland.
3   Approximately 22 km.
4   Late 1930s' initiatives to address the issue were suspended with the onset of World War II. Nothing of substance was done until after the end of the war.
5   Approximately 370 km.
6   In December, 1982.
7   Strictly speaking, the UN in general, and the FAO in particular, make a distinction between highly migratory fish stocks (tuna primarily) and straddling stocks, where the

latter term is a catchall for all other fishery resources to be found within the EEZ and the adjacent high seas. The distinction arose for political reasons within the Third UN Conference on the Law of the Sea, and is defensible neither on biological nor on economic grounds. Like many others, we merge the two and talk in terms of straddling stocks broadly defined. It should be emphasized that straddling fish stocks (B) and transboundary fish stocks (A) are not mutually exclusive.

8 One can reasonably ask why economists were analyzing the economics of transboundary – EEZ to EEZ – fish stock management as early as the late 1970s, in light of the fact that the UN Convention on the Law of the Sea was not available for signing until the last month of 1982. The answer lies in the fact that the Third UN Conference on the Law of the Sea covered much more than fisheries. Negotiations over fishery issues in the Conference were more or less completed early on, in 1975. As a consequence, several coastal states (e.g., those of North America) established EEZs during the last half of the 1970s, doing so on the basis of drafts of the Convention. The fisheries articles in the final version of the Convention were essentially unchanged from those to be found in post-1975 drafts of the Convention.

9 As a corollary to this proposition, if non-cooperating coastal states do in fact mismanage a transboundary stock, they deserve severe censure for their irresponsible behavior.

10 When the players are asymmetric. It should be added that, in international fishery games, asymmetry between and among players is the rule, not the exception.

11 The American legal expert Thomas Jensen defines a "fish war" as the deliberate overexploitation of the fishery resource for the purpose of denying harvest opportunity to the other party or parties (player or players) (Jensen 1986, p. 18).

12 For reasons that are not entirely clear, the Canadians, in particular, were adamantly opposed to side payments (Munro and Stokes 1989).

13 A very practical lesson in the validity of the Prisoner's Dilemma.

14 The Norwegian–Russian Barents Sea cooperative fisheries arrangement focuses primarily on several groundfish species, cod in particular. Among the side payments, like provisions, there is an allowance for quota swaps between the two. Furthermore, in light of the fact that the cod are at a juvenile stage in the Russian EEZ and are at an adult stage in the Norwegian EEZ, the Russian fleet is granted permission to take a substantial portion of its cod quota within the Norwegian zone (Stokke 2003).

15 Although, of course, the term side payments was never used. Two endowment funds were to be established to support scientific research and Pacific salmon enhancement in general to the benefit of the two states. While both Canada and the United States were, under the terms of the Agreement, to contribute, the contributions came overwhelmingly from the United States. The endowment funds thus constituted an implicit side payment (Miller *et al.* 2001, pp. 23–24).

16 For example, the renewed Treaty called for a reduction of Canadian harvests of Columbia River system-produced Chinook and coho salmon. Canada is to be allowed to access up to US$30 million "to help mitigate the impacts of the harvest reductions in Canada" (Canada, Department of Fisheries and Oceans, 2009, p. 2). Needless to say, the term side payments appears nowhere in the renewed Treaty.

17 And discrete high seas fish stocks.

18 Every DWFS is, of course, also a coastal state. Spain, Japan, and Poland are prominent examples of DWFSs. It used to be that DWFSs were almost exclusively developed states, but this is no longer the case. Developing states have now joined the DWFS ranks, examples of which are the People's Republic of China, Ecuador, Mexico, and Thailand.

19 The full title of the conference is: UN Conference on Straddling Fish Stocks and Highly Migratory Fish Stocks. The full title of the Agreement is: Agreement for the Implementation of the Provisions of the United Nations Convention on the Law of the Sea of 10 December 1982 Relating to the Conservation and Management of Straddling Fish Stocks and Highly Migratory Fish Stocks.

20 From Maine to North Carolina.
21 See Munro *et al.* (2004) for a thorough discussion of this issue.
22 That is, the analysis of the economic consequences of a breakdown of RFMO fisheries management.
23 The Northwest Atlantic proves an example. Canada and the U.S. share several transboundary stocks. Two-player games are obviously all that is required for analyzing the economics of the management of such stocks. NAFO, by way of contrast, has 12 members (NAFO 2011).
24 Suppose, for example, that a transboundary stock is shared by two coastal states, and does not extend out to the adjacent high seas. The two coastal states can be seen as owning the resource on a condominium basis (McRae and Munro 1989).
25 Pacta tertiis nec nocent nec prosunt.
26 The status of customary international law is gained by international use and recognition. Once a treaty, or part thereof, has gained this status, then, as noted, a non-party to the treaty can ignore the relevant provisions, only if it explicitly states its intention to do so (Buergenthal and Murphy 2002). Thus, for example, Part V, Exclusive Economic Zone, of the 1982 UN Convention is a part of customary international law and is effectively binding on non-parties to the 1982 UN Convention (e.g., the United States).
27 An intense effort is now underway to curb "laundering" of fish harvested by vessels engaged in unregulated fishing. The cooperation extends to non-RFMO member states (Munro and Sumaila 2011).
28 In a few of the tuna-based RFMOs, established before 1995, some relevant (developing) states were not included among the "charter" members. This is regarded as an anomaly to be corrected as rapidly as possible (Lodge *et al.* 2007). In all of the discussion to follow, new members will be seen as consisting exclusively of DWFSs.
29 There were significant delays in the publication of the Örbech *et al.* article. Kaitala and Munro were provided with an early pre-publication draft of the article.
30 In technical terms, the Kaitala–Munro argument runs as follows. Assume that the relevant RFMO is formed by but one coastal state and one DWFS, denoted by C and D_1 respectively, and assume further that the two players are symmetric. Characterize the threat point payoffs of C and D_1, assumed to be positive, as $J_i(x(0), E_C^N, E_{D1}^N), = C, D_1$, where N denotes *non*-cooperation, and where x denotes the biomass, or stock, level. Optimal resource management policy calls, it is assumed, for investing in the resource stock, x, at maximum speed by setting the harvest rate equal to zero, up to $t = T_R > 0$, at which time the optimal resource stock level, x^*, will have been achieved. At $t = T_R$, positive harvesting is to commence on a sustainable basis, and remain at this sustainable level until $t = \infty$ (Kaitala and Munro 1997).

It is anticipated that, at $t = T_R$, prospective new members, attracted by the profitable fishery, will apply for admission to the RFMO, agreeing to abide by the RFMO management regime. Suppose, for the sake of simplicity, that the new members are identical to C and D_1. The Örbech *et al. just and reasonable* allocation rule for the new members is applied. Recall that a seemingly appropriate interpretation is that each new member is to receive a share of the net economic returns from the fishery equal to those enjoyed by C and D_1. Denote the global net economic returns from the fishery expressed in present value terms and evaluated at $t = T_R$, as $\omega(x^*)$, and denote an equal share of $\omega(x^*)$ as $\bar{\omega}(x^*)$. The larger the number of new members, then obviously the smaller will be $\bar{\omega}(x^*)$.

Independent of the resource investment period T_R, one can find a number of new members such that the following will hold: $J_i\left(x(0), E_C^N, E_{D_1}^N\right) > e^{-\delta T_R} \bar{\omega}(x^*)$, $i = C, D_1$ where δ denotes the common social rate of discount. Thus, on individual rationality grounds, both C and D_1 would refuse to establish the RFMO, and non-cooperative resource management would reign (Kaitala and Munro 1997, p. 97).
31 The inequality in note 30 would not hold.
32 The inequality in note 30 holds. The Kaitala and Munro counter-example is as

follows. The analysis follows a strict Nash "split the difference" rule. Taking a characteristic function game approach should not, however, change the outcome. Once again there are two "charter" members, a coastal state C and DWFS, D_1. At $t=0$, the instant after the RFMO is formed, a new member D_2, appears on the horizon. D_2 is identical to D_1. C is identical to D_1 and D_2, except that it has lower fishing effort costs than D_1 and D_2. Side payments are feasible. Hence the global net economic returns from the fishery are not affected by D_2's accession to the club. D_2 is informed that it will begin receiving economic benefits from the fishery only from $t=T>0$ onwards.

It is now assumed that a three-player cooperative game is established and that, under the cooperative game, the global net economic benefits from the fishery, in present value terms, can be expressed as $\omega(x(0)) = \omega_C(x(0)) + \omega_{D_1}(x(0)) + \omega_{D_2}(x(0))$ where $\omega_{D_1}(x(0))$ is given by: $\omega_{D_2}(x(0)) = e^{-\delta T}\omega_{D_1}^T(x(T),T)$. Denote the cooperative surplus from the cooperative game as $\theta(x(0))$.

Employing the Nash "split the difference rule," we have:

$$e^{-\delta T}\omega_{D_2}^T(x(T),T) = \frac{\theta(x(0))}{3} + J_{D_2}\left(x(0), E_C^N, E_{D_1}^N, E_{D_2}^N\right)$$

where the second term at the end of the above equation denotes D_2's threat point payoff. The implication is that the length of the waiting period has no impact on D_2's payoff, and that hence the destabilizing threat of new members has not been mitigated (Kaitala and Munro 1997, pp. 99–100).

33 Argentina, Canada, Chile, Iceland, and New Zealand.
34 Bjørndal and Munro (2003). Let us recall the argument that the pre-1995 straddling stock fisheries management arose in part because the property rights to the high seas portions of straddling fish stocks were so ill defined.
35 Once again, the inequality in note 30 would not hold.
36 In this author's opinion, Pintassilgo and Costa-Duarte overstate the difficulty of introducing the Transferable Membership (quota) solution. They imply that each "charter" RFMO member state must be allocated harvest quota (correct), and that, second, each member state must then proceed to divide up its national quota among its fishers through an ITQ scheme. Member states may establish ITQ schemes, if they so wish, but there is absolutely no requirement for them to do so in order for the Transferable Membership scheme to be feasible (Pintassilgo and Costa-Duarte 2000, p. 365).
37 With all equations being safely relegated to appendices.
38 We might refer to this as the cat's paw strategy.
39 Which scientists often complain is too large to begin with.
40 Cited in Willock and Lack (2006, p. 27).
41 This carries with it the flavor of the Individual Rationality constraint. The report on the Norway–FAO Expert Consultation on the Management of Shared Fish Stocks actually put forth the Individual Rationality constraint in explicit form, which it described as a basic requirement for stable long-term cooperation:

> it has to be recognized that each and every participant in a cooperative arrangement must anticipate receiving long term benefits from the cooperative arrangement that are at least equal to the long term benefits, which it would receive, if it refused to cooperate. This fact, which should be obvious, is often ignored in practice.
>
> (FAO 2002, para. 47)

The author has seen this paragraph cited many times, often as an amazing revelation.
42 The article was well accepted by the legal experts on the Independent Panel on Recommendations for RFMO governance.
43 Meere's co-author is Mary Lack, who is in turn a colleague and co-author of Anna Willock. Anna Willock was a member of the Independent Panel, and the lead author of the report's chapter on allocations, which discussed RFMO quota trading at length.
44 Royal Institute of International Affairs.

References

Albiac, J., Sánchez-Soriana, J., and Dinar, A. (2008) "Game theory: A useful approach for policy evaluation in natural resources and the environment," in J. Albiac, J.J. Sánchez-Soriana, and A. Dinar (eds), *Game Theory and Policy Making in Natural Resources and the Environment* (pp. 1–11), London: Routledge.

Alexander, L. and Hodgson, R. (1975) "The impact of the 200-mile economic zone on the Law of the Sea," *San Diego Law Review*, 12: 569–599.

Australian Government, Australian Fisheries Management Authority (2012) "South Tasman Rise," available at: www.afma.gov.au/managing-our-fisheries/fisheries-a-to-z-index/south-tasman-rise/.

Bailey, M., Sumaila, U.R., and Lindroos, M. (2010) "Application of game theory to fisheries over three decades," *Fisheries Research*, 102: 1–8.

Bjørndal, T. and Martin, S. (2007) *The Relevance of Bioeconomic Modelling to RFMO Resources: A Survey of the Literature*, Recommended Best Practices for Regional Fisheries Management Organizations: Technical Study No. 3, Chatham House, London.

Bjørndal, T. and Munro, G. (2003) "The management of high seas fisheries resources and the implementation of the UN Fish Stocks Agreement of 1995," in H. Folmer and T. Tietenberg (eds), *The International Yearbook of Environmental and Resource Economics 2003/2004* (pp. 1–35), Cheltenham: Edward Elgar.

Buergenthal, T. and Murphy, S.D. (2002) *Public International Law: In a Nutshell*, third edition. St. Paul: West Group.

Canada, Department of Fisheries and Oceans (2009) "Pacific Salmon Treaty renewal," available at: www.dfo-mpo.gc.ca/media/back-fiche/2009/pr01-eng.htm.

Clark, C. (1980) "Restricted access to a common property resource," in P. Liu (ed.), *Dynamic Optimization and Mathematical Economics* (pp. 117–132), New York: Wiley Interscience.

Food and Agriculture Organization of the U.N. (2001) *International Plan Of Action to Prevent, Deter, and Eliminate Illegal, Unreported, and Unregulated Fishing*. Rome: FAO.

Food and Agriculture Organization of the U.N. (2002) *Report of the Norway-FAO Expert Consultation on the Management of Shared Fish Stocks Bergen, Norway, 7–10 October 2002*. Fisheries Report No. 695, Rome.

Franckx, E. (2000) "*Pacta Tertiis* and the Agreement for the implementation of the straddling and highly migratory fish stocks provisions of the United Nations Convention on the Law of the Sea," *Tulane Journal of International and Comparative Law*, 8: 49–81.

Jensen, T.C. (1986) "The United States-Canada Pacific Salmon Interception Treaty: An historical and legal overview," *Environmental Law*, 16: 365–422.

Kaitala, V. and Munro, G. (1997) "The conservation and management of high seas fishery resources under the New Law of the Sea," *Natural Resource Modeling*, 10: 87–108.

Levhari, D. and Mirman, L. (1980) "The great fish war: An example using a dynamic Cournot-Nash solution," *Bell Journal of Economics*, 11: 649–661.

Li, E. (1998) "Cooperative high-seas straddling stock agreement as a characteristic function game," *Marine Resource Economics*, 13: 247–258.

Lodge, M., Anderson, D., Løbach, T., Munro, G., Sainsbury, K., and Willock, A. (2007) *Recommended Best Practices for Regional Fisheries Management Organizations: Report of an Independent Panel to Develop a Model for Improved Governance by Regional Fisheries Management Organizations*, Chatham House, London.

McRae, D. and Munro, G. (1989) "Coastal state rights within the 200-mile exclusive economic zone," in P. Neher, R. Arnason, and N. Mollet (eds), *Rights Based Fishing* (pp. 97–112), Dordrecht: Kluwer.

Miller, K. and Munro, G. (2004) "Climate and cooperation: A new perspective on the management of shared fish stocks," *Marine Resource Economics*, 19: 367–393.

Miller, K., Munro, G., McDorman, T., McKelvey, R., and Tydemers, P. (2001) "The 1999 Pacific Salmon Agreement: A sustainable solution?" Occasional Papers: Canadian-American Public Policy No. 47, Canadian-American Center, University of Maine, Orono.

Munro, G. (1979) "The optimal management of transboundary renewable resources," *Canadian Journal of Economics*, 3: 271–296.

Munro, G. (2008) "Game theory and the development of resource management policy: The case of international fisheries," in J. Albiac, J.J. Sánchez-Soriana, and A. Dinar (eds), *Game Theory and Policy Making in Natural Resources and the Environment* (pp. 12–41), London: Routledge.

Munro, G. and Stokes, R. (1989) "The Canada-United States Pacific Salmon Treaty," in D. McRae and G. Munro (eds), *Canadian Oceans Policy: National Strategies and the New Law of the Sea* (pp. 17–35), Vancouver: University of British Columbia Press.

Munro, G. and Sumaila, U.R. (2011) "Lutter contre la pêche illégale," in P. Jacquet, R. Pachuari, and L. Tubiana (eds), *Regards Sur la Terre 2011: Océans La Nouvelle Frontière* (pp. 265–273), Paris: Armand Colin.

Munro, G., McDorman, T., and McKelvey, R. (1998) "Transboundary fishery resources and the Canada-United States Pacific Salmon Treaty," Occasional Papers: Canadian-American Public Policy No. 33, Canadian-American Center, University of Maine, Orono.

Munro, G., Van Houtte, A., and Willmann, R. (2004) "The conservation and management of shared fish stocks: Legal and economic aspects," FAO Fisheries Technical Paper 465, Rome.

Northwest Atlantic Fisheries Organization (2011) www.nafo.int.

OECD (2009) *Strengthening Regional Fisheries Management Organizations*. Paris: OECD.

Örbech, P., Sigurjonsson, K., and McDorman, T. (1998) "The 1995 United Nations straddling and highly migratory fish stocks agreement: Management, enforcement and dispute settlement," *The International Journal of Marine and Coastal Law*, 15: 361–378.

Orrego Vicuña, F. (1999) *The Changing International Law of High Seas Fisheries*. Cambridge: Cambridge University Press.

Pintassilgo, P. (2003) "A coalitional approach to the management of high sea fisheries in the presence of externalities," *Natural Resource Modeling*, 16: 175–197.

Pintassilgo, P. and Costa-Duarte, C. (2000) "The new member problem in the cooperative management of the high seas," *Marine Resource Economics*, 15: 361–378.

Pintassilgo, P. and Lindroos, M. (2008) "Coalition formation in straddling stock fisheries: A partition function game approach," *International Game Theory Review*, 10: 303–317.

Pintassilgo, P., Finus, M., Lindroos, M., and Munro, G. (2010) "Stability and success of Regional Fisheries Management Organizations," *Environmental and Resource Economics*, 46: 377–402.

Serdy, A. (2007) "Trading of fishery commission quota in international law," *Ocean Yearbook*, 21: 265–288.

Stokke, O. (2003) "Management of shared fish stocks in the Barents Sea," in *Papers*

Presented at the Norway-FAO Expert Consultation on the Management of Shared Fish Stocks Bergen Norway, 7–10 October 2002, FAO Fisheries Report No. 695 Supplement (pp. 181–191), Rome.

United Nations (1982) United Nations Convention on the Law of the Sea, UN Doc. A/Conf. 62/122.

United Nations (1995) United Nations Conference on Straddling Fish Stocks and Highly Migratory Fish Stocks, Agreement for the Implementation of the Provisions of the United Nations Convention on the Law of the Sea of 10 December 1982 Relating to the Conservation and Management of Straddling Fish Stocks and Highly Migratory Fish Stocks. UN Doc. A/Conf. 164/27.

U.S. Department of State (1999) Diplomatic Note No. 0225 from Canada to the United States; reply; attached Agreement, June 30. www.state.gov.

Willock, A. and Lack, M. (2006) *Follow the Leader: Learning from Experience and Best Practice in Regional Fisheries Management Organizations*. Sydney: WWF International and TRAFFIC International.

8 Haggling on the verge of disaster[1]

Jérémy Laurent-Lucchetti, Justin Leroux and
Bernard Sinclair-Desgagné

8.1 Introduction

Human societies rely on a number of indispensable ecological services, such as
water purification, livestock support, flood prevention, waste recycling, climate
stability, erosion avoidance and fresh air, for their economic activities and well-
being. These services are provided by forests, lakes, coral reefs, savannas, wetlands, oceans, the troposphere and other ecosystems that typically are
"common-pool resources" – that is, resources "…from which it is difficult to
exclude or limit users once the resource is provided, and one person's consumption of resource units makes those units unavailable to others" (Ostrom 1999,
p. 497). The impossibility to exclude potential beneficiaries while inevitable capacity constraints exist (at least in the short run) makes such ecosystems, and the corresponding ecological services, particularly prone to a "tragedy of the commons."

Over the last decades, significant research efforts have considered how human
societies can, and actually do, cope with this problem.[2] Taking stock of this literature, this chapter builds on two well-documented additional observations. First,
the provision of ecological services is subject to discontinuities, bifurcations or
threshold effects that may show up rather abruptly, following persistent abuses
of the involved ecosystems (Scheffer *et al.* 2001). In agriculture, for example, it
is often the case that "…no perceptible change in the environmental state occurs
unless a specified farming practice is applied with a minimal intensity and on a
minimal area in the zone of interest" (Dupraz *et al.* 2009, p. 613). In the literature on biodiversity, the so-called "rivet hypothesis" (Ehrlich and Ehrlich 1981;
Lawton 1993) alleges that:

> the functions of species in ecosystems can be analogous to the functions of
> rivets in an airplane. Both systems can afford continual extraction of its con-
> stituent components without experimenting a loss of function. However, after a
> certain point, this capacity is lost and only one additional species extinction
> (rivet popped) may cause a collapse in the functional properties of the system.[3]

Second, the inherent complexity of ecosystems usually makes it difficult to assess
threshold values with certainty.[4] Experts will therefore typically disagree about the
precise levels of these thresholds. This can lead to a peculiar information structure,

with the aggregation of different experts' opinion, often resulting in multimodal distributions.

As stated in the Millennium Ecosystem Assessment Report (2005), "The expansion of abrupt, unpredictable changes in ecosystems, many of which are with harmful effects on increasingly large numbers of people, is the key challenge facing managers of ecosystem services." Previous works have drawn attention to certain exogenous characteristics of agents, like risk aversion, willingness-to-pay and asymmetry of information, in driving the outcome.[5] Although these certainly are important items in understanding the conservation or depletion of common-pool resources, we emphasize here the role of interaction, endogenous communication and cooperation among agents in the presence of a specific type of uncertainty.

In sharp contrast with the literature so far, the type of uncertainty we introduce here does not always lead to lower collective demand for natural capital, even when all agents are risk averse. "Cautious equilibria," in which agents behave as if the worst-case scenario were certain, are found to coexist with "dangerous equilibria," in which the overall request of ecological services might lead to their collapse, and even "dreadful equilibria," in which agents collectively claim so much of the resource that no unilateral deviation by one agent can stop its exhaustion. This surprising phenomenon arises because the location of thresholds follows a multimodal probability distribution. An important implication is that, in some settings with uncertainty – but perfect information – strategic interaction can override the agents' primary characteristics (such as risk aversion).

Our framework is very similar to that discussed in Suleiman and Rapoport (1988). There, the distribution of thresholds is unconstrained, and the setting described up to now corresponds to what they call the "Bernoulli distributed source." Nevertheless, their approach is not a game-theoretic one

> partly because of the problem of multiplicity of equilibria [...] and partly because [they] suspect that the game theoretic approach [...] may not capture the cognitive processes that underlie the subjects' decision behavior. Rather, [they] have proposed a simpler individual choice behavior model in which social uncertainty is captured by a probability distribution that the subject has over the total request of the remaining group members.[6]

Hence, by providing a systematic analysis of the Nash equilibria of the corresponding game, our approach should be seen as a complement to that found in Suleiman and Rapoport (1988). This allows us to investigate the nature of the coordination problems at play, the robustness of multiple equilibria that arise and some welfare comparisons between them.

To handle multiple equilibria, we consider next the (realistic) possibility that agents communicate and cooperate via group deviations.[7] As one might expect, this rules out all dreadful equilibria. Somewhat more surprising, however, is the fact that dangerous equilibria may be vulnerable to group deviations, while cautious equilibria are not. Actually, dangerous equilibria are not coalition-proof when certain cautious equilibria exist. The upshot is that any cautious equilibrium is efficient and Pareto dominates all dangerous equilibria that can be reached from it by increasing every agent's claim on natural capital.

These results are initially derived with only two possible ceilings. To be precise, our model amends the well-known Nash demand game (Nash 1950; Malueg 2010), also called the "Divide-the-dollar game," by supposing that symmetrically informed players are splitting an uncertain amount (of natural capital) which follows a discrete or multimodal probability distribution. This setting seems to capture a number of stylized situations: in climate change negotiations, for instance, parties normally focus on a finite number of collective targets, such as 550 parts per million (ppm) of carbon dioxide (CO_2-equivalent) – a politically sensible objective that many think is unlikely to prevent major environmental disruptions, 450 ppm, which may limit global warming to a manageable level (thought to be 2°C), or 350 ppm, which some scientists and vulnerable countries regard as the upper bound on emissions that guarantees the preservation of the present biosphere.

We then explain how our results are qualitatively robust if uncertainty concerning the location of thresholds is captured by a continuous but multimodal probability distribution. The latter situation may reflect the fact that the models and approaches that scientists tend to adopt generally offer different confidence intervals or probability distributions rather than point estimates. Again, such continuous multimodal probability distributions are likely to emerge in climate change policy discussions (Jones 2003; Moss and Schneider 2000), from the aggregation of experts' opinions and the Bayesian weighting practiced by the Organization for Economic Cooperation and Development (OECD) and the Intergovernmental Panel on Climate Change (IPCC).

On a policy note, these findings support the creation of institutions and governance mechanisms that enhance collaboration among users of natural commons: For as long as agents can identify a cautious equilibrium in which they all consume less than in the current state, they should cooperate in moving to this precautionary, yet more efficient, situation. As the derivation of our results will show, however, a lower threshold will invite such a move only if the probability associated with it is sufficiently large; the collective adoption of a costly precautionary stance is therefore robust to the existence of baseless doomsayers.

The rest of the chapter unfolds as follows. The upcoming section covers some examples inspired by the Millennium Ecosystem Assessment Report (2005), which illustrate our approach. Section 8.3 lays out the basic model and the expected outcomes. Section 8.4 presents and proves our main propositions. Section 8.5 checks their robustness and generality, section 8.6 discusses some of their policy implications and section 8.7 brings concluding remarks.

8.2 Some examples

The Millennium Ecosystem Assessment Report (2005) contains numerous examples of systems characterized by threshold effects with uncertainty on these thresholds. We recall here some of these examples in order to demonstrate the kind of problem we address in this chapter.

8.2.1 Disease emergence

Spreads of infectious diseases regularly exhibit nonlinear behavior. As stated in Olinky and Stone (2004, p. 70):

> The notion of thresholds forms a central part of classical and current epidemiological theory and carries important implications for disease eradication and vaccination programs.... When modeling epidemics, it is convenient to formulate the population in terms of its underlying graph structure with nodes representing individuals, and potential contacts or connections between pairs of individuals as edges of the network. The connectivity of the graph naturally controls to a great degree the spread of an infection through a network. It is well understood that for a large and completely random graph, there is a threshold level of connectivity. Below the threshold, individuals are essentially disconnected from one another, all direct and indirect pathways being considered. However, for a critical number of edges the graph forms a "giant component" whereby nearly all individuals are connected to one another.

Of course, while scientists can often warn of increased risks of change, they cannot predict the thresholds where the change will be encountered. The Millennium Ecosystem Assessment Report (2005, p. 89) states that:

> The almost instantaneous outbreak of SARS (severe acute respiratory syndrome) in different parts of the world is an example of such potential, although rapid and effective action contained its spread: Within weeks, SARS spread from Hong Kong to infect individuals in 37 countries in early 2003.... During the 1997–98 El Niño, excessive flooding caused cholera epidemics in Djibouti, Somalia, Kenya, Tanzania, and Mozambique. Warming of the African Great Lakes due to climate change may create conditions that increase the risk of cholera transmission in surrounding countries. An event similar to the 1918 Spanish flu pandemic, which is thought to have killed 20–40 million people worldwide, could now result in over 100 million deaths within a single year. Such a catastrophic event, the possibility of which is being seriously considered by the epidemiological community, would probably lead to severe economic disruption and possibly even rapid collapse in a world economy dependent on fast global exchange of goods and services.

8.2.2 Fisheries collapse

Fish population collapses have been commonly encountered in both freshwater and marine fisheries. Fish populations are generally able to withstand some level of catch with a relatively small impact on their overall population size. As the catch increases, however, a threshold is reached after which too few adults remain to produce enough offspring to support that level of harvest, and the population may drop abruptly to a much smaller size. For example, the Atlantic cod stocks of the east coast of Newfoundland collapsed in 1992, forcing the closure of the fishery after hundreds of years of exploitation. As stated in Kennedy (1997, p. 304):

> The moratorium in 1992 marked the largest industrial closure in Canadian history. In Newfoundland alone, over 35,000 fishers and plant workers from over 400 coastal communities became unemployed. In response to dire warnings of social and economic consequences, the federal government intervened, initially providing income assistance through the Northern Cod Adjustment and Recovery Program, and later through the Atlantic Ground-fish Strategy, which included money specifically for the retraining of those workers displaced by the closing of the fishery. Newfoundland has since experienced a dramatic environmental, industrial, economic, and social restructuring.

8.2.3 *Changes in dominant species in coral ecosystems*

This example is related to the concept of "keystone species," a species that has a disproportionately large effect on its environment relative to its abundance. Such species play a critical role in maintaining the structure of an ecological community, affecting many other organisms in an ecosystem and helping to determine the types and numbers of various other species in the community. An ecosystem may experience a dramatic shift if a keystone species is removed, even though that species was a small part of the ecosystem by measures of biomass or productivity. The Millennium Ecosystem Assessment Report (2005, p. 89) states that:

> Some coral reef ecosystems have undergone sudden shifts from coral-dominated to algae-dominated reefs. The trigger for such phase shifts, which are essentially irreversible, is usually multifaceted and includes increased nutrient input leading to eutrophic conditions, and removal of herbivorous fishes that maintain the balance between corals and algae. Once a threshold is reached, the change in the ecosystem takes place within months and the resulting ecosystem, although stable, is less productive and less diverse. One well-studied example is the sudden switch in 1983 from coral to algal domination of Jamaican reef systems. This followed several centuries of over-fishing of herbivores, which left the control of algal cover almost entirely dependent on a single species of sea urchin, whose populations collapsed when exposed to a species-specific pathogen. As a result, Jamaica's reefs shifted (apparently irreversibly) to a new low-diversity, algae-dominated state with very limited capacity to support fisheries.

8.2.4 Regional climate change

Smith *et al.* (2001, p. 945) report that "Physical, ecological and social systems may respond in an abrupt, non-linear or irregular way to climate change." For example, in the Sahel region of North Africa, vegetation cover is almost completely controlled by rainfall. When vegetation is present, rainfall is quickly recycled back to the atmosphere through evapotranspiration, generally increasing precipitation and, in turn, leading to a denser vegetation canopy. Model results suggest that land degradation leads to a substantial reduction in water recycling and may have contributed to the observed trend in rainfall reduction in the region over the last 30 years. In tropical regions, deforestation generally leads to decreased rainfall. Since forest existence crucially depends on rainfall, the relationship between tropical forests and precipitation forms a positive feedback that, under certain conditions, theoretically leads to the existence of two "forest" steady states: rainforest and savanna (although some models suggest only one, stable climate–vegetation state in the Amazon).

8.2.5 Water resources

Another sharp illustration is the current fate of the Sea of Galilee, in Israel. In addition to having very high religious and historical value, the lake, which is located in Northern Israel, is the main provider of irrigation and drinking water and it is one of the sources of the Jordan River. However, salt-water springs at the bottom of the lake are a cause for concern. As long as the pressure from the above fresh water is sufficient, it will prevent salt springs from irreversibly over-salinating the lake (Gvirtzman *et al.* 1997). The amount of water still available to fill human needs is subject to diverging opinions, however, and the ongoing five-year drought might have pulled this threshold further down.

The examples will underlie the game-theoretic analysis that will now follow.

8.3 The model and its equilibria

Consider several agents (which can be firms, individuals or countries) who must simultaneously decide how much of a natural capital they will claim for themselves. Overall demand is sustainable up to a limit, but scientists disagree on the tipping point beyond which the available resource would collapse to 0, making it effectively useless to all. To keep matters simple, suppose some studies report the ceiling on total demand to be at 1, while others deem it to be $a \in (0, 1)$. These point estimates are given consensual and common-knowledge probabilities p and $(1-p)$, respectively.

Denote by x_i an agent i's claim, demand or request (we use these terms interchangeably throughout the chapter) on natural capital, $x = (x_i)_{i \in N}$ a request vector or profile, $X = \Sigma_N x_i$ total demand, and $X_{-i} = \Sigma_{j \neq i} x_j$ the sum of all agents' claims except agent i's. The utility that agent i derives from being delivered her request, x_i, is given by $u_i(x_i)$. We assume the agents are risk averse or risk neutral.[8]

Reaching this consumption level is of course conditional on total demand not exceeding the ecological threshold; otherwise each agent gets nothing ($u_i(0)=0$).

Concretely, x_i might correspond, for example, to a farming area encroaching on some endangered key species' habitat, a certain flow of wastewater being dumped into a lake, a quantity of fish caught or some level of carbon dioxide emissions accruing into the atmosphere. This brings agent i a positive utility level $u_i(x_i)$, provided an underlying key ecological service – in these cases, land fertility, water purification, livestock renewal or stable weather, respectively – is maintained. Otherwise, agent i's utility level drops to 0. Agent i's expected payoff in this game is thus given by $v_i(x_i, X_{-i})=u_i(x_i)I(X\leq a)+pu_i(x_i)I(a<X\leq 1)$, where $I(\cdot)$ indicates whether the condition within parenthesis holds ($=1$) or not ($=0$). Given this setup, the best response of each agent solely depends on the sum of the other agents' demands. In particular, if the other agents collectively demand $a<X_{-i}\leq 1$ they are effectively making the outcome uncertain; agent i's best response is therefore to demand $1-X_{-i}$, which grants her the largest (expected) payoff without making the outcome any riskier.[9] When $X_{-i}\leq a$, however, agent i becomes pivotal in possibly making the outcomes uncertain. Indeed, she could demand $a-X_{-i}$ and obtain this much with certainty, or demand more – it is then in her best interest to ask for $1-X_{-i}$ – at the cost of creating uncertainty for everyone involved. Ultimately, her individual decision will depend on whether $u_i(a-X_{-i})>pu_i(1-X_{-i})$. It is straightforward to show that under risk-neutrality or risk-aversion, agent i will opt for a sure outcome – by demanding $a-X_{-i}$ – only if X_{-i} is low enough. By contrast, if the other agents are collectively not generous enough, so that $a-X_{-i}$ is small, even a risk-averse agent i will prefer to take chances and force a risky outcome.

Proposition 1 The current game gives rise to three sorts of equilibria:

1 Cautious equilibria, in which agents collectively set total demand at the highest secure level $X=a$;
2 Dangerous equilibria, in which agents altogether request natural capital up to the risky upper ceiling $X=1$ and face a probability $1-p$ of exhausting the resource; and
3 Dreadful equilibria, wherein everyone's claim on ecological services is so high (i.e., $X_{-i}>1$ for all i) that no individual adjustment can avoid their collapse.

Note that no Nash equilibrium exists in which agents collectively ask for an amount of natural capital lower than a or strictly between a and 1. An agent can always increase his payoff if the aggregate demand is between a and 1, either by increasing his own consumption so that the total demand is 1 (thus consuming a higher amount with the same uncertainty) or by decreasing his consumption so that total demand is a, if possible, so as to consume a lower amount with certainty.

Note, moreover, that cautious, dangerous and dreadful Nash equilibria can coexist despite the fact that all agents are risk averse. The following example illustrates this.

Example 1. Let there be only two agents, with identical utility function $u_i(x_i)=\sqrt{x_i}$ for $i=1$, 2. Suppose $a=0.8$ and $p=0.8$. The strategy profile $x = (0.5, 0.5)$ is a dangerous equilibrium because $v_i(0.5,\ 0.5)=0.7*0.8=0.56>v_i(0.3, 0.5)=0.54$ for $i=1$, 2. At the same time, the profile $x'=(0.4, 0.4)$ is a cautious equilibrium, since $v_i(0.4,\ 0.4)=0.63>v_i(0.6,\ 0.4)=0.77*0.8=0.62$ for $i=1$, 2; and $x''=(1.5,\ 1.5)$ is also clearly an equilibrium, a dreadful one which brings each agent's payoff to 0. Although we exclude such risk attitudes, note that all three types of equilibria could exist as well with risk-loving agents. To see this, suppose that $i=1$, 2, $u_i(x_i)=x_i^2$, $p=0.4$ and $a=0.8$. One can check that $x=(0.5, 0.5)$ is a dangerous equilibrium, that $x'=(0.4, 0.4)$ is again a cautious one and that $x''=(1.5,\ 1.5)$ is a dreadful equilibrium.

The coexistence of cautious and dangerous equilibria contrasts with the findings reported so far in the literature (see Bramoullé and Treich 2009, for example).[10] Figure 8.1 illustrates the sets of equilibria predicted in the proposition, in the two-agent case.

If agent i becomes more risk averse, a secure amount of resources now yields relatively more utility than the higher but riskier amount: The set of cautious equilibria expands while the set of dangerous equilibria shrinks. A decrease in the probability p that the actual threshold on ecological services is 1 instead of a

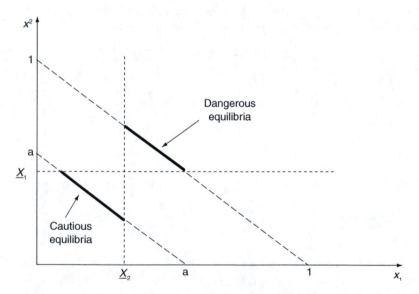

Figure 8.1 Coexistence of cautious and dangerous equilibria. $\underline{X}_1$ represents the demand of agent 2 above which agent 1's best response is to demand $x_1=1-x_2$, and below which agent 1's best response is to demand $x_1=a-x_2$. The quantity $\underline{X}_2$ is defined symmetrically.

leads to the same conclusion. Finally, consider an increase of the lower threshold from a to a': The set of dangerous equilibria gets smaller (unambiguously) but the set of cautious equilibria might not expand.

In view of the multiplicity of Nash equilibria, we shall now move on to examine what happens when group deviations (and not just individual ones) are permitted.

8.4 Allowing for communication and cooperation

Users of common-pool resources can normally communicate, negotiate and act collectively. The standard Nash equilibrium concept a priori discards this behavior, so one may cast doubts about their plausibility in the present context.[11] A direct consequence of allowing agents to talk to each other and eventually collude could be, for instance, that subgroups may form in which members prefer to jointly move away from some Nash equilibrium. This section will now examine whether the three types of equilibria defined above are immune to such deviations.

Recall that a Nash equilibrium x is strong if no coalition of agents can improve its members' respective payoff through a joint deviation. Allowing for this yields the following statement:

> **Proposition 2** Cautious Nash equilibria are strong, but dreadful Nash equilibria are not.

The intuition behind Proposition 2 is clear. Any group deviation from a dreadful equilibrium benefits all, including the members of the deviating coalition. Symmetrically, any group deviation away from a cautious equilibrium either entails a reshuffling of resource within the coalition – thus hurting at least one member – or threatens the availability of the resource. The latter is not profitable for anyone in the coalition because any agent could have unilaterally forced a risky outcome (by increasing its demand by $1-a$) without having to share the surplus but chose not to do so (since we are at a cautious equilibrium).

Proposition 2 has a straightforward welfare implication: All cautious equilibria are Pareto efficient (to see this, consider the grand coalition that includes all the agents). Furthermore, any cautious equilibrium Pareto dominates all dreadful ones. The status of dangerous equilibria is not so clear-cut, however. To analyze it, we shall invoke a weaker equilibrium notion that forbids certain improbable group deviations. Let us call a group deviation self-enforcing if it is not itself exposed to improving subgroup deviations. Following Bernheim *et al.* (1987), a Nash equilibrium is said to be coalition-proof if no self-enforcing group deviation can deliver an outcome that is Pareto improving. Clearly, any strong Nash equilibrium (hence any cautious equilibrium, by the last proposition) is coalition-proof.

Proposition 3 Dangerous equilibria are Pareto dominated by any cautious equilibrium in which no agent demands more, and are thus not coalition-proof should such a cautious equilibrium exist.

The general intuition behind Proposition 3 is germane to that underlying Proposition 2. Consider a dangerous equilibrium from which a cautious equilibrium may be reached by reducing some agents' demands while not increasing the demands of anyone else. Then, by definition of a cautious equilibrium, no single agent would subsequently want to deviate from it. But, because group deviations are less advantageous than unilateral ones (as the surplus must be shared somehow), coalitional deviations are not in any agent's best interest either. Hence, the welfare of the coalition members has improved; but the non-deviators are also better off, because their payoff is now certain. Therefore, this cautious equilibrium Pareto dominates the initial dangerous one. It follows that the latter is not coalition-proof.

When there are only two players, no dangerous equilibrium can be coalition-proof when cautious equilibria exist (this can readily be checked by looking at Figure 8.1). In general, however, coalition-proof dangerous equilibria and cautious equilibria do coexist. For example, consider a setting with three agents whose preferences are such that $u_i(a/3) > pu_i(1 - 2a/3)$ for $i = 1, 2, 3$, with $a < \frac{3}{4}$; it follows immediately that $x = (0, \frac{1}{2}, \frac{1}{2})$ is a coalition-proof dangerous equilibrium while $x = (a/3, a/3, a/3)$ is a cautious one.

Note that Proposition 3 is not a characterization of coalition-proof dangerous equilibria because such equilibria may exist even in the absence of a Pareto-dominating cautious equilibrium, as the following example illustrates.

Example 2. Let us add a third identical player to the previous Example 1, where $p = 0.8$, $a = 0.8$ and $u_i(x_i) = \sqrt{x_i}$ for $i = 1, 2, 3$. Clearly, the request profile $x = (\frac{1}{2}, \frac{1}{2}, 0)$ is a dangerous equilibrium because $(\frac{1}{2}, \frac{1}{2})$ was a dangerous equilibrium in the two-agent game. A profitable deviation for coalition $T = \{1, 2\}$ is to demand $(0.4, 0.4)$; this deviation is self-enforcing since $(0.4, 0.4)$ was a cautious equilibrium in the earlier game. But $x' = (0.4, 0.4, 0)$ is not a cautious equilibrium because the third agent gains by asking for 0.2 instead of zero.

The above example illustrates the well-known shortcoming of coalition-proofness: A self-enforcing group deviation may be exposed to some outsiders repositioning.[12] More importantly, it also suggests (as Figure 8.1 somewhat does) that a group deviation from a dangerous to a cautious equilibrium can only occur when claims on natural capital are "not too asymmetric" across agents. This observation has ramifications for public policy and climate change negotiations that will be discussed in section 8.6.

8.5 The aggregation of experts' opinions

In the game considered thus far, the demand threshold could take only two possible values. This scenario may be interpreted as one in which two experts disagree on the value of the threshold, and their perceived relative accuracy is measured by the probability p. In other words, agents believe that the expert who says "the value of the threshold is 1" is right with probability p and that the other expert (the one announcing "a") is correct with probability $1-p$. In practice, however, there may be more than two experts. Moreover, predictions rarely come in the form of point estimates, but are usually accompanied by confidence intervals. One would then often contemplate a situation with a continuum of possible thresholds randomly spread according to a multimodal probability distribution. This case could stem from acknowledging measurement errors and aggregating various interval or probabilistic estimates (instead of point estimates) of thresholds, as it is common in many scientific fields (see, for example, Weigel *et al.* 2010, for the climate modeling case). However, one can check that our analysis yet produces qualitatively similar results.

Let us consider a situation in which the ceiling on ecological services, r, is located according to a common-knowledge distribution function F with density f such that $F(0)=0$.[13] Focusing on our interpretation of different experts' opinions, we view F as an aggregate of various interval or probabilistic estimates of an ecological threshold and assume it is multimodal. Each mode might correspond to an experts' (unimodal) belief over the threshold, while the probability weight attributed to each distribution is exogenously given.

Being at a Nash equilibrium requires of course that each player be at a global maximum, given the other players' claims. Such an outcome will be called cautious (dangerous) when total demand is at the lowest (highest) level. It turns out that both types of equilibria may coexist, even in this continuous framework. A notable difference with the discrete case analyzed above is that there can be only one Nash equilibrium of a kind. It also happens, nevertheless, that the cautious equilibrium in this continuous setting is still a strong Nash equilibrium that dominates a dangerous equilibrium in which no agent claims less.[14]

8.6 Policy implications

The existence of an ecological threshold, and the fact that its exact level is uncertain, raise specific policy issues. An important one is whether to then adopt precautionary measures. The feasibility and social desirability of such actions have been widely debated in policy circles and remain an active research topic (see Wiener *et al.* 2011; Barrieu and Sinclair-Desgagné 2006, and the references therein). In the present context, choosing a precautionary stance would mean to avoid claiming natural capital beyond the lowest possible threshold, in order to safeguard those vital and irreplaceable ecological services. Contrary to the current literature, which assumes a benevolent planner or representative agent with the proper kind of risk or ambiguity aversion, Proposition 1 above shows that this outcome can actually be achieved in a decentralized (or *laissez faire*) fashion: It corresponds to what we called a "cautious" equilibrium.

Propositions 2 and 3 entail, moreover, that precautionary outcomes would arise rather naturally as a result of fostering communication and collaboration between agents, since cautious equilibria are robust to group deviations (and are, thus, also Pareto optimal), while dreadful equilibria are not and dangerous equilibria may not be.

There is, however, one caveat to Proposition 3 that is worth mentioning. In that proposition, the coalition that departs from the dangerous equilibrium, thereby implementing a precautionary outcome, bears all the cost while outsiders retain their initial claim (which will moreover materialize with certainty). This could create an incentive for agents to stick to their original request and free-ride on deviating coalitions, so dangerous equilibria might not be that vulnerable after all. One way around this situation is to seek a grand coalition in which everybody settles for less natural capital. This is the approach chosen notably in the post-Kyoto negotiations over national reductions in carbon dioxide emissions. It might be the only sensible one when agents are fairly similar in their respective preferences and requests, but the effort then spent in drawing everybody together might be daunting. Alternatively, if there is "enough asymmetry" between agents at some dangerous equilibrium outcome x (but not too much, in light of the discussion that follows Example 2 above), a coalition of the willing, ready to implement a precautionary outcome, might come about.

8.7 Concluding remarks

This chapter has analyzed the behavior of rational agents sharing a non-excludable ecosystem that may not deliver some key services beyond an uncertain ecological threshold. We modeled this situation as a version of the well-known "Divide-the-dollar" game in which the amount to be split follows a discrete probability distribution. This brought about two new insights for the economics of common-pool resources. First, strategic interaction can have much more impact on the outcome than individual features: Whatever the agents' respective degree of risk aversion, for instance, "cautious" equilibria, in which agents altogether behave as if the lowest (and safest) threshold were certain, were found to coexist with "dangerous" equilibria, in which the agents' request of ecological services up to a higher threshold might lead to an ecosystem breakdown, and even "dreadful" equilibria, in which so much natural capital is claimed collectively that no single player's actions can prevent its exhaustion. Second, allowing agents to cooperate and form deviating coalitions would eliminate all dreadful equilibria and several dangerous equilibria, while cautious equilibria were shown to be robust to such deviations. These results support the emphasis currently put by the common-pool resources literature on social capital, governance and institutions. The latter also captures the recurrent empirical observation that some resource-sharing communities were able to avoid a tragedy of the commons through communication and cooperation (Ostrom 1999); its derivation indicates, moreover, which dangerous equilibria will be discarded and which situation a successful deviating coalition will then prefer.

The above analysis and conclusions may apply to other contexts as well. Abusing natural capital might trigger severe social unrest instead or in addition to a loss of ecological services (as in Diamond's (2005) tale of the Mayas collapse through drought and warfare), for instance, or the agents' actions might directly encroach on social (rather than natural) capital until some uncertain borderline is crossed and civil war erupts (as in André and Platteau's (1998) account of the rising tensions in social and family relations that increasing land scarcity engendered in the 1980s in Rwanda, which partly paved the way for the bloody civil war that broke out in 1994).

Another immediate step from this chapter, considering the relative simplicity of the present game, would be to check whether the above results hold as well in the laboratory. In such a setting, we expect the presence of focal points, or the subjects' usual preference for equality and fairness (as reported in Ostrom 2000), to then reduce the initial sets of equilibria but affect as well the extent to which deviating coalitions may form. Other theoretical insights could additionally be obtained by relaxing some informational assumptions. For example, agents might be allowed to hold different beliefs about the location and distribution of thresholds or have access (at some cost) to a privately observable warning signal (of the type discussed, say, in Scheffer *et al.* 2009). The issue of asymmetric information has already been considered in the common-pool resource literature (see Lindahl and Johannesson 2009, and the references therein), but not with various discrete thresholds or when the distribution of thresholds is multimodal, as above. One should also examine rigorously how agents communicate and coordinate with each other. To be sure, for the above equilibrium outcomes to locate where potential thresholds precisely lie, some means of coordination must already exist (particularly in large-scale natural commons, such as open seas or the earth's atmosphere). It would be worthwhile to investigate what they are, and to explore when and how they can support cooperation. In a dynamic setting, finally, one might introduce learning (exogenous or endogenous) and investigate the robustness of cautious and dangerous equilibria under various information acquisition scenarios.

Notes

1 This chapter is a non-technical version of "Splitting an uncertain (natural) capital" by the same authors. We are grateful to Olivier Bochet, Joseph Harrington, Michael McBride, Alan Miller, Hervé Moulin, Nicolas Sahuguet, Maher Said, Carlos Seiglie, Gunter Stefan, Ekaterina Turkina, Jonathan Wiener and Georges Zaccour for useful conversations or advice. We also acknowledge valuable feedback from participants to the Montréal Natural Resource and Environmental Economics Workshop, the Montréal Economic Theory Group, the Société canadienne de sciences économiques 2010 conference, the 2010 World Congress of Environmental and Resource Economists, the 2011 American Economic Association Meeting, the 8th Game Theory Practice Meeting and seminars at the University of Bern, Humboldt University, the European School of Management and Technology in Berlin, Rice University and the University of Norwich, as well as financial support from the Social Sciences and Humanities Research Council of Canada (SSHRC).

2 For an exhaustive literature survey and appraisal, see Elinor Ostrom's (2010) lecture, delivered when she received the 2009 Bank of Sweden Prize in Economic Sciences in Memory of Alfred Nobel.

3 This statement is drawn from Muradian's (2001, p. 11) benchmark discussion of ecological thresholds.
4 For a discussion of this general point, together with an overview and appraisal of
   available statistical methods, see Andersen *et al.* (2008).
5 Most economic analyses of natural commons involving uncertainty, regime shifts and
   strategic interaction have done so in a public good provision context (see, e.g.,
   Boucher and Bramoullé 2010, and the references therein).
6 Suleiman and Rapoport (1988, p. 111).
7 Formally, this means that we use the strong and coalition-proof equilibrium concepts
   developed respectively by Aumann (1959) and Bernheim *et al.* (1987).
8 The function $u_i(.)$ is concave and nondecreasing.
9 If $X_{-i} > 1$, agent i will receive nothing no matter the realized value of the ceiling. Her
   best response is then degenerate, and any demand level will do. As we shall see
   below, this case gives rise to so-called "dreadful" equilibria.
10 We refer the reader to Laurent-Lucchetti *et al.* (2011) for the formal conditions characterizing the coexistence of cautious and dangerous equilibria.
11 Quoting Ostrom (2010, p. 648), for instance, on why the Prisoner's Dilemma game
   might not fully capture what goes on in the sharing of common-pool resources:
   "Public investigators purposely keep prisoners separated so they cannot communicate.
   The users of a common-pool resource are not so limited."
12 In fact, if we strengthen the requirement of a self-enforcing deviation to include possible deviations from outsiders, we obtain the following characterization result: "A
   dangerous equilibrium is coalition-proof if and only if there does not exist a cautious
   equilibrium in which no agent demands more."
13 In the binary framework discussed in the previous sections, the threshold level, r,
   could take on only two values, a and 1. The corresponding probability density function, f, took on the value zero everywhere on [0, 1] except for $f(1) = p$ and $f(a) = 1 - p$.
14 We refer the reader to Laurent-Lucchetti *et al.* (2011) for numerical examples illus-
   trating this fact.

References

Andersen, T., Carstensen, J., Hernandez-Garcia, E. and Duarte, C.M. (2008) "Ecological
    thresholds and regime shifts: Approaches to identification," *Trends in Ecology and
    Evolution*, 24: 49–57.
André, C. and Platteau, J.-P. (1998) "Land relations under unbearable stress: Rwanda
    caught in the Malthusian trap," *Journal of Economic Behavior and Organization*, 34:
    1–47.
Aumann, R.J. (1959) "Acceptable points in general cooperative n-person games," in R.D.
    Luce and A.W. Tucker (eds), *Contributions to the Theory of Games IV, Annals of
    Mathematical Studies, vol. 40* (pp. 287–324), Princeton: Princeton University Press.
Barrieu, P. and Sinclair-Desgagné, B. (2006) "On precautionary policies," *Management
    Science*, 52: 1145–1154.
Bernheim, D., Peleg, B. and Whinston, M.D. (1987) "Coalition-proof Nash equilibria: I
    concepts," *Journal of Economic Theory*, 42: 1–12.
Boucher, V. and Bramoullé, Y. (2010) "Providing global public goods under uncer-
    tainty," *Journal of Public Economics*, 94: 591–603.
Bramoullé, Y. and Treich, N. (2009) "Can uncertainty alleviate the commons problem?"
    Journal of the European Economic Association, 7: 1042–1067.
Diamond, J. (2005) *Collapse: How Societies Choose to Fail or Succeed*. London: Penguin
    Books.

Dupraz, P., Latouche, K. and Turpin, N. (2009) "Threshold effect and coordination of agri-environmental efforts," *Journal of Environmental Planning and Management*, 52: 613–630.

Ehrlich, P. and Ehrlich, A. (1981) *Extinction: The Causes and Consequences of the Disappearance of Species*. New York: Ballantine Books.

Gvirtzman, H., Gavern, G. and Gvirtzman, G. (1997) "Hydrogeological modeling of the saline springs at the Sea of Galilee, Israel," *Water Resource Research*, 33: 913–926.

Jones, R. (2003) "Managing climate change risks," paper delivered at the OECD Workshop on the Benefits of Climate Policy: Improving Information for Policymakers, Paris.

Kennedy, J. (1997) "At the crossroads: Newfoundland and Labrador communities in a changing international context," *The Canadian Review of Sociology and Anthropology*, 34(3): 297–318.

Laurent-Lucchetti, J., Leroux, J. and Sinclair-Desgagné, B. (2011) "Splitting an uncertain (natural) capital," mimeo, available for download at: www.cirpee.org/fileadmin/documents/Cahiers_2011/CIRPEE11-05.pdf.

Lawton, J. (1993) "The role of species in ecosystems: Aspects of ecological complexity and biological diversity," in A.D. Schulze and H. Mooney (eds), *Biodiversity: An Ecological Perspective* (pp. 215–228), Germany: Springer.

Lindahl, T. and Johannesson, M. (2009) "Bargaining over a common good with private information," *Scandinavian Journal of Economics*, 111(3): 547–565.

Malueg, D. (2010) "Mixed-strategy equilibria in the Nash demand game," *Economic Theory*, 44: 243–270.

Millennium Ecosystem Assessment (2005) Millennium Ecosystem Assessment Synthesis Reports.

Moss, R.H. and Schneider, S.H. (2000) "Uncertainties in the IPCC TAR: Recommendations to lead authors for more consistent assessment and reporting," in R. Pachauri, T. Taniguchi and K. Tanaka (eds), *Third Assessment Report Guidance Papers* (pp. 33–51), Geneva: World Meteorological Organization.

Muradian, R. (2001) "Ecological thresholds: A survey," *Ecological Economics*, 38: 7–24.

Nash, J.F. (1950) "The bargaining problem," *Econometrica*, 18: 155–162.

Olinky, R. and Stone, L. (2004) "Unexpected epidemic thresholds in heterogeneous networks: The role of disease transmission," *Physical Review*, 70: 030902.

Ostrom, E. (1999) "Coping with tragedies of the commons," *Annual Review of Political Science*, 2: 493–535.

Ostrom, E. (2000) "Collective action and the evolution of social norms," *Journal of Economic Perspectives*, 14(3): 137–158.

Ostrom, E. (2010) "Beyond markets and states: Polycentric governance of complex economic systems," *American Economic Review*, 100: 641–672.

Scheffer, M., Bascompte, J., Brock, W.A., Brovkin, V., Carpenter, S.R., Dakos, V., Held, H., van Nes, E.H., Rietkerk, M. and Sugihara, G. (2009) "Early-warning signals for critical transitions," *Nature*, 461(3): 53–59.

Scheffer, M., Carpenter, S.R., Foley, J.A., Folke, C. and Walker, B. (2001) "Catastrophic shifts in ecosystems," *Nature*, 413: 591–596.

Smith, J.B., Schellnhuber, H.-J. and Mirza, M.M.Q. (2001) "19.6.1. The irregular face of climate change," in J.J. McCarthy, K.S. White, O. Canziani, N. Leary and D.J. Dokken (eds), *Vulnerability to Climate Change and Reasons for Concern: A Synthesis* (pp. 945–946). Cambridge: Cambridge University Press.

Suleiman, R. and Rapoport, A. (1988) "Environmental and social uncertainty in single-trial resource dilemmas," *Acta Psychologica*, 68: 99–112.

Weigel, A.P., Knutti, R., Liniger, M.A. and Appenzeller, C. (2010) "Risks of model weighting in multimodel climate projections," *Journal of Climate*, 23: 4175–4191.

Wiener, J., Rogers, M.D., Hammit, J.K. and Sand, P.H. (eds) (2011) *The Reality of Precaution: Comparing Risk Regulation in the United States and Europe*. Washington, DC: Resources for the Future (RFF) Press.

9 The dynamics of collective actions that protect the environment against the worst effects of globalization

Paloma Zapata-Lillo

9.1 Introduction

Globalization and the resulting fierce competition over natural resources have dramatically increased the over-exploitation of natural resources, such as water, land, and forests. This has led to deforestation, environmental pollution, and climate change, among other deteriorating effects. The free-trade agreements increase land plundering and common resources, and forced displacement of people from their homes (Havice 2004). In Mexico, according to official data from SAGARPA in 2008 (The Ministry of Agriculture, Cattle Raising, Rural Development, Fishing, and Nutrition) in the few years after the North American Free Trade Agreement came into effect, emigration from Mexican rural communities toward the United States doubled. Perhaps one of the most serious consequences of globalization is the breaking of both the intra-community social bonds and the virtuous interaction between the communities and their environment. It has led to the depopulation of entire small towns, whose former environment-protecting inhabitants were transformed into individuals who do not have any interest in foreign environments where they emigrate to, and tend to attack them.

As it has been shown in the work of E. Ostrom (Gibson *et al.* 2000; Costanza *et al.* 2000) and in numerous examples around the world (Maathai 2009; Gutiérrez 2009; Harvey 2000; Rosas 1997), many communities are able to govern their common resources in a sustainable way, preventing the members from selfishly squandering them. They are able, in some cases, to notably rescue their local environment, as is the case of the Mixteca community in Oaxaca, which was awarded the Goldman prize in 2008. The Goldman Environmental Prize is awarded annually to grassroots environmental activists, one from each of the world's six geographic regions: Africa, Asia, Europe, Islands and Island Nations, North America, and South and Central America. Typically, local communities can be the main source of resistance against the destructive action of corporations. They might promote the imposition of environment – protecting rules (we may mention as an example the Mexican cases of Tepoztlán, Morelos, of Cabo Pulmo, and Baja California Sur, the Zapatista communities in Chiapas, and recently the community of Cherán in Michoacán that defends its forest against a criminal cartel). By encouraging and generalizing this kind of behavior around the world, it would be possible to stop and reverse such environment-destructing global trends. In this chapter, the conditions for resistance emergence and the patterns they taken are studied. Those questions are important in order to know if it is possible to prevent communities from disintegration, and how to do so.

There are two main paths for the resistance against the globalization impact. On the one hand, in many cases, it is done by forming a nucleus of members who organize the rest of the community in order to carry out the different necessary collective actions, leading to a lasting virtuous interaction with the environment (such as the cases of the Mixteca region and Chiapas). On the other hand, in many other cases, the resistance is in the form of social movements that cyclically form large organizations and carry out strong actions during certain periods, while remaining relatively apathetic in other periods (such as the case of Tepoztlán and Chiapas). When this second pattern takes place, communities may achieve considerable improvements in the environment-protecting legislation that rules the local natural resources (e.g., establishment of ecological reserves). Both patterns are not necessarily mutually exclusive. Often communities have permanent nucleoli that are in charge of daily problems, but when a large threat appears, a cyclical pattern might emerge. Then, in apathetic periods of the cycle, the regular nucleus recovers its place. If the permanent organization characteristic of the first pattern is not reached, the achieved improvements may be lost. It is important that those kinds of patterns, movements, and permanent community organization are linked so that apathetic periods are not too destructive.

The conditions that enable communities to organize themselves to protect the environment are studied in Zapata-Lillo (2008). In this chapter, the behavioral patterns that emerge and the role of social stock in that emergence will be studied. The kind of conflicts facing communities, the dynamics of their resistance, and the social protective stock accumulation (environmental protecting rules) are modeled in a simplified way. Two dynamics will be considered: (a) the emergence of organizations in a stage that leads to collective actions that protect the environment; and (b) the accumulation of social protective stock. For the first of these dynamics, a version of Ostrom's game (1990) is used, assuming that it is repeated with a learning dynamic as in Young (1998), and the long-term trends will be investigated. On the other hand, in the accumulation dynamics, the corresponding long-run patterns will be studied. Both processes will be modeled as perturbed Markov processes, and the stochastic stable states will be found. In those dynamics, time is considered in two senses: (1) to study the accumulation of social protective stock, and (2) for the people of the community to learn. In the first sense, the history of the process is the history of the development, stagnation, and retrocession in laws, protocols, and people's awareness; that is, the history of the public good stock accumulation and depreciation in the long run. That is, accumulation and depreciation of protective rules. It is also the history of community organizations, the movements that have occurred, and the changes in permanent organization. The establishment of laws or decrees related to the environmental protection is considered as a sort of accumulation of an environmental-protecting stock (we also consider social awareness as part of that stock). That long-run process goes through stages. Time, in the second sense, is shorter. It is expressed by different periods within a stage. First, in each of those stages, the repetition of the collective action game and the learning dynamics occur again and again through short periods of time. Second, during a stage, the stock level does not change. Third, people learn from previous periods in a limited way because they are only able to obtain a small part of social experience and they make mistakes. Then, a stochastically stable state might be reached or the stage would be over before one of those stable states is reached. In the first case, that stable state determines how many groups (maybe none) participate and what the stock level is in the next stage (that is, the effectiveness of protective laws and social conscience). In the second case, there would be a probability for each efficient number of groups that participate. In both cases, at the end of each stage *t*, the stock might be accumulated, or not. Fourth, the public good that protects the environment is accumulated at the end of each stage. Then, it will be considered that the passing time, from the beginning of a stage until the beginning of another, is much longer than the passing time between two consecutive periods inside a stage. It will be studied why one of two different behavior accumulation patterns might happen: (1) The process, in the long run, leads to a set of actions that achieve a stock *k*, and then keeps it forever, only accumulating to produce depreciation compensation. The emergence of cycles in the size of the nucleus linked to *k* is considered in this case. (2) The process follows a kind of cycle with effervescent stages and apathy stages. In the last case, a cycle in the stock sizes emerges. The stages of disorganization are very upset because, in that time, the protective rules might be violated or become worse, and community disintegration might take place.

The time when a stochastic stable state is achieved could be extremely long in relation to the time of duration of a stage. Then, the possibility that any stochastically stable state is not achieved at the end of a stage is considered and another form of accumulation dynamics is introduced.

The chapter will be developed as follows: In the first two sections, the game, its properties, and the dynamics in a stage when the community has reached a stock *k* are studied. Those sections are very similar to the corresponding sections of Zapata-Lillo (2008); however, some changes are introduced, such as the existence of social stock, as well as more general payoff functions. Besides, the dynamic that is considered here is Young's adaptation play (Young 1998). In the third section, the social stock accumulation dynamic is studied in two scenarios: the assumption that a stochastically stable state is reached in each stage, and the assumption that it is not.

9.2 The model

9.2.1 Collective action game

There are some typical situations in the global world that affect common resources: (a) the activities of large corporations polluting water resources or deforesting a region, and people from the community have the dilemma of leaving home to go out and find a job or taking collective actions to rescue their commons; (b) a corporation (or a criminal organization) that wants to exploit a community's resources may be buying or renting (or grabbing) them. As a result, the community members might sell/rent (or permit robbery of) those resources or resist in order to protect them.

In order to build the model, let us consider one of those situations: A community N is involved in a conflict about its water resources (or another kind of resource). A multinational corporation Λ, taking advantage of certain matters not covered by statute law, intends to develop a project (a tourism or industrial complex) that would affect the amount and the quality of water supplied to members of the community, as well as possible grave environmental damage produced by construction of the complex. However Λ's project has other meanings for the community members. Many people expect that they would find jobs during construction and in the future when it is in operation. Other people wish to sell their products, extend their businesses, and so on. Therefore, there is a social dilemma in the community. The conflict affects all aspects of community life, and so people frequently have to make decisions about opposing or supporting the company's project. It is usual that communities are partitioned into different social groups $\{M_j\}$, such as neighborhoods, small merchants, and peasants. Each of those social groups M_j has representation in the community assembly that makes community decisions about opposing or supporting the project. If opposition to the company is the majority opinion, people have to take different collective actions, such as sending petition letters, distributing pamphlets, and organizing demonstrations. People from each social group must decide whether or not to participate in those actions by majority. Each collective action is carried out if a sufficient number of those social groups has decided to participate, and then they can form an efficient organization. The social groups that choose P form an effective organization, if each member of the community obtains a larger payoff than he obtains without any organization, and the project proceeds.

Elinor Ostrom (1990) introduced an extensive game with two players to express the dilemma inside communities. It is an alternative to the Prisoners' Dilemma. Figure 9.1 presents the game that has two parts: In the first part, both players simultaneously decide whether (A) or not (−A) to accept a compromise to cooperate. The second part is a Prisoners' Dilemma, which occurs if at least one of the players does not accept the compromise. C and NC are Cooperation and Defection, respectively.

Assuming that there are n groups in the community, the conflict can be modeled as a n-players version of Elinor Ostrom's alternative game (Ostrom 1990). It is assumed that the community has accumulated a social stock of size k. Each player is a social group in the game. The game has two parts. In the first one, each player M_j (social group) has two options: to participate in the collective action (P) or to act alone (NP). In the subgames, in the second part, each of the players has to decide if it supports Λ (NC) or opposes it (C). There are two kinds of subgames, depending on how many groups have decided P in the first

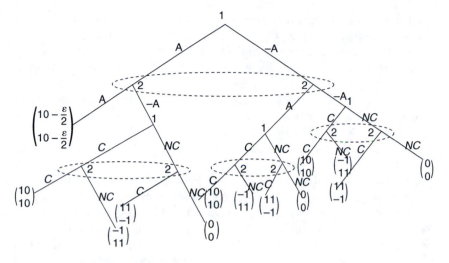

Figure 9.1 Ostrom's alternative game.

part of the game: (a) *s* groups in {M_j} have decided *P* and they are able to form an effective organization; (b) collective actions are not possible due to the small number of participants. In this last case, each subgame is a tragedy of the commons (Hardin 1968).

It is assumed that M_j is homogenous in the utility function of its members. Furthermore, since all individuals are homogenous, all M_js have the same payoff function.

Future works could consider different functions for different M_js, in order to introduce the links between permanent and cyclic organizations, which appear in many communities in real life.

Simple payoff functions are introduced as follows. Cooperation improves protective forces in different ways:

1   Past cooperation has accumulated a kind of stock (laws, social conscience) that gives individual rights to each person and each group M_j over resources (e.g., water). The resource is a public good (or a common) in the sense that it is non-excludable. The *k* size of the stock measures the effectiveness of the protection rules to give enough clean water to individuals in the community. Because those rules prohibit monopolizing and polluting water, they grant common property rights to community members regarding these sources and give community decision power over them. Those rights and prohibitions take different shapes, which may be more or less effective. The size of the stock can be defined (laws, regulations, and ruling social awareness) by, for example, establishing a preference relationship among the different laws, protocols, and community vigilance that can be set up. Let *k* be the stock that has been accumulated until a stage *t*. Each group that chooses

NC, in the second part of the game, earns $f_{NC}(k)$ whatever its decision was in the first part, and whatever others' decisions are. Each group M_j of the community that has decided (P, C) – that is, P in the first part and C in the second – obtains an extra payoff $f_P(k)$ if there is an effective organization S. Each M_j of the community that has decided (NP, C) obtains an extra payoff $f_C(k)$. Groups can cooperate in an isolated way if they do not choose P or if there is not an effective set of groups that choose P. Individuals who belong to a group M_j that choose P spend time and money to support collective actions, while members of groups that support a collective action, but are not engaged with other groups in an organization S, only act when they want, and they spare less time than people in groups who belong to S. But most important is that every group that chooses C cannot take the advantages that Λ supplies. Those advantages are larger, as k is larger because stronger rights make stronger power for M_js. Finally, people who do not cooperate and do not spare any time in collective actions can benefit overall from the mentioned advantages. Then, $f_{NC}(k) > f_C(k) > f_P(k)$. $f_{NC}(k) - f_P(k)$ and $f_{NC}(k) - f_C(k)$ are the costs of cooperation, in each case. Those costs depend on k, but they do not depend on how many groups choose P. It is also assumed that $f_P(0) = 0$, and $f_{NC}(0) > 0$.

2 Participation of s groups in the collective action implies that laws and social consciences are effective, as many people keep a watchful eye on law enforcement. Then, a function g expresses the payoff function of s, $g(s)$ if s is large enough. It is assumed that $g(0) = 0$, and $g(s+1) - g(s) < f_{NC}(k) - f_C(k)$, for each k and each s. Besides, in the case that, for some k, $g(n) > f_{NC}(k) - f_P(k)$, there is a tragedy for people from the community if everybody defects. Let s_k^* be the size of the minimum number of groups in $\{M_j\}$ such that they are able to act collectively (an efficient organization). That is, s_k^* is the minimum integer number such that $g(s_k^*) > f_{NC}(k) - f_P(k)$. So $g(s) = 0$, for each $s < s_k^*$. If s_k^* exists, it is an increasing function of k. If s_k^* does not exist or it is larger than n, it is impossible that the community acts collectively.

3 Let S be the set of groups that choose P in the first part of the game, and $|S| \geq s_k^*$. It is assumed that M_j in S suffers a punishment if it chooses NC in the second part. The punishment is a positive real ω, and it means that a group M_j in S, which has defected from a collective action, loses the community's trust.

4 People know, when they make decisions, that not forming an organization is a tragedy not only because everybody's cooperation is better than everybody's defection, but because cooperation will achieve improvements of protective laws in the future (accumulation), and that is important for people. However, it is not included in the payoff function for simplification. Most important, we do not think people from a community act as in a repeated game, considering future payoffs and discounts in a precise way, as is usual in those games. It is assumed that people only have naive perceptions about the future, and results do not change by introducing those perceptions.

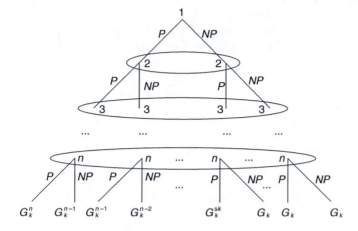

Figure 9.2 Collective action extensive game.

Figure 9.2 illustrates the game that was explained above. G_k^s means that s groups have decided to participate, while G_k means that no group will participate.

Let f_P, f_{NC}, and f_C be strictly increasing functions of the stocks, and g an increasing function of the number of groups that choose C.

There are two kinds of subgames. In what follows, the reader can find the development of their payoff functions and the Nash equilibria.

a   In the first kind of subgames, people from a $S \subseteq \{M_j\}$ have decided P, and S is large enough to collectively act in an efficient way – that is, $|S| \geq s_k^*$. So, S is an active nucleus inside the community. The subgame is denoted by G_k^s. The set of actions of each player M_j is $D_{kj}^s = \{C, NC\}$, where C means cooperation with the community – that is to say, opposition to Λ – and NC means no cooperation (support Λ). A σ profile is a vector of actions (C or NC), one for each group. The M_j's choice is denoted by σ^j. Then, the payoff obtained by any M_j in G_k^s when groups have chosen a profile σ is denoted by $\varphi_{kj}^s(\sigma)$. It is defined as

$$\varphi_{kj}^s(\sigma) = \begin{cases} f_P(k) + g(s_\sigma + 1) & \text{if } j \in S \text{ and } \sigma^j = C, \\ f_{NC}(k) + g(s_\sigma) - \omega & \text{if } j \in S \text{ and } \sigma^j = NC, \\ f_C(k) + g(s_\sigma + 1) & \text{if } j \notin S \text{ and } \sigma^j = C, \\ f_{NC}(k) + g(s_\sigma) & \text{if } j \notin S \text{ and } \sigma^j = NC. \end{cases}$$

$$s_\sigma = \left| \{M_i | i \neq j, \sigma^i = C\} \right|.$$

In a subgame such that an organization S with s groups is formed, NC is dominant for every group that is not in S.

Let us assume that $|S| > s_k^*$. If the payoff improvement by S' participation and the punishment cannot make M_j participate, that is, if $f_{NC}(k) - f_P(k) > g(s_\sigma + 1) - g$

$(s_\sigma)+\omega$, then NC is also dominant for every group that is in S. This means that the organization is not stable in a Nash equilibrium, and it disappears. On the other hand, if the punishment is large enough, that is, $f_{NC}(k)-f_P(k)<g(s_\sigma+1)-g(s_\sigma)+\omega$, then C is dominant for groups in S. Finally if $s=s_k^*$, due to the definition of s_k^*, C is dominant for each M_j that is in S, whatever the value of ω is.

b   If the number of M_j wanting to cooperate is smaller than s_k^*, the subgame would be $G_k=(\{M_j\}, \{D_k^j\}, \varphi_k)$, where $D_k^j=\{C, NC\}$. The payoff obtained by any M_j is defined as

$$\varphi_{k_j}(\sigma)=\begin{cases} f_C(k)+g(s_\sigma+1)\text{if } \sigma^j = C \\ f_{NC}(k)+g(s_\sigma)\text{if } \sigma^j = NC \end{cases}$$

$$s_\sigma = \left|\{M_i|i \neq j, \sigma^i = C\}\right|$$

If, for each s, $g(s+1)-g(s)>f_{NC}(k)-f_C(k)$, then for each M_j, it is better to cooperate, without anyone forcing them to do it. The fact that everybody cooperates would be, then, the only Nash equilibrium of that subgame, and organizations will not be useful. That case is valid for some groups in the community, such as elderly people and sometimes women's group. This would be considered in future work. But here, it has been assumed that everybody has the same utility function. Hence, only the case of $g(s+1)-g(s)<f_{NC}(k)-f_C(k)$ for each $0\leq s\leq n$ that happens much more frequently is considered and extended as an output of the globalization and the fierce competition resulting from it. Therefore, the strategy Defection (NC) is dominant and the only Nash equilibrium is $(NC, NC,\ldots, NC)$. In this situation, if $g(n)<f_{NC}(k)-f_C(k)$, it could not be expected that any group M_j would cooperate, and it would not represent a tragedy for the community. On the contrary, it is the case where people from the community can be compensated against the benefits that company Λ offers, since $g(n)$ is larger than $f_{NC}(k)-f_C(k)$. Otherwise that community would be facing a similar tragedy to the Hardin one. Globalization makes such tragedy more frequent, since some of the globalization effects reduce protective laws and people cooperation effectiveness.

9.2.2 The collective action reduced game $\hat{G}_k$

After analyzing the collective action extensive game by a backward induction (that is, assuming players choose actions according to Nash equilibria in all of the subgames), one arrives at the reduced game $\hat{G}_k$. This game is the first part of the collective action game, but now, instead of the subgames G_k^s or G_k, there are payoffs according to Nash equilibria of those subgames. The reduced game summarizes the whole game after analyzing all of the possible second parts.

Then $\hat{G}_k$ is a game with simultaneous moves (strategic game) that is formalized as follows:

$$\hat{G}_k =\left(\{M_j\},\{D_j = \text{Participation}(P),\text{No participation}(NP)\},\hat{\varphi}_k\right).$$

According to subgames Nash equilibria, groups that choose *NP* in the first part do not cooperate in the second, then $f_{NP}(k)=f_{NC}(k)$, the payoff function of player M_j is defined as

$$\hat{\varphi}_{k_j}(\sigma) = \begin{cases} f_P(k) + g(s_\sigma + 1) \text{ if } s_\sigma + 1 > s_{k^*} \text{ and } \sigma^j = P; \\ f_{NC}(k) + g(s_\sigma) \text{ if } s_\sigma \geq s_{k^*} \text{ and } \sigma^j = NP; \\ f_{NC}(k) \text{ otherwise.} \end{cases}$$

Where s_σ is $|\{M_i | i \neq j \text{ and } \sigma^i = P\}|$, that is the same notation we used in the second part of the subgames, but it is now being used for *P*.

The proof of the next proposition is very similar to the correspondent proof in Zapata-Lillo (2008).

> **Proposition 1** If $n \geq s_k^*$, then $\hat{G}_k$ is weakly acyclic, and a profile of pure strategies σ^* is a strict Nash equilibrium of the game $\hat{G}_k$ if and only if the number of players choosing *P* in σ^* is s_k^*. If s_k^* does not exist or $n s_k^*$, there is not a strict Nash equilibrium of the game.

A game is weakly acyclic if each pure strategy profile is joint with a strict Nash equilibrium in the graphic of best reply. It is a technical result that has importance because it determines a noncyclical behavior in many dynamics.

The second result tells whether or not there are enough people in the community (or they are effective enough). A strict Nash equilibrium means that a nucleus of people will be formed who will take charge of resisting dangerous projects and maintain the fulfillment of environmental protection rules. Otherwise the community does not resist and it might be disintegrated. The relationship between *n* and s_k^* depends on the sizes of *n* and *k*.

9.3 Learning process within a stage

It is necessary to model the organizational process using adequate dynamics. Many conflicts similar to the collective action game take place, in a period τ, in which the decision to act isolated or in an organized way is involved. The relationships between people happen mainly at the local level. Decisions made in local assemblies involve members of the groups M_j. Representatives of local assemblies meet in higher-level assemblies, where decisions made at a local level are discussed.

The project of interest to the community has many different effects on the community, and each M_j has to adopt a position on the issue, often changing their way of thinking and acting according to their own and others' experiences over time. Of course, each group does not have full information about others' behavior or attitudes; rather, partial information is gathered from gossip in the neighborhood, market, or church, from attendance at local assemblies, from

watching television or listening to the radio. Nobody gathers information sys-
tematically; instead, it is received at random. According to the obtained information, people make the best decisions they can, although sometimes they make
mistakes. That is, it is assumed that people from the community learn by experience, but they have limitations (obtain small information and make mistakes),
then groups have the limitations that make Young and other authors say people
are myopic. Formally, the model assumes that people have access to only a small
sample of available information and the groups also have access to those
samples. So a group has to act according to that information. Besides, in each
period, there is a small probability that each group will make mistakes in the
decision-making process. Young (1993, 1998) expressed that as a perturbed
Markov process and studied the stochastically stable states, which are the unique
states of the process that happen with positive probability in the long run. This
approach will be applied to the collective action game in the following sections.

9.3.1 The emergence of collective actions

An accumulation process goes through different stages. In this section, the
dynamics within a given stage are studied. A stage t is determined by water protection rules that are established in that stage. These rules form a stock that does
not change during the stage. When a stochastic stable state (sss) is reached, it
means that a number of groups might fight in order to achieve better protective
rules and social concerns, so the stock will be accumulated. If, in the achieved
sss no group participates, there will not be accumulation, and the stock is always
depreciated, so a new stage begins and the size of stock might change. We will
also consider the case when the time to reach an sss is too long.

In stage t, many collective actions are decided, one for each period τ within t.
Then, the game $\hat{G}_k$ is repeated period after period. As was explained in section 9.2,
N is divided into n "social groups" $M_1,\ldots, M_n$. Each group is a player. Each decision
(P or NP) of player M_j is determined by interests, beliefs, and the information of past
decisions that the members of such group make. The strength of the action depends
on the amount of groups deciding to participate in it. The assumption is that individuals follow learning dynamics with a lot of limitations, such as in Young (1998).
The whole community keeps the information that happened in the last κ periods, but
each person and each M_j has access to only a sample of this information. According
to the information obtained, M_j makes the best decisions it can, although sometimes
it experiments and makes mistakes. The emergence of an organization that makes
collective actions in a stage is a spontaneous order caused by a limited learning
process. Two possible scenarios might happen in the process: (1) a stochastically
stable state is reached, and the stage ends because of that, and (2) the stage is over
before one of these stable states has been reached, and each organization of s groups
has a positive probability of happening. The participation of s groups would determine the stock accumulation that might be achieved at the end of each stage. Figure
9.3 illustrates the dynamics within one stage, while the relation between accumulation and the beginning of new stages is illustrated in Figure 9.4.

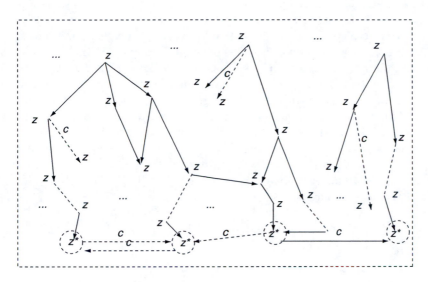

Figure 9.3 Learning dynamics in a stage.

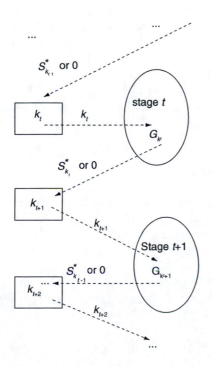

Figure 9.4 Accumulation dynamics.

The adaptive play: $\hat{G}_k$ is repeated once in each period τ. The set of states Z is $(D^n)^\kappa$, $D=\{P, NP\}$. That is, $z=(z(1),\ldots, z(\kappa))$, $z(\tau)=(\sigma^1(\tau),\ldots, \sigma^n(\tau))$, where $\sigma^j(\tau)$ is P or NP for each period τ. So, the state $\mathbf{z}$ is a vector that registers the chosen actions in each of the κ periods that the community remembers. That is, $\mathbf{z}$ is a vector of information of the group's behavior in κ periods. Young called history to each one of these states. A social convention is a history $z=(\sigma^*,\ldots, \sigma^*)$ such that σ^* is a strict Nash equilibrium. Each group M_j is only able to take into account a sample of size λ from the state z. That is, a vector with λ of the coordinates (registers) of $\mathbf{z}$. The group chooses the best response according to such a sample with probability $1-\eta$, and with probability η, it is deviated from the best response. This deviation may be due to mistakes, experiments, or attempts to influence the rest of the groups with its decision.

So, a sample is a vector as follows:

$$z(\lambda) = \left(z(r_1) = \left(\sigma^1(r_1),\ldots,\sigma^n(r_1) \right),\ldots, z(r_\lambda) = \left(\sigma^1(r_\lambda),\ldots,\sigma^n(r_\lambda) \right) \right).$$

Then, $\hat{z}(\lambda) = \dfrac{1}{\lambda}\left((x^1,\lambda - x^1),\ldots,(x^n,\lambda - x^n) \right)$ expresses the frequencies where individuals have chosen actions (x^j is the number of P that the group M_j has chosen according to $z(\lambda)$). Each M_j chooses a best response with probability $1-\eta$, and any other strategy with probability η. Each $z(\lambda)$ might be selected as a sample with positive probability.

Definition 1. A learning dynamics without mistakes is a correspondence π from Z to Z such that if z' is in $\pi(z')$, $z'(i-1)=z(i)$, for $i=2, 3,\ldots, \kappa$. Besides, $z'(\kappa)=(\sigma'^1(\kappa),\ldots, \sigma'^n(\kappa))$ is such that, for each player M_j, $j=1,\ldots, n$, there is a sample $z(\lambda)$, and $\sigma'^j(\kappa)$ is a best reply to $\widehat{z}(\lambda)$ for M_j.

The learning dynamics is considered as a finite Markov process: A Markov matrix Q, whose order is $|Z|$, represents the learning dynamics without mistakes π if, for each couple (z, z'),

$$Q_{zz'} = \begin{cases} q_{zz'} \text{ if } z' \in \pi(z), \\ 0 \text{ if } z' \notin \pi(z), \end{cases}$$

where $q_{zz'}$ is the probability of choosing a combination of samples of z that determines z'.

Then, each group makes mistakes with a small probability. The mistakes of each M_j are independent of the mistakes of the others.

Let J be a subset of $\{M_j\}$. For each $\eta \in (0, a]$, $a<1$, if Q is a learning dynamics without mistakes and x and x' are states, $\alpha_{xx'}^J$ is the probability of moving from x to x' when only the groups in J make mistakes, J_{xx} is such that $\alpha_{xx'}^{J_{xx'}}$ is positive, then a perturbation of Q with rate η is the following Markov matrix

$$Q_{zz'}(\eta) = (1-\eta)^n Q_{zz'} + \sum_{y\in\pi(z),y\neq z}\sum_{J_{yz'}\neq\varnothing} \alpha_{yz'}^{J_{yz'}}\, \eta^{|J_{yz'}|}(1-\eta)^{n-|J_{yz'}|} Q_{zy}.$$

It obtained a perturbation of the dynamics π, which allows reaching any z' from each z, through a finite number of periods (at most κ periods). Then, the perturbed dynamics is irreducible. It is clear that $Q(\eta)$ has the following properties:

Proposition 1 For each $\eta \in (0, a]$:

a $Q_{zz'}(\eta)$ tends to $Q_{zz'}$ as η tends to 0, for each couple (z, z');

b   there is a unique distribution vector $q(\eta)$ such that $q(\eta)Q(\eta) = q(\eta)$;

c   there is a non-negative integer number $\xi_{zz'}$ such that the limit of

$$\frac{Q_{zz'}(\eta)}{\eta^{\xi_{zz'}}},$$

as η tends to 0 exists and is positive for each couple (z, z') such that $Q_{zz'}(\eta) > 0$.

Young (1998) defines a regular perturbation B^{η} of B if it satisfies a, b, and c. Let μ^{η} be the unique vector such that $\mu^{\eta}B^{\eta} = \mu^{\eta}$, Young proves that μ^*, the limit of μ^{η}, as η tends to 0, exists, and it is one of the vectors that satisfies $\mu B = \mu$. He defines stochastically stable states as those states z such that $\mu_z^* > 0$. The concept of stochastic potential of each state of the process allows him to characterize the stochastically stable states of the process. The stochastic potential of the state z is the minimum of the costs of all the z-trees in the graphic $(V, \vec{A})$, where $V = Z$ and $\vec{A} = \{(x, x') | B_{xx'}^{\eta} > 0\}$. The cost function is $c(x, x')$ that is equal to the minimum number of mistakes while moving from x to x'. Then, the cost of a z-tree is the sum of all the $c(x, x')$ of the arrows in the z-tree. The set of all those trees is denoted by T_z.

Theorem 1 (Young 1998). Let B^{η} be a regular perturbed Markov process, and μ^{η} the unique stationary distribution of B^{η} for each $\eta > 0$. Then $\lim_{\eta \to 0} \mu^{\eta} = \mu^*$ exists, and μ^* is a stationary distribution of the unperturbed process B. The stochastically stable states are those that have minimum stochastic potential.

Which states are the stochastically stable states of the adaptive play in the reduced collective action game that has been considered in this chapter? The following theorem helps to answer this question. Consider a weakly acyclic game and the graphic of best replies of that game. Let L_{Γ} be the number of vertexes of the largest trajectory joining a profile of pure strategies to a strict Nash equilibrium in that graphic.

Theorem 2 (Young 1993). Let Γ be a weakly acyclic n-person game, and let Q be the unperturbed adaptive play with sizes of memory and sample κ and λ, respectively. If $\lambda < \dfrac{\kappa}{L_{\Gamma} + 2}$, the process converges, from any initial state, to one of the social conventions $(\sigma^*, \ldots, \sigma^*)$, with probability one. The stochastically stable states are those states that correspond to strict Nash equilibria with minimum stochastic potential.

What is the interpretation of that theorem? In the graphic of best replies of a weakly acyclic game, there is a trajectory that joins any pure strategy profile to a strict Nash equilibrium. Then, if the players of those games learn with Young's dynamics, it is possible that they move from any state of the process to a convention. Which convention? The convention that is possible to achieve, from everywhere, with the minimum mistakes of the players. The theorem suggests something more: The process reaches that social convention in a number of periods that is smaller or equal to $\dfrac{\kappa}{L_\Gamma + 2} \cdot\cdot$.

Then, we have that:

Theorem 3. For $n \geq s_k^*$ and $\lambda < \dfrac{\kappa}{L_\Gamma + 2}$, a state z is a stochastically stable state if, and only if, it is such that all the registers of exactly s_k^* groups of the $\{M_{ij}\}$ (always the same) are P and the rest of the registers are NP. If $n < s_k^*$, no one chooses P in any of the periods that the community remembers in a stochastically stable state. $\dfrac{\kappa}{L_\Gamma + 2}$ is the maximum number of periods to reach a stochastically stable state.

That is, if water resources give enough community benefits, a stochastically stable state means the emergence of a nucleus that is in charge of keeping the commons (the emergent social convention). On the contrary, if the community has lost the ability to govern the commons, or these commons have become too impoverished, no nucleus emerges, and the community might begin to disintegrate.

9.4 Accumulation and organization in the long run

Each stochastically stable state suggests that in each stage, if the groups that are involved in conflicts are effective enough according to the accumulated stock k, people tend to act collectively so that they make stock (laws and social concerns) more effective. They also tend to achieve a larger "accumulated stock" at the end of the stage, and the community tends to arrive at a collective action game that might involve a different stock. If those groups are relatively weak, there is no stock accumulation in that stage. The stochastic stable states are very important for determining which game tends to be played in the next stage. However, the number of periods to achieve one of those states might be too long, so it may exceed the regular time in which a stage occurs within a community in the real world. Therefore, the studied state might not mean anything in the community's real life. This chapter considers both scenarios: (i) a process such that in each stage a stochastically stable state is reached, and (ii) a process in which none of those states is reached in each stage. In case (ii), there is a need to establish the probability for each possible number of cooperating groups, and then the probability for the different accumulation stock sizes.

In both cases, it is logical to assume that the passing time, from the beginning of a stage until the beginning of another, is much longer than the passing time between two consecutive periods inside a stage. The dynamics in the scenarios (i) and (ii) are analyzed next.

Scenario (i). A stochastically stable state is achieved in each stage. So far, we have considered how people, after stage t, might accumulate a new stock (more effective rules and social concerns) that will act in the next stages. Now, assume that the stock that existed at the beginning of t depreciates before stage $t+1$ begins, and the stock that was acquired during t stays. The conflict in the stage t is the game $\hat{G}_k$ if k is the stock that has been accumulated until t. At the end of t, if $s_k^* \leq n$, the stock is accumulated by the cooperation of s_k^* groups; otherwise, there is no accumulation. But, in both cases, k has suffered depreciation. The stock depreciates due to laws and social concerns becoming out-dated over time.

Let us further discuss the accumulation and depreciation processes.

Accumulation. As has been explained earlier, the participation of s groups enables the accumulation of new stock. Let us denote that new stock by $ac(s)$. When, at the beginning of stage t, the accumulated stock is $k(t)$, and $s_{k(t)}^*$ is smaller than or equal to n, it implies the participation of $s_{k(t)}^*$ groups, in stage t. Otherwise, people do not accumulate any new stock in that stage.

The accumulation of new stock function $h(k) = \begin{cases} ac\left(s_{k(t)}^*\right) \text{if } s_{k(t)}^* \leq n, \\ 0 \text{ otherwise.} \end{cases}$

The function h is increasing in the interval $[0, \hat{k}]$, where $\hat{k}$ is such that $s_{\hat{k}}^* = n$. However, if $k > \hat{k}$, then $h(k) = 0$.

Depreciation. Let us assume that the accumulated stock is depreciated by a rate ρ, $\rho \in (0, 1)$. If at the beginning of stage t, there were $k(t)$ units of stock, and $h(k)$ units are accumulated during t, in $t+1$ there will be k' equal to $(1-\rho)$ $k(t) + h(k)$ units of stock. However, in order to keep the state space finite, only integer stocks will be considered as follows:

$$k(t+1) = \begin{cases} \left[k(t)(1-\rho) + h(k(t))\right]^+ \text{ if } s_{k(t)}^* \leq n, \\ \left[k(t)(1-\rho)\right]^+ \text{ otherwise.} \end{cases} \tag{1}$$

$[a]^+$ is the integer number nearest to a. If there are two integer numbers that are nearest to a, $[a]^+$ is the largest.

Let us consider the accumulation–organization process stage by stage as the following process. The set of possible states is $F = \{(k, s_k^*)|k = 0, 1, 2, \ldots, k_m\}$, where k_m is the largest stock that is possible to reach from 0 according to the stock's dynamics equation 1.

$s_{k(t+1)}^* \leq n$ leads to the dynamics $(k(t), s_{k(t)}^*) \rightarrow (k(t+1), s_{k(t+1)}^*)$ otherwise, $(k(t), s_{k(t)}^*) \rightarrow (k(t+1), 0)$. It is possible to express the process as a Markov matrix $\hat{Q}$, where each row is a unitary vector such that $\hat{Q}_{ww'} = 1$, if $w = (k(t), s_{k(t)}^*)$ and $w' = (k' = [k(t)(1-\rho) + h(k(t))]^+, s_k^*)$, s_k^* and/or $s_{\hat{k}}^*$ might be zero.

It is possible to establish perturbations as in section 9.2. But now perturbations due to "nature" are considered. These perturbations provoke, with small probability, the disappearance of stock units (each one disappears with probability ε independently of the others). Why is it possible for stock to disappear? As it was stated previously, the stock is formed by laws, rules, and people's concerns. It has been assumed that the stock depreciates, at a rate ρ, because laws and social concerns wear out and become outdated over time. But part of those laws and concerns can also disappear, in a stochastic way, when people lose their expectations or particular interests concerning common goods. It is also possible that commons might deteriorate suddenly (they become uncompetitive) in the global world. On the other hand, some protective laws become dead words, when it is possible to avoid them to build forbidden projects. Then, it is assumed that, in each period, each unity of stock, in an independent way, can disappear with a small positive probability ε.

It is possible to express this process as a regular perturbed Markov process and study their stochastic stable states. That is a process that satisfies the conditions a, b and c of the Proposition 2.

For each $w = (k_w, s_{k_w})$ and $w' = (k'_w, s_{k'_w})$ in F, where s_{k_w} and $s_{k'_w}$ are some s_k^* (s_k^*) or 0, let v be $(k_v = [k(t)(1-\rho) + h(k(t))]^+, s_{k_v}^*)$. Then we build the matrix, $\hat{Q}_{ww'}(\varepsilon) = (1-\varepsilon)^{k_w} \hat{Q}_{ww'} + \varepsilon^{k_v - k_w} (1-\varepsilon)^{k_w} \hat{Q}_{wv}$ if $k_v > k_{w'}$, otherwise $\hat{Q}_{ww'}(\varepsilon) = 0$.

It is obvious that the limit of $\hat{Q}(\varepsilon)$, as ε approaches 0, is equal to $\hat{Q}$. It is also obvious that, for each (w, w') such that $\hat{Q}_{ww'}(\varepsilon) > 0$, there is a non-negative integer $v_{ww'}$ such that the limit of $\dfrac{\hat{Q}_{ww'}(\varepsilon)}{\varepsilon^{v_{ww'}}}$, as ε approaches 0, exists and is positive.

Then, $\hat{Q}(\varepsilon)$ satisfies properties a and c in the Proposition 2. To show that $\hat{Q}(\varepsilon)$ is regular, property b has to be satisfied. This property is implied by the following proposition.

Proposition 1 For each k and k', there is a sequence $\{k_0 = k, \ldots, k_l = k'\}$ such that, for $t = 0, \ldots, l$, $\hat{Q}w_t w_{t+1}(\varepsilon) > 0$, where

$$w_t = \begin{cases} (k_t, s_{k_t}^*) \text{ if } s_{k(t)}^* \le n, \\ (k_t, 0) \text{ otherwise.} \end{cases}$$
k_m is the largest stock that is possible to reach

from 0 according to the stock's dynamics. Proposition 3 means that the process can reach a level stock $k' \le k_m$ from any stock level k. k' is smaller than or equal to k_m, so it is always possible to reach $k'' \ge k'$ ($k'' \le k_m$) from k through the process without mistakes. If $k'' = k'$, the sequence is complete. If $k'' > k'$, we have to add to the mentioned sequence some moves without accumulation, only depreciation, until it reaches k'.

Therefore, the perturbed Markov process $\hat{Q}(\varepsilon)$ is regular, and it implies the following theorem.

Theorem 4. There are stochastically stable states of the perturbed process $\hat{Q}(\varepsilon)$. They are the states with minimum stochastic potential.

Recurrent communication classes (rcc) of the unperturbed process can be defined as usual. All of the states in a rcc Y have the same stochastic potential. Some rcc might be composed of stochastically stable states (they have minimal stochastic potential). In some of them, an efficient number of groups might remain organized, although the number of those participating groups might increase or decrease when the process moves from one state to another inside the rcc. There would be a cycle in the nucleus size that is not destructive due to the fact that the community remains organized during it. This is the case when the stock k is such that $s_k^* \leq n$, but $[k(1-\rho)+k(s_k^*)]^+ \leq k$. In the case that $[k(1-\rho)+k(s_k^*)]^+$ is equal to k, Y would have only one state. On the other hand, when a stock k is such that $s_k^* > n$ is reached, there is no group inside the community that can allow people to earn more than $f_{NC}(k)$. Then, periods of apathy will occur until depreciation leads to a stock k' such that $s_{k'}^* \leq n$; that is, a participation cycle would be provoked, when the process goes from one state to another inside Y. There would be an organization–disorganization cycle that might be dangerous for the community, as was explained earlier.

The following simple example demonstrates both kinds of stochastically stable states, depending on the parameters.

Example. Let $f_{NC}(k)=\gamma+\beta k, f_P(k)=\gamma+\beta k-d_P$, and $g(s)=\beta(s-(\gamma+\beta k))$. Besides, $h(k)=s_k^*$ if $s_k^* \leq n$, and $h(k)=0$ otherwise. Then,

$$h(k) = \begin{cases} s_k^* \text{ if } k \in \left[0,\hat{k}\right], \\ 0 \text{ if } k > \hat{k}, \end{cases}$$

$$s_k^* = \left[\frac{d_P}{\beta}+\gamma+\beta k\right]^+, \text{ and}$$

$$k(t+1) = \begin{cases} \left[k(t)(1-\rho)+s_k^* - \beta(\gamma+\beta k)\right]^+ \text{ if } s_k^* \leq m, \\ \left[k(t)(1-\rho)\right]^+ \text{ otherwise.} \end{cases}$$

The behavior of the sizes of the stock and of the organization emerging in the stochastic stable states, according to some sets of parameters, are analyzed below.

Example 1. Consider the set of parameters as: $\gamma=1$, $\rho=.3$, $d_P=.6$, $\beta=.2$, and $n=15$.

Figure 9.5 presents part of the graphic of the dynamics without mistakes in Example 1. The first number of each pair means the accumulated stock and the second one the minimum number of groups that form an efficient organization according to that stock. The graphic does not start in one of the pairs; it illustrates how the movement is when the community is in any possible pair. The graphic only has a stochastic stable state (28, 10). When the process reaches such state it remains in it, because there are no mistakes. This is the meaning of the bold arrow under (28, 10).

The unique stochastic stable state is $(k=28, s_k^*=10)$. That is, a nucleus has emerged in the community, in this stable state, and it is formed by ten groups. Besides, the level stock that is reached is 28. In this case, in the long run, with high probability, part of the community remains organized. They reach a satisfactory level of stock, and then the organization allows that stock to be kept. There would be free-riders because there are 15 groups in the community and ten is the minimum number that forms an effective organization, while five groups only obtain benefits, but do not cooperate. The community and each group would obtain more benefits if there were no free-riders, but the total participation would not be a stable state because any group's payoff would improve if it defects.

Example 2. Consider that the parameters change as follows: $\gamma=2$, $\rho=.1$, $d_p=1.6$, $\beta=.5$, and $n=10$. Figure 9.6 expresses the dynamics without mistakes.

The unique rcc is the set {(10, 0), (9, 10), (15, 0), (14, 0), (13, 0), (12, 0), (11, 0)}, and each one of the elements in the rcc is a stochastic stable state. That is, after some stages, all people from the community participate in the organization and reach a stock that is satisfactory to them. Then, the organization disappears for some stages, until depreciation brings the stock to an unsatisfactory level, so they get organized again. In Figure 9.6, the stock level 9 is the trigger that brings organization.

The stable states of a process are defined considering mistakes; however, in both examples (Figures 9.5 and 9.6), there is only one ccr, and the states in this are the sss. Then it is not necessary to introduce mistakes to find them. Of course, when mistakes are considered, stable states are stochastic. That is, the stable states are not always present. Other states appear with small probability.

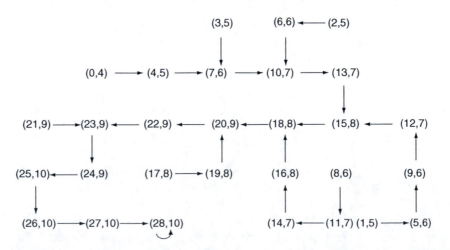

Figure 9.5 Accumulation dynamic where community remains organized.

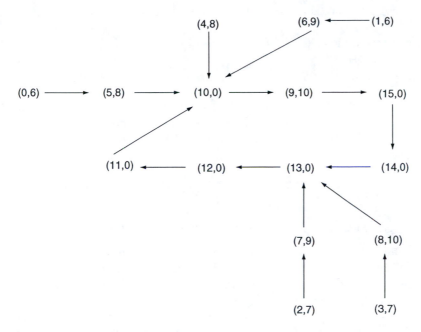

Figure 9.6 Accumulation dynamic in which a community falls in an organization–disorganization cycle.

Scenario (ii). The number of periods to reach a stochastically stable state is
too large. Then, the question is: Which is the probability for an emerging organization with size s at the end of the stage? In order to answer, we consider Freidlin and Wentzell's theorem (1984). The theorem says that the stationary
distribution μ of an irreducible Markov process as $Q(\eta)$ has the property that the
probability of each state z is proportional to the sum of the costs of its z-trees.
That result allows us to calculate the probability for an emerging organization
with size s outside the limit.

A stochastically stable state is reached when the rate of mistaking η reaches
0. Then, if it is assumed that the stage t ends in a period τ, before a stochastically
stable state has been reached, there would be a positive rate of mistaking η_τ, after
those τ periods. So, at the end of the stage t, the learning process would be $Q(\eta_\tau)$,
which is an irreducible Markov process. Due to the Freidlin and Wentzell
theorem, the stationary distribution $q(\eta_\tau)$ of $Q(\eta_\tau)$ is such that the probability of a

state z is $q_z(\eta_\tau) = \dfrac{\sum_{T \in T_z} \prod_{(x,x') \in T} Q(\eta_\tau)_{xx'}}{\sum_{w \in Z} \sum_{T \in T_w} \prod_{(xx') \in T} Q(\eta_\tau)_{xx'}}$. Each state z registers how

many times an organization of size s was formed in the last κ periods. Then, it
determines a probability of each efficient organization with size s. Let us denote
it by $p(s|z)$ that frequency. $p(s|z)$ and $q_z(\eta_\tau)$ determine the probability that an

efficient organization with size $s \geq s_k^*$ ($\sum_{z \in Z} q_z(\eta_\tau) p(s|z)$) might emerge and

provokes a new accumulation of $ac(s)$. Then,

$$\hat{Q}_{kk'} = \begin{cases} \sum_{z \in Z} \sum_{s \geq s_k^*} q_z(\eta_\tau) p(s|z) \text{if } k' = \left[(1-\rho)k + ac(s)\right]^+, \\ 0 \text{ otherwise.} \end{cases}$$

It is clear that a regular perturbed stochastic accumulation process $\hat{Q}(\varepsilon)$ can be established in the same way as in scenario (i). Then, $\hat{Q}(\varepsilon)$ has stochastically stable states.

9.5 Summary

9.5.1 Effects of globalization and community's opposition to them

Globalization has dramatically increased the over-exploitation of natural resources such as water, land, and forests. Perhaps one of the most serious consequences of globalization is the breaking of both the social bonds and the virtuous interaction between the communities and their environment. Such communities are among the most important agents to stand against threats to nature from globalization. They protect natural resources, claiming for laws, social awareness, etc. We observe in communities some patterns, which we exemplify next.

In communities of the real world, there emerge nuclei that are in charge of the common problems, particularly natural resources protection. Many communities are able to govern their common resources in a sustainable way, preventing the members from selfishly squandering them. They can also be the main source of resistance against the destructive action of corporations and are able, in some cases, to notably rescue their local environment. This is the case of the Green Belt Movement formed by Kenyan women who have spent decades working in rural Kenya planting and sustaining millions of trees. Their key focus now is on "Saving Lake Chad," one of the continental lakes facing the threat of drying up as a result of the worsening effects of climate change and desertification (Maathai 2009). Another case is that of the Mixteca community in Oaxaca. Since the early 1980s, the Center for Integral Small Farmer Development in the Mixteca (CEDICAM), a local environmental organization, has been leading an unprecedented land renewal and economic development program that employs ancient indigenous agricultural practices to transform this barren, highly eroded area into rich, arable land. They have planted more than one million native-variety trees, built hundreds of miles of ditches to retain water and prevent soil from eroding, and adapted traditional Mixteca indigenous practices to restore the regional ecosystem (Clark 2008).

A permanent organization that has lasted a very long time is characteristic of communities in these examples. In many other cases, communities might promote the imposition of laws and rules that protect the environment and establish the community-governing of their commons. Their histories are full of hard struggles that they have endured to reach those goals. We have several examples. There is the Bolivian waters war that is narrated in Raquel Gutiérrez' book *Los Ritmos del Pachakuti. Levantamiento y movilización en Bolivia* 2000–2005' (Gutiérrez 2009). There are also the Mexican cases of Tepoztlán, Morelos, Cabo Pulmo in the sea of Cortez and the Zapatista communities in Chiapas, which achieved important improvements in laws and rules, locally and nationally. Histories of those communities are cycles of effervescence followed by calm.

The whole region of Morelos has a long history of struggles. It has been famous since the Mexican revolution due to Emiliano Zapata and the South Army. In particular, Tepoztlán, which is in Morelos, has not come back. The hills (the Tepozteco) contain a forest of pines and holms oaks and also a jungle, with great diversity of flora and wildlife. It also accumulates rainwater and irrigates a great part of the state of Morelos. The zone is the communal property of the Tepoztlán community. There have been several attempts to transform this zone into a tourist destination, which threatens to seriously damage the environment and natural resources, but the community's opposition has thus far prevented this. They have had several victories. In 1937, the hill was declared a national park, and in 1988 it became part of a protected zone within the Ajusco-Chichinautzin Biological Corridor. The end of 1994 saw the last attempt to build a large tourism project – a golf club as part of a tourist, industrial, and residential project – but due to a hard struggle by the community, the government officially prohibited construction of projects inside the protected zone (Rosas 1997). After each of these projects was abandoned due to struggles, the community came back to the usual organization that is not strong enough to stop future threats.

The history of the Cabo Pulmo is very similar to that of Tepozteco. The Cabo Pulmo coral reef is an ecological wonder. It is one of just three of its kind on the Pacific coast of America. It is in the Sea of Cortez in the southern Baja California Sur. Many of the 800 species of marine animals seek refuge in the reef, and it plays an important role in the ecology of the region. Cabo Pulmo has been under serious threat due to the intense fishing that has damaged the marine life. The communities located there have protected the reef, and they have been supported by international organizations and scientific communities. The preservation of Cabo Pulmo is full of victorious struggles. In 1995, the state of Baja California Sur made Cabo Pulmo a Natural Protected Area. In 2000, Mexico appointed it as a National Marine Park. In 2005, it was designated a UNESCO World Heritage Site as one of the "Islands and Protected Areas of the Gulf of California." In 2008, Cabo Pulmo became a Ramsar International Wetlands Site. However, Cabo Pulmo is now under serious threat again. The Mexican government has opened the door to one of several large tourism projects that threaten to harm Cabo Pulmo's coastal and marine life. Communities are again fighting to stop those projects (Letter from scientists to the director of World Heritage Centre United Nations Educational, Scientific and Cultural Organization, May 23, 2011).

Among the stories of the resistances of the Mexican communities, Zapatista communities in Chiapas are the most well-known, and a large collection of literature is available on the subject. The history of the struggles of Chiapanecan communities is very old, dating from the sixteenth century, at the time of the colony. There were important struggles over centuries, many of which were harshly repressed and followed by calm times (Benjamin 1989). Let us consider only the most modern stages of this history that, in addition to the traditional struggle for land, begins to explicitly make the claim of indigenous autonomy involving the indigenous government over their territories and natural resources. Those claims are for Chiapas, but also for all communities in the country. Then, we will consider Zapatism from 1994 and come up to the present moment (Harvey 2000; Aubry 2005). Zapatism history is full of stages of effervescence, in which support and recognition were accomplished for the many problems indigenous people have endured and the hard struggles they toiled through to achieve their rights. First, the outbreak in January 1994, when they forced the Mexican government to accept a dialogue that, after a few years, culminated in the signing of the San Andrés Agreements, which signified the recognition of indigenous autonomy. However, in turning these agreements into national law, the Mexican government did not fulfill the agreements and approved a very diminished law without real recognition of the rights of indigenous peoples in their territories. The Zapatistas had to continue making large mobilizations to unify the indigenous communities from across the country and other social sectors and put pressure on recognition of the San Andrés Agreements. External support is fading and they are focused on developing facts, plus real autonomy, by increasing strategies on decision making within the communities, in the areas of education, health, and protecting natural resources. At present and for the last few years, Zapatista communities have remained in one of these stages (Baronnet *et al.* 2011; González-Casanova 2006).

Our model is a tool to study a community's behavior patterns and reflect them in a simplified way.

9.5.2 A short summary of the model

a   We have considered a collective action game in which the players are the social groups forming the community. In the game, these social groups have to decide if they should act collectively to protect the common natural resources or if they will remain indifferent. The payoff function of the game depends on the protective laws that are established and the real rules that govern the common natural resources (social awareness also affects this). s_k^* is the minimum number of groups that are able to obtain a better payoff than that of indifference of everybody. If $n \geq s_k^*$, a profile of pure strategies σ^* is a strict Nash equilibrium if and only if the number of players choosing P in σ^* is s_k^*. Those Nash equilibria mean the emergence of an organization nucleus in the community. If s_k^* does not exist or $< s_k^*$, the Nash equilibrium is that everybody remains indifferent.

b   Protective laws, real rules, and social concerns are considered in this chapter as public good stock.

c   The game is repeated many times in Young's learning dynamics, in which each player chooses its decisions, taking into account the past experience of people's behavior. Each social group has only a small sample of information of that experience and also will make mistakes with a small probability that provokes a deviation from a best response. When an equilibrium of that dynamics (a stochastic one) is reached, an organization is formed (if there are enough people). That is, a nucleus emerges inside the community, and it can improve the laws and rules, so there is accumulation of stock. If there are few people to compensate the community's effort to protect the natural resources, the stochastic stable state means no organization is formed, and there is no stock accumulation.

d   Then, the game is repeated with different stock in each stage. The histories of accumulation and community organization happen in the long run of this other dynamic. It provokes the emergence of patterns as communities that remain organized (communities have stable organization nuclei and similar sizes of stock) or communities that have a cyclic behavior (different sizes of nuclei and of stocks) may have periods of total disorganization.

9.6 Conclusion and policy implications

The model developed in this chapter supports the opinion that communities that are in contact with natural resources may be the main actors in facing the worst effects of globalization – in particular, environmental and natural resource catastrophes. Those people may act by forcing themselves to change their own environment-damaging activities and stopping those of the big corporations and state powers. If the direct payoff that members of the communities receive from the common resources is very small compared with protection and organization costs, they will act aggressively against those resources, either directly by wasting them or indirectly by abandoning them. If, on the other hand, the benefit is large enough (the larger, the more effective), a nucleus in charge of protecting the environment and other communal interests will emerge from within the community. The model reflects real facts, such that some communities tend to maintain their organization for a very long time. The nucleus that is the organization soul may increase or decrease stage by stage. Nature and environmental protection become part of their cultures. They reach obligatory protective conditions (laws and social concerns) and keep them working. In contrast, other communities or social groups act as movements. That is to say, an organization of a large part of the population fights to reach those obligatory protective rules. When those conditions are met, people lose expectations regarding organization and cooperation, and they think that everything will remain in good order. However, laws and social concerns wear out over time and, after some periods of apathy, people realize that laws have become ineffective; common natural resources are desirable for corporations, and it is necessary to do something against it. An organization–disorganization cycle appears as a result. Both patterns can appear in the same community. If a community is not able to follow the first pattern (organization around a nucleus), it might lose its achievements. The soul of that kind of nucleus is formed by people who appreciate commons more than the benefits that corporations offer. In future works, it would be very important to introduce different payoff functions in order to study those cycles that have an effective nucleus in apathetic stages. The breakdown of the community bonds and the loss of its governance of the common are behind the increase in migration and the difficulty for communities to face the criminal cartels. Models such as those presented in this chapter may be useful tools for measuring the environmental impact of the community property and governing over their common resources. They would help in estimating the increase in environmental protection in a community when the benefits people receive from the common resources improve. They can also help in studying how some policies can endanger the existence of many communities that have an important role to play in the protection of ecology and the environment by stopping the worst effects of globalization. From the citizens' viewpoint, the model implies that not all economic and political activities are valid and that relevant international treaties should be enforced. It is also clear that it is necessary to protect communities around the world against the expropriation of their resources.

The last remark has importance that needs to be applied to the model. The number of periods to achieve one of the stochastic stable states might be too long, so it may exceed the regular time in which a stage occurs within a community in the real world. Therefore, the studied state might not mean anything in the community's real life. We think that is often the case. In order to study a real community, we have to estimate the mistake rate in a period and work with the process that we called scenario (ii), utilizing the probability that we built there.

References

Aubry, A. (2005) *Chiapas a Contrapelo. Una Agenda de Trabajo para su Historia en Perspectiva Sistémica*. México: Contrahistorias, La otra mirada de Clío.

Baronnet, B., Mora Bayo, M., and Stahler-Sholk, R. (2011) *Luchas "muy otras." Zapatismo y Autonomía en las Comunidades Indígenas de Chiapas*. México: Colección Teoría y Análisis, Universidad Autónoma Metropolitana.

Benjamin, T. (1989) *A Rich Land, a Poor People. Politics and Society in Modern Chiapas*. Albuquerque: University of New Mexico Press.

Clark, J. (2008) "Oaxaca man seeks sustainability in devastated Mixteca alta area," Special to the *Herald/Review*, April 13.

Costanza, R., Low, B., Ostrom, E., and Wilson, J. (eds) (2000) *Institutions, Ecosystems and Sustainability*. Cleveland, OH: CRC Press.

Freidlin, M. and Wentzell, A. (1984) *Random Perturbations of Dynamical Systems*. New York: Springer-Verlag.

Gibson, C., McKean, M., and Ostrom, E. (eds) (2000) *People and Forests. Communities, Institutions and Governance*. Cambridge, London: MIT Press.

González-Casanova, P. (2006) "El zapatismo y el problema de lo nuevo en la historia," *Contrahistorias*, 6: 31–40.

Gutiérrez, R. (2009) *Los Ritmos del Pachakuti – Levantamiento y Movilización en Bolivia (2000–2005)*. Puebla: Bajo Tierra Ediciones, ICSH-BUAP.

Hardin, G. (1968) "The tragedy of the commons," *Science*, 12: 1243–8.

Harvey, N. (2000) *La Rebelión en Chiapas, la Lucha por la Tierra y la Democracia.* México: Ediciones ERA.

Havice, E. (2004) "Free trade of labour? The relationship among migration, development and free trade in rural Mexico," University of California-Berkeley Human Rights Center, Human Rights Research Report 2004.

Maathai, W. (2009) *The Challenge for Africa.* New York: Pantheon Books, Random House, Inc.

Ostrom, E. (1990) *Governing the Commons: The Evolution of Institutions for Collective Action.* Cambridge: Cambridge University Press.

Rosas, M. (1997) *Tepoztlán Crónica de Desacatos y Resistencia.* México: Ediciones ERA.

Young, P. (1993) "The evolution of conventions," *Econometrica*, 61: 57–84.

Young, P. (1998) *Individual Strategy and Social Structure: An Evolutionary Theory of Institutions.* Princeton: New Jersey University Press.

Zapata-Lillo, P. (2008) "How does environment awareness arise? An evolutionary approach," in J. Albiac, A. Dinar, and J. Sánchez-Soriano (eds), *Game Theory and Policymaking in Natural Resources and the Environment* (pp. 278–306), London: Routledge.

10 Informal agreements in transboundary water resources

Antonio Lloret[1]

10.1 Introduction

Governance of transboundary (international) water resources (TWR) requires a thorough understanding of both institutions and the interplay of formal and informal agreements. Many freshwater resources are located across national boundaries, so nations must rely on institutional schemes of cooperation to manage shared resources. These schemes are formalized by institutional agreements such as treaties. Treaties are not isolated institutions that operate independently; rather, treaties are just one part of a complex array of formal agreements, both domestic and international, that govern transboundary water resources and that must be analyzed in an integrated way.

Transboundary river basins are subject to variable socio-demographic conditions and hydrologic conditions that often have large inter-annual variability and perhaps are non-stationary. When the rate of change of the conditions governing the natural resource is faster than the rate at which formal institutions adapt, the chance of domestic and international disputes is likely to increase (Giordano and Wolf 2003; Wolf *et al.* 2003, 2003b).

While flexible formal institutions are desirable, the transaction costs associated with negotiation, implementation, and renegotiation, as well as the power structure among countries, make them static. One alternative to make agreements more flexible is to create informal agreements. Informal agreements are policy instruments used by governments to overcome crises, uncertain events, or variable conditions (including water flow variability or changes in demand and supply of the resource) that are not always considered in formal agreements. In what follows, I develop the notion of an informal agreement as a feasible solution to TWR problems, and model the potential benefits of informal schemes in 39 bilateral water basins.

Extensive work on transboundary water resources[2] suggests that when two or more countries share a basin, they have to work jointly in terms of economic development, infrastructural capacity, management, and the resolution of political differences (Wolf *et al.* 2003b). Tensions are likely to arise when countries have asymmetric benefits from the use of the water they share. Possible ways of reducing these tensions are through joint management, institutional building, preventive diplomacy, and joint welfare maximization, among others (Wolf *et al.* 2003a).

According to the Atlas of International Freshwater Agreements (UNEP 2002), there are 263 international basins. Most international basins are shared between two countries, but some are shared by more than two nations and up to 17 (Giordano and Wolf 2003; Wolf *et al.* 2003b). The complexity of TWR requires that cooperation and joint management be reflected in their institutional arrangements.

In regional transboundary water resources, models of cooperative behavior are more common than non-cooperative models (Dinar *et al.* 1992). At the international level, water resources have characteristics that tend to induce cooperation (Wolf and Hamner 2000). There are some examples of institutional arrangements showing that, at the international level, transboundary water resources have followed cooperative schemes. Examples of these arrangements include the International Commission for the Protection of the Danube, the International Borders and Water Commission between Mexico and the United States, or the International Joint Commission that oversees water issues between the United States and Canada.

Cooperative schemes tend to be formalized with international water treaties. More than 350 treaties have been signed since 1850 (UNEP 2002). A detailed analysis of 157 international water agreements by Wolf and colleagues (Giordano and Wolf 2003; Wolf *et al.* 2003, 2003b) found that water allocation between riparian states is rarely reflected in water treaties and, in those cases in which the agreements specify quantities, allocation is often in fixed amounts. Also, many treaties ignore hydrological variation and the likely changes in values and needs of the river basin. They also found that "...the likelihood and intensity of conflict rises as the rate of change [of socioeconomic conditions or hydrologic conditions] within the basin exceeds the institutional capacity to absorb that change"; and that most of the disputes (86 percent) are related to issues of water quantity and water infrastructure. More recent work on cooperative schemes in transboundary water resources addresses scarcity as an issue often cited in formal agreements in four key themes: water allocation, water quality, hydropower, and flood control (Dinar 2009).

A solution to the problem of conflict is a more flexible formal institution (Dietz *et al.* 2003; Kilgour and Dinar 2001). However, changing or redesigning formal agreements is not always feasible; often the transaction costs associated with renegotiation exceed the net benefits from the renegotiated formal agreements.

To capture cooperative behavior among countries, I assume that countries behave rationally and that their decisions account for the other countries' decisions; countries have very well-defined objectives and they have developed expectations over their behavior. I suppose that: (1) the model considers the joint net benefits of the whole basin; and (2) assuming that an agreement leads to cooperative gains, these benefits are preferred over the single benefits of a country. In the next section, I discuss an alternative analytical tool that may help address some of the problems found in transboundary water resources.

10.2 Informal agreements

Informal institutions are an alternative to formal institutions for adapting faster to changes. Informal institutions are policy instruments used among nations, regions, or states within a country. Informal institutions take several forms: from the most basic signaled or non-spoken communications to outspoken joint declarations or written rules and statements. The main characteristic that makes institutions informal is that they lack the full authority, given by a legislative body such as congress, of the government they represent (Lipson 1991).

Informal agreements are broad in scope and can take many forms. In the simplest form, it could be a memorandum of understanding between two nations in order to show policy directives to solve a conflict; for example, a policy directive to solve a trading dispute. In its most complex form, an informal institution is some social norm that has existed over time and that induces some type of behavior; for example, non-written norms in cattle grazing or fisheries harvested by cooperatives (North 1990; Ostrom 1990; Young 2002). For the purpose of this chapter, I limit the analysis to those informal agreements in TWR that are used to solve one very particular issue. For example, in the context of water resources, an informal agreement would be the so-called Picnic Table Talks between Israel and Jordan (Dinar *et al.* 2011), or a joint declaration between two nations to solve an extended drought.[3]

In matters of international law, transboundary water resources agreements rarely have binding conditions that limit behavior. Any country may breach the agreement if they can without penalty. However, most countries abide by formal agreements mainly because of reputation. Informal agreements are generally less reliable and convincing because less reputation is at stake (Lipson 1991; Sigman 2002; Tesler 1980).

Informal agreements have the advantages over formal agreements of being more easily created and renegotiated and less costly to abandon than formal agreements (Lipson 1991). An agreement can be sustained over time depending on how well the agreement accommodates uncertain events. If the formal agreement is not designed to accommodate changes, it may become unsustainable, mostly because of the transaction costs involved in the renegotiation process. Under such circumstances, informal agreements may serve as policy directives to address changes due to uncertain events or to reduce some asymmetries, at least temporarily, at a lesser transaction cost (Lipson 1991; Tesler 1980).

In the context of TWR, this flexibility may be useful if there is water flow variability or uncertainty about the future benefits under a formal agreement. This is precisely the working hypothesis of this chapter. In what follows, I argue that cooperation schemes are relevant for the study of transboundary water resources, and that a cooperation model is optimal for solving questions of bilateral negotiations of natural resources.

10.3 Modeling bilateral international cooperation

The model used in this chapter has two main elements quite common in allocation schemes of natural resources. The first element is the choice of the total amount of water to be distributed between two countries, and the second element is the method in which allocation takes place. In the formal agreement, the total amount of water is based on the expected value of water flow. The informal agreement is the realization of water flow for a given year. As far as the method of allocation, in both the formal and the informal agreements, the allocation scheme is that which maximizes the joint net benefits between both countries as a function of water flow and the bargaining parameter. By choosing such model, I attempt to capture the idea that a formal agreement can be sustained over time because, when problems arise, informal agreements serve as temporary solutions.

The scarcity of water resources is perhaps the main problem that countries sharing a river face because they receive the asymmetric benefits from use of water resources in a transboundary basin. Increasing demand for the resource and fewer resources to share may indeed bring the question of strategic behavior and the need, if the benefits are to be shared, to agree upon some scheme of cooperation (Dinar 2009; Dinar *et al.* 2011).

The transboundary water resources literature closely analyzes the bargaining power parameter in terms of its link to water conflicts and the power asymmetry between two or more countries. Scholars argue that levels of conflicts may arise due to poor institutional arrangements as well as political, sovereignty, or boundaries problems. Other elements that make the bargaining power parameter significant are military power, economic strength, infrastructure development, and geographical position. All these elements ultimately determine to whom and how the resources are allocated (Conca *et al.* 2006; Dinar 2004; Dinar and Dinar 2003; Giordano and Wolf 2003; Just and Netanyahu 1998; Wolf 1998, 1999; Wolf *et al.* 2003b; Yoffe and Fiske 2002; Zeitoun and Warner 2006).

The bargaining power parameter represents a weight and/or strength in the negotiation process that one country has over another country. It can be measured by issue-specific power strength, military might, geographical position, sovereignty, economic strength, institutional capacity, and infrastructure, to name a few (Jonsson 1981). Bargaining is used as a form of negotiation of outcomes when countries have different preferences for how to use or benefit from a resource. Two countries with the same preferences over the resource but different strengths will have a distribution of benefits according to that strength. A country with a high bargaining parameter may deny another country the resource if that country sees fit.

Often, bargaining outcomes are a reflection of an issue linkage or a political strategy to add flexibility to the bargaining process (Fischhendler and Feitelson 2003; Fischhendler *et al.* 2004). Issue linkages may be mechanisms to adapt to uncertain events, but they tend to be nested in the formal agreements. The effect that issue linkages have in establishing informal and formal agreements is not always clear and can be difficult to measure.

The strength reflected in the bargaining parameter means that the country with such strength has perhaps a higher level of development so that it can benefit more with one single unit of the resource than can the country with less development. That is why it is important to have a cooperative scheme that allows for a redistribution of benefits. In contrast with a non-cooperative scheme, a country that has more power may limit access to the less powerful country to the resource (Parrachino *et al.* 2006), thus a higher bargaining power parameter may derive in a non-cooperative behavior unless there are some constraints, such as formal agreements.

In the context of this chapter, however, the bargaining power parameter is a measure that weights preferences. Preferences are represented by payoff functions. A water basin's joint benefit function is the sum of each country's payoff function weighted by its respective bargaining power parameter. The model scheme uses a bargaining parameter in the range of [0–1]. A bargaining power parameter of one means full strength, whereas a bargaining power parameter of zero means no strength at all. In any of the extremes (0 or 1), the preferences from the strongest member are represented and would drive the relationship in the exploitation of the resource, whereas in the interior of the range there is a shared management scheme. The model I chose has a solution for the optimal jointly managed resource given the bargaining power parameter. However, I do not calculate the bargaining power parameter but rather assume it takes a given value, and then I estimate the gains of informal agreements for each value of the bargaining power parameter.

The next section develops the analytical model and illustrates empirically the gains for establishing informal agreements to 39 bilateral international basins.

10.4 Analytical method

The analytical method estimates the formal and informal agreements and then compares the joint net benefits of each type of agreement to find the potential gains of establishing informal agreements. The model incorporates a bargaining parameter for each country in each basin. First, it develops a general model that considers the bargaining power parameter within the range of 0–1 to measure the potential joint net benefits of informal agreements relative to the joint net benefits of formal agreements. Second, I show that informal agreements have greater than or equal net benefits than those of formal agreements for different values of the bargaining parameter. Third, I analyze particular cases for which the general model is limited by considering the cases in which a country has all the bargaining power – that is, when $\theta=0$ or $\theta=1$. The analysis results in a bilateral agreement that could be sustained over time for all bargaining parameters. And finally I analyze the relationship between gains and water flow variability.

10.4.1 Model

Definition 1: Main assumptions

a   There are two countries sharing a river; an upstream country and a downstream country.
b   All water originates upstream.
c   Governments' decisions are to maximize joint welfare equal to the sum of the net benefits of each country.

Let W be a random variable that represents the total water flow available for the upstream country. The random variable is independently and identically distributed across time.

X_u be upstream consumption of water.
X_d be downstream consumption of water.
$U_u(X_u) = U_u(W - X_d)$ be the upstream country's net benefits, assumed to be strictly concave.
$U_d(X_d)$ be the downstream country's net benefits, assumed to be strictly concave.
θ be the bargaining power parameter given to the upstream country, with $(1 - \theta)$ being the bargaining power parameter for downstream country.

To make the problem tractable, I use a quadratic benefit function of the form $U_i(X_i) = a_i X_i - b_i X_i^2$.

The model identifies the water flow relationship to each country. Sharing takes place when the upstream country does not consume the entire volume available and instead passes some of it to a downstream country by means of a treaty or a formal agreement. In the absence of treaties or other arrangements, the upstream country will consume $X_u \leq W_t$ that maximizes its utility before sharing any water with a downstream country.

Definition 2: The formal agreement

The formal agreement is a rule agreed upon by the upstream user to release a fixed quantity to the downstream user. I model a fixed[4] allocation scheme to show the gains of informal agreements over formal agreements with a specification that allows for a bargaining parameter in the range $0 < \theta < 1$.

Suppose that two countries negotiate a fixed quantity $\tilde{X}_d$ for downstream country that maximizes the expected joint net benefits $E[J(\theta, W - X_d, X_d, W)]$. The solution to the maximization problem of expected net benefits is:

$$J_F\left(\theta, \tilde{X}_d, W\right) = \theta U_u(W - \tilde{X}_d) + (1 - \theta)U_d(\tilde{X}_d)$$

That is the policy that becomes the formal agreement, and it is compared with the informal agreement.

Definition 3: The informal agreement

The informal agreement is a temporary fixed allocation agreed upon by upstream user to downstream user. It is a one-time policy based on the optimal allocation X_d^* that maximizes the joint net benefits given a realization of the random variable W. The problem is to maximize the joint net benefits $J[\theta, W-X_d, X_d, W]$ with solution:

$$J_I\left(\theta, X_d^*, W\right) = J\left[\theta U_u(W - X_d^*) + (1-\theta)U_d(X_d^*)\right]$$

That is the policy that becomes the informal agreement, and it is to be compared with the formal agreement.

Definition 4: The satiation point

The satiation point of each country is that in which the marginal benefits of a given country is equal to zero as estimated by finding the first-order condition of the benefit function. Thus $\phi_d = \dfrac{a_d}{2b_d}$ is the satiation point of downstream country and $\phi_u = \dfrac{a_u}{2b_u}$ the satiation point of upstream country.

Proposition 1: Under general conditions, there are always positive gains from establishing informal agreements with a bargaining power parameter in the range $0<\theta<1$ for some W_t.

Analysis of formal and informal agreement when the bargaining power parameter is in the extremes: Given the setup of the model, it is possible that one country has all the bargaining power, in which case the negotiation outcome will depend solely on the best possible outcome for the most powerful country, and the gains of establishing informal agreements will be either zero or positive depending on such bargaining parameter.

Corollary 1.1: The formal and informal agreements may not be sustained when $\theta=0$ for any level of water flow W_t for some t. The formal agreement is now $\min[W_t, \tilde{X}_d]$ and the informal agreement is now $\min[W_t, \tilde{X}_d]$ and the gains of establishing informal agreements are always equal to zero when the bargaining parameter is $\theta=0$ for any level of water flow W_t for all t.

Corollary 1.2: The formal and informal agreements estimated in the general model may not be sustained when $\theta=1$ for any level of water flow W_t for some t. The formal agreement is now $\min[W, \max(0, \tilde{X}_d)]$ and the informal agreement is now $\max[0, \tilde{X}_d(W)]$ and the gains of establishing informal agreements when $\theta=1$ are greater than or equal to zero for all levels of water flow W_t for all t.

Proposition 2: The policies for the agreements for all levels of water flow W_t for all t and all bargaining power parameters in the region $[0, 1]$ are for the formal agreement $\min[W_t, \max(0, \tilde{X}_d)]$ and for the informal agreements $\min[W_t, \max(0, X_d^*(W))]$. These policies guarantee that the gains due to establishing informal agreements are always $G(\cdot)\geq0$.

Proposition 3: The average gains of establishing informal agreements increase as the variance increases for the bargaining power parameter in the region (0, 1) and are zero when $\theta=0$ as well as when $\theta=1$.

To illustrate the analytical method, the next section applies the model to 39 bilateral basins and calculates the gains for establishing informal agreements.

10.5 Empirical analysis

In what follows, I apply the analytical methodology for 39 bilateral basins by estimating the formal and informal agreements in each dyad and by comparing their joint net benefits. To do so, first I compile the demand of each country, then I estimate for each basin the formal and the informal agreements for a range of bargaining power parameters in the interval [0–1.] Then, for each year, I average out the gains for each parameter and find the maximum gains due to establishing informal agreements in each dyad.

I constructed a database with water resources variables and institutional variables for multiple countries and basins in order to estimate the demand functions, the benefit functions, and the formal and informal agreements over time. All variables in the database are based on public information available in the literature (GRDC 2006; Owen *et al.* 2004; Shiklomanov 1999; UN 2006; UNDP 2006; WRI 2005).

I estimate a linear demand function based on empirical data from each country in the database. The choice of a linear demand is threefold. First, it is analytically tractable and helps to understand the phenomena of water allocation that otherwise may be entangled with other types of water demand. Second, a linear demand has different levels of elasticity, and a linear demand accounts for that since there are multiple users such as domestic, urban, and agricultural. Constant demand elasticity does not account for all users. And third, a linear demand implies that there is a satiation point for each country and, as such, there is only so much water one country can use in a given year.

The demand functions for each country in each basin may differ. The reason is that demand is endogenously generated by the amount of water available in a basin.[5] To account for this, I estimate the demand functions with real data and calculate first the average amount of water available in a given basin. Then, I multiply the water average by the geographical share of that country in the basin. The average amount of water in each country per basin was used to estimate the demand function with price and elasticity. The price of water per country per basin was estimated by using the percentage of water used for agriculture, domestic, and industrial users in each country. Each of these users has a particular price for water and elasticity per country. For the cases in which prices, percentage of use, or elasticity were not available, I used regional data to approximate such variables. Table 10.1 shows the elasticities used to construct the demand function (Rosegrant *et al.* 2002, p. 141).

With the variables of price per user (domestic, industrial, and agricultural) percentage use of water, average water, and price elasticity, I constructed the

Table 10.1 Water price elasticities for selected countries and regions

Region/country	Water price elasticities		
	e-Domestic	*e-Industrial*	*e-Agriculture*
United States	−0.40	0.59	−0.11
China	−0.45	−0.68	−0.13
India	−0.43	−0.65	−0.12
European Union	−0.16	−0.45	−0.04
Japan	−0.22	−0.45	−0.06
Australia	−0.45	−0.67	−0.11
Other Developed Countries	−0.31	−0.53	−0.08
Eastern Europe	−0.24	−0.44	−0.06
Central Asia	−0.45	−0.77	−0.11
Rest of Former Soviet Union	−0.35	−0.67	−0.09
Latin America	−0.45	−0.75	−0.11
Sub-Saharan Africa	−0.50	−0.70	−0.13
West/Asia North Africa	−0.52	−0.80	−0.15
South Asia	−0.40	−0.70	−0.10
Southeast Asia	−0.35	−0.73	−0.11

Source: Rosegrant *et al.* (2002, p. 141).

Note
Calculations by the author of values in Rosegrant *et al.* (2002, p. 141).

demand by estimating the slope and intercept for each user. Next, I sum up the users' demands to find the aggregate demand function of a country in a given basin. Finally, I find the inverse demand function and integrate it to get the benefit function of a country. Table 10.2 shows the benefit functions of the countries in the analysis.

10.6 Analysis of results

In the analytical method, I have shown that there are always gains to be made by establishing informal agreements, regardless of the bargaining parameter, and that there is a maximum that can be achieved. I found that the maximum gains could be up to 53 percent and a minimum of 0.2 percent. The average across all basins is about 6.5 percent. The gains depend on two main factors: 1) the variability of water flow; and 2) the relative bargaining power parameter between countries. Table 10.3 and Figure 10.1 summarize the main results of the empirical analysis.

Gains from establishing informal agreements depend on a number of factors, in particular water flow, satiation point of upstream user, and the value of the bargaining power parameter.

Figure 10.1 arrays the maximum gains by basin, regardless of the bargaining parameter. This figure shows how gains in several basins are little. The reason some of these basins do not present much gain is because the variability of water

Table 10.2 Benefit functions per country in each basin

Basin characteristics			Benefit functions			
River basin	Upper basin	Lower basin	Upper basin intercept	Upper basin slope	Lower basin intercept	Lower basin slope
Amur	Russia	China	4.05	(0.01)	1.67	(0.00)
Cavally	Ivory Coast	Guinea	3.56	(0.17)	2.30	(0.07)
Colorado	USA	Mexico	3.23	(0.04)	2.41	(0.03)
Columbia	USA	Canada	3.23	(0.01)	1.05	(2.68)
Corubal	Guinea-B	Guinea	0.21	(0.01)	0.15	(0.02)
Cross	Cameroon	Nigeria	3.16	(0.24)	3.25	(0.13)
Don	Russia	Ukraine	7.17	(0.06)	3.05	(0.29)
Douro	Spain	Portugal	6.52	(0.08)	5.93	(0.42)
Elbe	Germany	Czech Republic	4.12	(0.09)	1.99	(0.05)
Essequibo	Venezuela	Guyana	3.47	(0.02)	2.96	(0.01)
Fraser	USA	Canada	3.23	(0.01)	1.05	(2.68)
Gambia	Gambia	Senegal	5.54	(0.36)	2.27	(0.59)
Geba	Guinea-B	Senegal	5.71	(79.39)	2.27	(20.83)
Glama	Sweden	Norway	4.51	(0.06)	2.03	(0.05)
Grande	USA	Mexico	3.23	(0.29)	2.41	(0.40)
Irrawaddy	China	Myanmar	3.04	(0.08)	3.00	(0.01)
Juba	Kenya	Ethiopia	0.24	(0.02)	1.44	(0.16)
Kelantan	India	Myanmar	0.22	(0.01)	0.19	(0.01)
Kemi	Russia	Finland	0.39	(0.02)	0.16	(0.01)
Lempa	Guatemala	El Salvador	0.35	(0.01)	0.12	(0.01)
Mira	Colombia	Ecuador	0.14	(0.02)	0.08	(0.01)
Mississippi	USA	Canada	0.14	(0.01)	0.06	(0.01)
Negro	Honduras	Nicaragua	0.11	(0.01)	0.77	(0.01)
Nelson	USA	Canada	0.14	(0.01)	0.06	(0.01)
Ob	Kazakhstan	China	4.95	(0.01)	1.90	(0.00)
Orinoco	Colombia	Venezuela	0.14	(0.00)	0.07	(0.00)
Oulojoki	Russia	Finland	0.22	(0.01)	0.16	(0.01)
Ravama	Tanzania	Mozambique	5.71	(0.57)	2.25	(0.28)
Rhône	France	Switzerland	3.97	(0.02)	1.81	(0.02)
San Juan	Nicaragua	Costa Rica	3.65	(0.02)	1.73	(0.05)
Sassandra	Ivory Coast	Guinea	3.12	(0.06)	2.30	(0.09)
Stikine	USA	Canada	0.02	(0.00)	0.10	(0.10)
Taku	USA	Canada	0.27	(0.01)	1.00	(0.71)
Tana	Finland	Norway	3.76	(0.27)	1.30	(0.29)
Tano	Ivory Coast	Ghana	0.34	(0.03)	0.18	(0.02)
Tejo	Spain	Portugal	0.51	(0.01)	4.30	(0.25)
Tuloma	Russia	Finland	0.22	(0.01)	0.10	(0.01)
Vuoksa	Russia	Finland	4.05	(0.04)	1.13	(0.04)
Yukon	USA	Canada	5.72	(0.02)	1.05	(0.01)

Source: Estimated by author from information from database.

Table 10.3 Summary of gains of establishing informal agreements for multiple basins

Basin characteristics			Gains at theta (in percentages)												Time series		
River basin	Upper basin	Lower basin	0	0.1	0.2	0.3	0.4	0.5	0.6	0.7	0.8	0.9	1	Maximum gains	Average	Variance	C. Var (in %)
Amur	Russia	China	0.00	2.79	4.60	5.71	6.31	6.59	6.67	6.63	6.52	6.38	6.21	6.67	359.65	5,400.0	20.43
Cavally	Ivory Coast	Guinea	0.00	2.97	5.83	8.47	10.80	12.66	13.93	14.58	14.76	14.67	14.44	14.76	14.58	14.2	25.89
Colorado	USA	Mexico	0.00	0.40	0.88	1.48	2.07	2.39	2.39	2.33	2.28	2.23	2.18	2.39	19.99	30.1	27.45
Columbia	USA	Canada	0.00	0.28	0.02	0.02	0.02	0.03	0.04	0.05	0.07	0.14	4.86	4.86	237.81	1,820.0	17.94
Corubal	Guinea-B	Guinea	0.00	0.28	0.49	0.66	0.81	0.95	1.10	1.25	1.40	1.61	1.88	1.88	9.78	2.6	16.61
Cross	Cameroon	Nigeria	0.00	2.13	4.19	6.24	8.32	10.49	12.82	15.37	18.28	21.84	27.02	27.02	16.36	9.7	19.01
Don	Russia	Ukraine	0.00	0.71	1.00	1.19	1.36	1.53	1.77	2.08	2.54	3.26	4.54	4.54	25.92	95.1	37.62
Douro	Spain	Portugal	0.00	0.53	1.04	1.55	2.05	2.53	2.98	3.52	4.31	5.56	7.83	7.83	16.95	74.3	50.87
Elbe	Germany	Czech Republic	0.00	2.22	3.77	4.84	5.56	6.04	6.34	6.52	6.60	6.63	6.61	6.63	34.71	32.0	16.30
Essequibo	Venezuela	Guyana	0.00	1.40	2.64	3.81	4.94	6.09	7.31	8.66	10.22	12.17	15.33	15.33	202.98	922.1	14.96
Fraser	USA	Canada	0.00	0.00	0.00	0.00	0.00	0.00	0.00	0.01	0.01	0.02	0.66	0.66	114.35	224.7	13.11
Gambia	Gambia	Senegal	0.00	2.84	4.45	5.43	6.02	6.39	6.68	7.04	7.45	7.91	8.42	8.42	5.24	4.0	38.32
Geba	Guinea-B	Senegal	0.00	3.83	6.47	8.00	8.69	8.85	8.73	8.46	8.13	7.77	7.42	8.85	0.05	0.0	57.17
Glama	Sweden	Norway	0.00	0.44	0.82	1.06	1.17	1.19	1.16	1.15	1.13	1.11	1.09	1.19	21.14	12.3	16.56
Grande	USA	Mexico	0.00	2.27	5.39	13.18	39.51	47.16	46.09	47.66	49.34	51.15	53.09	53.09	1.48	2.8	113.08
Irrawaddy	China	Myanmar	0.00	0.19	0.40	0.62	0.85	1.06	1.26	1.44	1.59	1.70	1.79	1.79	253.09	924.2	12.01
Juba	Kenya	Ethiopia	0.00	0.02	0.06	0.11	0.19	0.32	0.54	0.95	1.78	3.64	7.78	7.78	5.91	2.5	26.99
Kelantan	India	Myanmar	0.00	0.04	0.10	0.17	0.24	0.29	0.32	0.37	0.43	0.52	0.65	0.65	16.77	14.5	22.69
Kemi	Russia	Finland	0.00	2.87	5.17	6.59	7.19	7.24	7.02	6.67	6.29	5.97	5.69	7.24	7.97	4.1	25.39
Lempa	Guatemala	El Salvador	0.00	1.24	2.15	2.48	2.50	2.51	2.52	2.53	2.55	2.56	2.57	2.57	11.70	14.2	32.23
Mira	Colombia	Ecuador	0.00	1.20	2.10	2.76	3.23	3.57	3.81	3.96	4.06	4.13	4.16	4.16	4.47	0.6	17.16
Mississippi	USA	Canada	0.00	0.24	0.44	0.55	0.59	0.63	0.66	0.70	0.75	0.86	0.86	0.86	512.00	13,653.3	22.82
Negro	Honduras	Nicaragua	0.00	0.01	0.02	0.04	0.08	0.13	0.22	0.42	0.94	2.29	3.33	3.33	26.29	48.5	26.49
Nelson	USA	Canada	0.00	0.22	0.27	0.31	0.36	0.42	0.49	0.59	0.75	1.03	1.62	1.62	95.70	323.7	18.80
Ob	Kazakhstan	China	0.00	0.08	0.13	0.16	0.17	0.18	0.20	0.22	0.24	0.27	0.30	0.30	403.82	3,935.1	15.53
Orinoco	Colombia	Venezuela	0.00	1.95	3.39	4.44	5.20	5.76	6.15	6.44	6.63	6.77	6.86	6.86	1,006.52	23,934.8	15.37
Oulojoki	Russia	Finland	0.00	0.36	0.74	1.11	1.43	1.68	1.84	1.94	1.98	2.01	2.05	2.05	7.99	1.8	16.91
Ravama	Tanzania	Mozambique	0.00	2.61	5.26	6.80	6.79	6.34	5.94	5.59	5.28	5.00	4.75	6.80	2.07	0.8	43.83
Rhône	France	Switzerland	0.00	0.48	0.89	1.15	1.28	1.31	1.32	1.34	1.35	1.37	1.38	1.38	65.06	186.6	20.99
San Juan	Nicaragua	Costa Rica	0.00	0.39	0.59	0.73	0.84	0.94	1.03	1.12	1.22	1.34	1.48	1.48	70.74	104.7	14.46
Sassandra	Ivory Coast	Guinea	0.00	0.30	0.70	1.17	1.60	1.83	1.92	2.01	2.12	2.24	2.37	2.37	10.01	9.9	31.41
Stikine	USA	Canada	0.00	0.00	0.00	0.00	0.00	0.00	0.00	0.00	0.00	0.01	0.57	0.57	48.59	31.1	11.49
Taku	USA	Canada	0.00	0.00	0.00	0.00	0.00	0.00	0.00	0.00	0.01	0.02	0.19	0.19	13.11	1.3	8.79
Tana	Finland	Norway	0.00	1.25	2.52	3.53	4.10	4.28	4.20	3.99	3.85	3.71	3.59	4.28	5.16	1.0	18.94
Tano	Ivory Coast	Ghana	0.00	0.11	0.43	0.90	1.42	1.89	1.96	1.38	0.85	0.57	0.39	1.96	4.50	1.1	23.01
Tejo	Spain	Portugal	0.00	0.01	0.03	0.07	0.12	0.21	0.39	0.77	1.76	4.89	14.48	14.48	9.62	34.7	61.26
Tuloma	Russia	Finland	0.00	0.81	1.43	1.82	2.02	2.08	2.06	2.02	1.98	1.95	1.91	2.08	5.87	1.2	18.27
Vuoksa	Russia	Finland	0.00	0.37	0.56	0.60	0.60	0.60	0.60	0.60	0.60	0.59	0.59	0.60	18.51	13.2	19.65
Yukon	USA	Canada	0.00	11.93	14.63	14.69	14.01	13.16	12.34	11.58	10.90	10.29	9.75	14.69	196.27	2,459.6	25.27

Source: Author, with information in database.

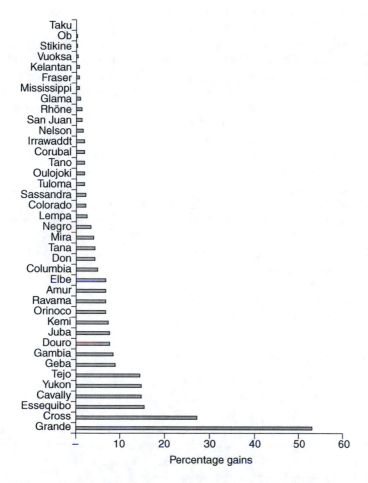

Figure 10.1 Maximum gains per basin (source: analysis by author using the analytical method and the variables in database).

flow is too small or because asymmetries among countries are really not that relevant. For instance, Taku, Stikine, Fraser, and Mississippi are basins shared between Canada and the United States. These four basins, given their particular characteristics, are basins in which the countries have similar marginal water prices and price elasticities and therefore redistribution of gains in the basin does not have an impact as reflected in the difference between formal and informal agreements. In addition, variability of water flow is relatively small with a coefficient of variation of approximately 10 percent in most of these basins (except Mississippi, which has 23 percent coefficient of variation).

However, gains increase as water flow variability increases. Consider the extreme cases in which there are more gains, such as in the Rio Grande and Cross basins. In the former, the variability is very large with a coefficient of variation of 113 percent. In this basin, there was a structural change in water flow because of the infrastructure that was in place back in the 1960s and 1970s. This basin has been contentious ever since, because most of the flow is regulated and because of drought issues. There was extreme drought in the region that brought about many conflicts during the 1990s, which explains the variability in water flow. As for the Cross Basin, the flow variability is just 19 percent in the range of most basins, and yet this basin presents the second largest gains by establishing informal agreements. One possible explanation is that there are asymmetries between Cameroon and Nigeria, which share the basin, and the bargaining power parameter between Cameroon and Nigeria is driving the gains.

The main driver of the gains from establishing informal agreements is water flow variability. The gains increase as water flow variability increases. This result is due to the fact that the formal agreement, when it exists, is based on the expected value of water flow, and the informal agreement considers a realization of current water flow.

This difference is relevant because, when there is small variability, the formal agreement will capture most of the benefits and give little chance for improvement to create gains with establishing informal agreements as temporary solutions. However, should the formal agreement indeed represent a fair distribution of benefits, then variability may not necessarily represent a problem in the basin.

10.7 Conclusions and policy implications

I developed a method of analysis of the potential gains of establishing informal agreements in transboundary water resources. I used a cooperative model that maximizes the joint net benefits between countries that share water resources. In doing so, I used a model that accounts for the benefits of each country in a basin weighted by the bargaining power that each country has in relation to another country. By using the bargaining power parameter bounded between 0 and 1, I found a hybrid of a formal agreement that has a fixed part in the extremes, when the bargaining parameter is close to 0 or 1, and a variable part that becomes indispensable to account for issues of low water flow. I have shown that there are always gains to be made by establishing informal agreements, regardless of the bargaining parameter. I also found an increasing relationship between the variance of water flow and the net gains of informal agreements.

The value of this research is its empirical application: It extends previous analysis in the literature by adding water demand functions and benefit functions to 39 transboundary water basins. In the analysis, I estimate formal and informal agreements for various years and for several bargaining parameters. I estimate the maximum gains associated with establishing informal agreements and ranked them. The average gain in the study of 39 basins was approximately 6.5 percent. I found that basins that have the lowest water flow variability have the least gain from informal agreements, and these small gains are concentrated when the bargaining power parameter is one. Further research is necessary to analyze determinants of the bargaining parameter, such as the effect of infrastructure and the level of development of the basin, or linkages that could explain particular outcomes.

Notes

1 I would like to thank the Asociación Mexicana de Cultura A.C. for their financial support.
2 For an extensive analysis of the topic on Conflict and Cooperation over International Fresh Water resources, the interested reader should approach the work by Dinar and Dinar (2003) and Just and Netanyahu (1998), and more recent work by Dinar (2009) and Dinar *et al.* (2011).
3 For example, in March 2001, following discussions between presidents from the United States and Mexico, the two governments announced an agreement under which Mexico would repay 600,000 acre-feet of water by 31 July 2001. The informal agreement was then included as Minute No. 307 to the 1944 treaty.
4 I chose to model a fixed allocation since it is the most common type of scheme used in transboundary water resources. However, the model could be extended to include other types of allocation, such as variable allocation.
5 For example, a country that has two basins, one in an arid region and one in a wet region, will have a demand function for each basin. Think of the case of the United States where the demand for water in the wet region of the northern boundary with Canada will be different than the demand for water in the arid region of the southern border where the United States shares its water with Mexico.

References

Conca, K., Wu, F., and Mei, C. (2006) "Global regime formation or complex institution building? The principled content of international river agreements," *International Studies Quarterly*, 50: 263–285.

Dietz, T., Ostrom, E., and Stern, P.C. (2003) "The struggle to govern the commons," *Science*, 302: 1907–1912.

Dinar, A. (2004) "Exploring transboundary water conflict and cooperation," *Water Resources Research*, 40: W05S01.

Dinar, A., Ratner, A., and Yaron, D. (1992) "Evaluating cooperative game theory in water resources," *Theory and Decision*, 31(1): 1–20.

Dinar, S. (2009) "Scarcity and cooperation along international rivers," *Global Environmental Politics*, 9(1): 109–135.

Dinar, S. and Dinar, A. (2003) "Recent developments in the literature on conflict negotiation and cooperation over shared international fresh waters," *Natural Resources Journal*, 43(3): 1217–1287.

Dinar, S., Dinar, A., and Kurukulasuriya, P. (2011) "Scarcity and cooperation along international rivers: An empirical assessment of bilateral treaties," *International Studies Quarterly*, 55: 809–833.

Fischhendler, I. and Feitelson, E. (2003) "Spatial adjustment as a mechanism for resolving river basin conflicts: U.S.–Mexico case," *Political Geography*, 25(5): 547–573.

Fischhendler, I., Feitelson, E., and Eaton, D. (2004) "The short and long term ramifications of linkages involving natural resources: The U.S.–Mexico transboundary water case," *Environment and Planning C*, 22(5): 633–650.

Giordano, M.A. and Wolf, A.T. (2003) "Sharing waters: Post-Rio international water management," *Natural Resources Forum*, 27: 163–171.

GRDC (2006) The Global Runoff Data Centre, D – 56002, Koblenz, Germany.

Jonsson, C. (1981) "Bargaining power: Notes on an elusive concept," *Cooperation and Conflict*, XVI: 249–257.

Just, R.E. and Netanyahu, S. (eds) (1998) *Conflict and Cooperation on Trans-boundary Water Resources*. Norwell, MA: Kluwer Academics Publishers Group.

Kilgour, D.M. and Dinar, A. (2001) "Flexible water sharing within an international river basin," *Environmental and Resource Economics*, 18: 43–63.

Lipson, C. (1991) "Why are some international agreements informal?" *International Organization*, 45(4): 495–538.

North, D.C. (1990) *Institutions, Institutional Change and Economic Performance*. Cambridge: Cambridge University Press.

Ostrom, E. (1990) *Governing the Commons. The Evolution of Institutions for Collective Action*. Cambridge: Cambridge University Press.

Owen, T., Furlong, K., and Gleditsch, N.P. (2004) "Codebook for the shared river basin gis and database," Center for the Study of Civil War, IPRI (vol. 2006). Oslo, Norway.

Parrachino, I., Zara, S., and Patrone, F. (2006) *Cooperative Game Theory and its Application to Natural, Environmental and Water Resource Issues: 1. Basic Theory*, unpublished manuscript, Washington DC.

Rosegrant, M., Cai, X., and Cline, S. (2002) *World Water and Food to 2025: Dealing with Scarcity*. Washington, DC and Colombo, Sri Lanka: International Food Policy Research Institute and International Water Management Institute.

Shiklomanov, I.A. (1999) "Observation data on monthly and annual river runoff from major stations located in different countries in each continent: International Hydrological Programme," Paris: UNESCO.

Sigman, H. (2002) "International spillovers and water quality in rivers: Do countries free ride?" *The American Economic Review*, 92(4): 1152–1159.

Tesler, L.G. (1980) "A theory of self-enforcing agreements," *The Journal of Business*, 53(1): 27–44.

UN (2006) *Water: A Shared Responsibility*. Nairobi, Kenya: United Nations.

UNDP (2006) *Human Development Report 2006. Beyond Scarcity: Power, Poverty and the Global Water Crisis*. New York, New York: United Nations.

UNEP (2002) *Atlas of International Freshwater Agreements*. Nairobi, Kenya: United Nations Environment Programme.

Wolf, A.T. (1998) "Conflict and cooperation along international waterways," *Water Policy*, 1(2): 251–265.

Wolf, A.T. (1999) "Criteria for equitable allocations: The heart of international water conflict," *Natural Resources Forum*, 23(1): 3–30.

Wolf, A.T. and Hamner, J. (2000) "Trends in transboundary water disputes and dispute resolution," in Green Cross International (ed.), *Water for Peace in the Middle East and Southern Africa* (pp. 55–66), Geneva: Green Cross International.

Wolf, A.T., Stahl, K., and Macomber, M.F. (2003a) "Conflict and cooperation within international river basins: The importance of institutional capacity," *Water Resources Update*, No. 125.

Wolf, A.T., Yoffe, S.B., and Giordano, M. (2003b) "International waters: Identifying basins at risk," *Water Policy*, 5: 29–60.

WRI (2005) *Water Resources and Freshwater Ecosystems*. Washington, DC: World Resources Institute.

Yoffe, S.B. and Fiske, G. (2002) "Use of GIS for analysis of indicators of conflict and cooperation over international freshwater resources," draft. Submitted for publication to Water Policy, World Water Council.

Young, O. (2002) *The Institutional Dimensions of Environmental Change: Fit, Interplay and Scale.* Cambridge, MA: MIT Press.

Zeitoun, M. and Warner, J. (2006) "Hydro-hegemony: A framework for analysis of trans-boundary water conflicts," *Water Policy*, 8: 435–460.

11 Efficient use of the Mekong River Basin

A joint management approach

Xueqin Zhu, Harold Houba, and
Kim Hang Pham-Do

11.1 Introduction

The Mekong River (MR) is the major water source in Southeast Asia, flowing through or forming the borders of six countries: China, Myanmar, Laos, Thailand, Cambodia, and Vietnam. The MR is not only the source of food, water, and transport for more than 70 million people from more than 90 distinct ethnic groups, the river basin is also home to more than 1,300 species of fish, creating one of the most diverse fisheries in the world (Campbell 2009; Osborne 2010). Over the years, there has been conflict and cooperation on water-resource management aimed to accommodate population growth, climate change, and economic development. Although the four downstream nations in the Lower Mekong (Thailand, Laos, Cambodia, and Vietnam) signed the 1995 Mekong Agreement[1] and formed the Mekong River Commission (MRC) to promote development and management of the river and its resources in a sustainable manner (MRC 2005), the sustainable development provision remains largely ambiguous due to the lack of a legal framework and procedural elements for management (Phillips *et al.* 2006; Bearden 2010; Osborne 2010). Water allocation is one of the increasingly important interdependency concerns in the Mekong River Basin (MRB), and is a source of tensions between the countries that share it (Campbell 2009).

In many transboundary water-resource sharing problems, allocation outcomes are determined not only by economic considerations but also by the distribution of political and bargaining power. Hence, water accrues more often simply to the most powerful riparian state within a basin. For the Mekong River, developments that are taking place in upstream and downstream tributaries are expected to affect the downstream communities at different levels. Moreover, the upstream country, China, has unquestionably greater political power. Much of the debate among the member countries is related to the operation of current dams and plans for drastic expansion of dam capacity. Therefore, there is a need for designing proper policies that can help manage the upstream–downstream water use to satisfy all the countries involved.

The literature on water resources management, based on game theory approaches (Dinar *et al.* 1992; Dinar and Dinar 2003; Madani 2010 and references therein), shows that sharing the total economic benefits from cooperation among the river basin countries, if it is attainable, gives rise to Pareto improvement. That is, either every country is better off or none is worse off. Even if some countries are not better off, there is still a possibility to be compensated if the total gain is larger than without cooperation. This implies that one can hope to bring agreement(s) and thereby cooperation on how to mitigate conflicts over water.

In this study, we view the MRB as a transboundary water resource, shared by two regions: upstream (China)[2] and downstream (the MRC). Currently, the cooperation between upstream and downstream regions is still lacking, and the MRC has weak policy instruments. Our aim is to investigate the welfare improvements arising: 1) from strengthening the governance of the MRC without cooperation with China; 2) from the MR's joint management by the MRC and China; and 3) the effects of improved governance by the MRC (before it engages in negotiations with China) on the distribution of welfare gains of the MR's joint management. For these purposes, we use a bargaining framework, in which an international transfer of funds from international institutions can be incorporated in order to provide stronger incentives for joint management of resources. This allows us to analyze the welfare changes from non-cooperation to cooperation. We consider the following major economic issues in the MRB: increasing dam capacity for hydropower generation and mitigation of flood damage, industrial and households' activities, irrigated agriculture, and the environmental services or damages (i.e., wetland benefits or damage from saltwater intrusion in the estuary during the dry season). In addition, it is believed that the highly centralized Chinese government has more grips on its water resources than the fragmented MRC with less effective management. We will, therefore, analyze the implications of the different bargaining powers when a joint management approach is proposed. For analyzing the welfare and the implication of strengthening the MRC's governance, we consider both weak and strong governance structures in our framework.[3] Particularly, the current situation represents "weak" governance in which the different water users maximize their own profits without taking into account externalities they cause. Strong governance is represented by a structure in which the MRC's regional welfare will be optimized. This allows comparing the welfare gains from improved river management of the MRC.

This chapter is organized as follows: The next section briefly describes the model elements, including the water balances, economic values, the disagreement points, and the Nash bargaining solution. Section 11.3 presents the simulation results of our model, including water quantity accounts and economic values under different scenarios. In section 11.4, we discuss the policy implications and the opportunities that can enhance effective regional cooperation. Finally, in section 11.5, we provide some concluding remarks.

11.2 The model

11.2.1 Water balances and economic values

Our model represents the physical hydrological basin reality with a unidirectional water flow from upstream to downstream. Basin-wide water availability is determined by precipitation or water (in)flows. We distinguish two seasons: wet and dry, and two regions: upstream and downstream. In each region, water users are aggregated into three representative water uses: industry and households, hydropower generators, and agricultural irrigators. For simplicity of modeling, we aggregated fishing into hydropower generation because both use the instream function of water. We neglect navigation in this version of modeling because most part of the river is un-navigable. Transboundary flows from upstream to downstream are sensitive to changes in water use and storage management.

Our model is built upon the work of Haddad (2011), in which both dam capacity and hydropower generation are considered, but we extend it by including other water uses (industrial and households, irrigation), flood damages, and wetland benefits or damages of saltwater intrusion. The model has an explicit representation of space (i.e., up- and downstream) and time (wet and dry seasons). We assume that irrigation takes place only in the dry season. As such, we are able to represent the detailed water balances in different seasons in different regions. Like Haddad (2011), our model is a static annual model in which two seasons are distinguished. The reservoir is filled in the wet season for usage in the dry season. Investment in dam capacity is therefore instantaneous, but we interpret it as long-term capacity.

Specifically, during the wet season, upstream water resources can be used for industrial and household activities, storage for use in the dry season, hydropower generation that is reusable further downstream, and passing through a dam (if there is one) to downstream. Outflow from upstream in the wet season, which might cause flooding upstream, runs directly to downstream. During the dry season, water inflow plus the (fraction of) stored water can be used for the similar purpose as in the wet season. River outflow in the dry season either can be used for irrigation or runs to downstream. Similarly, for downstream, water inflow plus the outflow from upstream can be used for the similar economic activities of industry and households, and hydropower generation. In the wet season, however, the river's outflow may cause flooding and can be stored directly by farmers or in the reservoirs and used for irrigation in the dry season (further details can be found in Houba *et al.* 2011). Dam capacity is endogenous. The river basin, including water flows and uses in space and time, is presented in Figure 11.1.

In the upstream–downstream case, upstream decisions may generate externalities affecting downstream water availability and the economic values. These externalities are positive to downstream when upstream stores more water in the wet season (i.e., reduced flood damage downstream), and negative when upstream decisions reduce downstream water inflow in the dry season, leading to

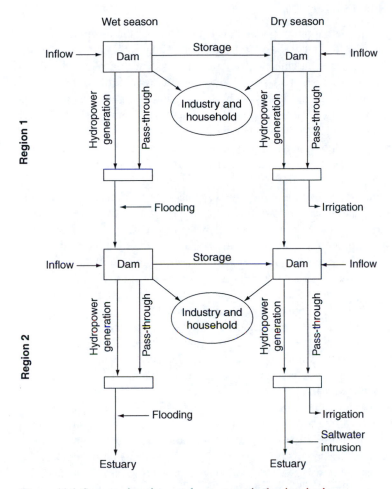

Figure 11.1 Seasons, locations, and water uses in the river basin.

increased water scarcity and saltwater intrusion. Joint management of the MRB has to internalize all such externalities. Such management is currently lacking for the whole MRB. For decades, the World Bank, the Asian Development Bank, and other international donor organizations have been active in talks between the MRB's governments about joint management of the MRB. One way to intervene is to introduce an exogenous budget (b) to provide stronger incentives for joint management of the MRB. Under such budget, each region would receive an additional external transfer, provided they reach an agreement on joint river management. The total economic value or welfare in each region is the sum of the net benefits (benefits minus costs) of water uses, plus the transfer received.

11.2.2 The disagreement point

We use an axiomatic bargaining approach in the form of the asymmetric Nash bargaining solution (for details, see Nash 1950; and Kalai 1977) for our analysis. This solution maximizes an objective function that depends on regions' utilities (i.e., net benefits), disagreement points, and bargaining weights reflecting the relative power of the regions. The Nash bargaining solution allows an underpinning through the strategic alternating-offers model in Rubinstein (1982) (for details, see Binmore *et al.* 1986; and Houba 2007, 2008).

The disagreement point plays an important role in the Nash bargaining solution. In the MRB, upstream China is a highly centralized economy with a strong government, whereas downstream MRC can be regarded as a rather politically divided government with weak policy instruments. For that reason, we assume that upstream maximizes its own regional welfare and internalizes its own regional externalities but not the downstream regions' externalities. For downstream, we assume that the current river management is ineffective in the sense that dam operators and agricultural users in this region optimize their own benefits without taking into account any regional externalities at all and taking externalities caused by upstream as given. Hence, we treat the model as a game in normal form and take its unique Nash equilibrium (NE) as the disagreement point. Due to the directional manner of externalities in which upstream influences downstream but not vice versa, we may solve the Nash equilibrium sequentially, similar to Ambec and Ehlers (2008). First, the upstream region maximizes its regional welfare subject to the water balances constraints. The maximal welfare for upstream is the disagreement point in the negotiations for a joint river basin management. Second, given the Nash equilibrium quantities for upstream, the downstream dam operator solves his decision problem (the dam capacity for the joint use of industrial and household water use and hydropower generation) before the downstream agricultural sector makes its irrigation decision. This represents downstream river management with weak governance, due to the sequential rather than comprehensive solution. Downstream disagreement utility under weak governance is given by the sum of the maximal utilities of the dam operators and the agricultural users.

However, if downstream would have strong governance (e.g., effective comprehensive river basin management),[4] the disagreement point should be derived similarly to that of the upstream, which is the maximal regional welfare. The difference between maximal welfare and the sum of utilities of the agricultural users and dam operators under weak governance yields the welfare loss of ineffective river basin management downstream. The Lagrange multipliers of the water balances are the shadow prices of each particular water use.

11.2.3 The Nash bargaining solution

The disagreement levels play an important role in the Nash bargaining solution. We denote $\alpha \in [\frac{1}{2}, 1)$ as the upstream bargaining weight and $1 - \alpha \in (0, \frac{1}{2}]$ as the downstream weight. These bargaining weights reflect that upstream China has more bargaining or political power than downstream MRC. The asymmetric Nash bargaining solution is given by maximizing the unique Nash bargaining objective function with the bargaining power of α and $1 - \alpha$ for upstream and downstream, respectively. We derive how the external budget b accrues to upstream and downstream, due to the bargaining powers (for details, see Houba *et al.* 2013).

The Nash bargaining solution shows that the negotiated transfers depend upon the exogenous budget and bargaining power. The stronger region, here by assumption upstream, obtains a larger share of the external budget. The final gain in economic welfare each region obtains from cooperation includes the direct effects of the external budget and the indirect effects through the utility function of that region. The magnitudes of the direct and indirect effects of increased economic efficiency will be investigated in our numerical analysis.

11.3 Numerical analysis for joint MRB management

For the numerical analysis, we specify the model according to Figure 11.1. Recall that our model is a static annual hydrologic model with given water inflows in the dry and wet season. In this section, we present our numerical results for the joint MRB management under different scenarios. First, we present our baseline or benchmark that represents the most realistic scenario for the actual disagreement point. The baseline analysis consists of the model results, based on the 1995 data. Due to the limitation of official data availability, we have to rely on a relatively old data source in the current study. Improved sharing and dissemination of official data could be a first, small but essential step in achieving cooperation. Our methodology developed in this study remains applicable and can contribute to better understanding of the joint management issue in the MRB, as long as more recent and better data become available. Then, we present the results on economic values, water balances, and shadow prices under non-cooperation between upstream and downstream; additionally for the case in which downstream has strong governance that shows the implication of the MRC's governance structure in terms of economic costs. Next, we discuss the results for several scenarios of upstream and downstream cooperation: with weak or strong downstream governance representing the disagreement point, different levels of bargaining powers, and with or without an exogenous budget. This provides information on the implications of cooperation.

11.3.1 Benchmark: non-cooperation

The yearly water inflows due to precipitation and the water withdrawals for industrial and household use (i.e., the so-called consumptive use) are given in Table 11.1.

The Mekong River is known for its large seasonal variability, with the ratio of 9:1 for water availability in the wettest and driest seasons. Using this ratio, we

Table 11.1 Yearly water inflows and water withdrawal in 1995 (km^3)

	Water inflows	Water withdrawal
Upstream	2,812	500
Downstream	1,492	104

Source: Adapted from Ringler (2001).

Table 11.2 Profits from different types of water uses in 1995 in million US$

	Upstream	Downstream
Irrigation	20	893
Industrial and households	11	159
Hydropower incl. fisheries	0.05	589
Wetlands	0	134
Total	31	1,778

Source: Adapted from Ringler *et al.* (2004).

can easily obtain the water inflows in both seasons. Table 11.2 shows the economic values generated from different types of water use in the two regions.

The economic value generated downstream is the aggregate of the MRC members. The ratio of the profit of one type of water to the total profit of all water reflects the relative importance or the weight of the value of that particular type of water in the economy.

To calibrate the model, we use the profit ratio of each category of water to generate the coefficients of the value functions for both upstream and downstream regions. Besides, we also use the water withdrawal in 1995 as the benchmark for the total consumptive use of industry and households. Lacking data, we set the costs of saltwater intrusion equal to zero, because there is a constant river flow from Tonle Sap in Cambodia to the estuary that already reduces saltwater intrusion. Further, we assume values for parameters of reserving costs, flooding costs, dam-building costs, and irrigation costs to make the model completely specified. These parameters can be adjusted during calibration in GAMS software.[5] This allows us to solve this model numerically and obtain results on water allocation to each type of water use. For calibration, we adjust the parameter for reserving costs in numerical simulation such that the model results reflect the current water use. The baseline results, including the possible expanding dam capacity and the shadow prices for each type of water, will be presented below.

11.3.2 Upstream under non-cooperation

In the baseline scenario, there is no cooperation, and upstream maximizes its own economic value (or welfare) subject to its regional water balances, for which we refer to the column "Non-cooperation" in Table 11.3. In such an

Table 11.3 Water balances under non-cooperation and cooperation in two seasons (km³)

	Non-cooperation		Cooperation	
	Wet	Dry	Wet	Dry
Upstream				
Water inflows (precipitation)	2,530.8	281.2	2,530.8	281.2
Water stored	649.2	−649.16	2,007.2	−2,007.2
Consumptive use	329.3	170.7	520.8	210.9
Hydropower generation	1.5	759.7	2.8	2,077.5
Outflows from dams	1,552.3	759.7	2.8	2,077.5
Irrigation	0	759.7	0	1,419.7
Outflows to downstream	1,552.3	0	2.8	657.8
Downstream (strong governance)				
Water inflows (precipitation)	1,342.8	149.2	1,342.8	149.2
River flow from upstream	1,552.3	—	2.8	657.8
Water availability	2,895.1	149.2	1,345.6	807.0
Water stored	295.7	−295.7	0.2	−0.2
Consumptive use	75.9	28.1	125.7	38.9
Hydropower generation	331.3	416.8	621.9	768.3
Outflows from dams	2,523.5	416.8	1,219.8	768.3
Irrigation	0	416.8	0	768.3
Outflows to the estuary	2,523.5	0	1,219.8	0
Downstream (weak governance)				
Water inflows (precipitation)	1,342.8	149.2	—	—
River flow from upstream	1,552.3	0	—	—
Water availability	2,895.1	149.2	—	—
Water stored	1.0	−1.0	—	—
Consumptive use	37.2	21.1	—	—
Hydropower generation	456.1	129.1	—	—
Outflows from dams	2,856.9	129.1	—	—
Irrigation	0	129.1	—	—
Outflows to the estuary	2,856.9	0	—	—

economy with the given technologies, hydrological parameters, and value functions, the river flow to downstream in the wet and dry season are 1,552 and 0 km³, respectively. In the wet season, the upstream region uses 329 km³ of water for consumptive use of industry and households, reserves 649 km³ for irrigation (or other use) in the dry season as its first priority, and distributes a small amount for hydropower (1.5 km³ water) according to the marginal values of these usages.

The shadow prices under non-cooperation are shown in Table 11.4. Under the current water inflows and existing technologies, the irrigation sector upstream has a very high shadow price, which means that it would benefit from further water use in the dry season. Given the storage costs, upstream does not want to reserve more than 649 km³ in the wet season for use in the dry season. The shadow price of the consumptive use of industry and households in the wet season is zero, implying that there is sufficient water for this purpose.

Table 11.4 Shadow prices per water use in baseline (non-cooperation) US$/m³

Water use	Upstream		Downstream (weak)		Downstream (strong)	
	Wet	*Dry*	*Wet*	*Dry*	*Wet*	*Dry*
Industry and households	0.0	0.2	0.0	256.5	0.0	79.5
Hydropower generation	105.0	Positive but very small	72.6	0.0	100.0	Positive but very small
Irrigation	—	55.0	—	338.9	—	70.5

However, the shadow price of water (see Table 11.4) for consumptive use of industry and households in the dry season is non-zero (0.2 upstream, 256.5 downstream), implying that there is water scarcity. The shadow price of water for hydropower generation in the wet season is very large (105) because the existing capacity of dams is very small in the upstream region. However, the shadow price of irrigation in the dry season is also very large (55), implying large demand for irrigation from the stored water of the reservoirs. Therefore, it is more efficient to reserve water for irrigation in the dry season than using water for hydropower generation in the wet season, considering the limited capacity of dams and high building costs. Furthermore, the high shadow price of hydro-power water in the wet season also explains the need for expanding dam capacity under the given reservoir building costs, because it can achieve the highest profit. The shadow price of hydropower water in the dry season is positive but very small, because all water that passes the dam is used for hydropower generation and later returned to the river or used for irrigation.

11.3.3 Downstream under non-cooperation

Water outflow, from upstream to downstream, is an externality for downstream and has to be taken as given. In order to check the welfare gains from better governance by the MRC, we solve the downstream problem under weak and strong governance. Weak governance, which is the current situation, means that there is no joint management between the dam operator and the agricultural sector for internalizing regional externalities. The Nash equilibrium is obtained by maximizing the dam operator's value function first and then solving the problem of the agricultural users. For strong governance, the equilibrium is obtained by maximizing the regional welfare, subject to the constraints of water balances.

As shown in Table 11.3, under strong governance, there will be 333.4 km³ less water outflow from the dam in the wet season than under weak governance (i.e., 2,523.5 versus 2,856.9 km³), which mitigates flood damages, because strong governance internalizes some externalities at the regional level. This is accomplished by expanding dam capacity by 208.6 km³ and storing 295.7 km³ more water and encouraging more consumptive use of 38.7 km³ water. For the same reason, hydropower generation is reduced by 124.8 km³ (from 456.1 to 331.3) in the wet season under strong governance to reduce flood damage. The stored water is used to increase hydropower generation and irrigation in the dry season. So, the economic costs of dam building, storing water, and less hydropower generation in the wet season are compensated by reduced flood damages and increased consumptive use in the wet season, and by increased hydropower generation and irrigation in the dry season.

The shadow price of consumptive use by downstream industry and households in the wet season under both weak and strong governance is zero, implying that there is sufficient water. They store water for the dry season because they can use it for irrigation. The shadow price of hydropower in the dry season is unknown because water is reserved for irrigation although it passes through the dam first for hydropower generation. In the dry season, the fact that the shadow prices for industry and households and irrigation under weak governance are higher than under strong governance implies that water scarcity is reduced by stronger governance.

Table 11.5 shows the existing dam capacity and the potential expansion under the non-cooperation situation. Downstream has more dam capacity (e.g., 494 km³), compared to a capacity of 4.5 km³ in the upstream region. This is probably due to the fact that the river is longer, it has many tributaries to the main stem, and it is shared by several countries in the Lower Mekong, compared with the Upper Mekong. Upstream has the potential to expand its dam capacity considerably for its economic development. Under weak governance, there is no expansion of dam capacity in the Lower Mekong because it has achieved the limit, but under strong governance there would be a potential expansion (209 km³), although it is relatively small compared to the upstream potential expansion (975 km³). This also leads to a lower relative shadow price of hydropower generation downstream than upstream in the wet season (100 versus 105).

Note that we calibrated the model with data from 1995 when upstream China did not have many dams installed in the MR. China has started expanding dam capacity rapidly since then, and has completed three dams with an aggregate capacity of 40.0 km³ and planned to build 13 dams in the near future (Osborne 2010). Our model results show the long-term development trend that already goes on in China, although we are aware that our results may overestimate these developments because our model does not place any cap on the maximal physically feasible dam capacity related to landscape considerations. While downstream has

Table 11.5 Existing dam capacity and expansion potential under non-cooperation (km³)

Dam capacity	Upstream	Downstream	
		Weak governance	*Strong governance*
Existing	4.5	494.3	494.3
Expansion	975.5	0	208.6
Total	980.0	494.3	702.9

already built many dams, its expansion potential in the future from an economic point of view may be relatively modest. Under weak governance, it has even reached its maximal level and no expansion will take place.

If there is no cooperation or water basin agreement, the two regions only care about their own economic values and allocate water according to their value functions. The upstream users will not consider the externalities they generate upon the downstream users and the downstream users just take this externality as given in their economic activities. This is not economically efficient because water is not used to its possible highest value. Without joint management, the economic value of upstream is US$316 million, while the downstream values are US$190 million and US$234 million, respectively, under weak and strong governance. The economic costs of weak governance are US$44.2 million (i.e., US$190 versus US$234.2 million; see Table 11.6). We turn now to show how cooperation through bargaining can achieve the more efficient use of the river basin (i.e., obtaining higher economic values in the two regions).

11.3.4 Upstream–downstream cooperation

In the bargaining model, the two regions have the possibility of bargaining, aiming to achieve the highest cooperative profit. We run the model for four scenarios with the upstream bargaining power α being 0.5 and 0.75, and the exogenous budget b being US$0 or 100 million. Table 11.6 shows the economic values for the upstream and downstream region under the four scenarios when downstream governance is weak or strong.

From Table 11.6, we can observe three findings. First, there are large welfare gains from cooperation for both regions, but the size and distribution depends upon the bargaining power and the international transfers. For equal bargaining power and no international budget transfers, the gain for downstream is US$143 million (from US$189.967 to 333.037 million), and US$121 million (234.161 to 355.129), depending on whether disagreement is characterized by weak or strong

Table 11.6 Economic values for non-cooperation and four scenarios of cooperation under weak and strong downstream governance (million US$)

| | Scenarios | | Upstream | | Downstream | |
	α	b	Weak gov. downstream	Strong gov. downstream	Weak gov. downstream	Strong gov. downstream
Non-cooperation	—	—	316.092	316.092	189.967	234.161
Cooperation	0.5	0	459.152	437.060	333.037	355.129
	0.5	100	509.152	487.060	383.037	405.129
	0.75	0	530.687	497.549	261.502	294.640
	0.75	100	605.687	572.549	286.502	319.640

downstream governance, respectively. Similarly for unequal bargaining power (e.g., 0.75), the gains are US$71.5 (from 189.967 to 261.5) and 60.5 million (from 234.161 to 294.640) for downstream, with the economic values being US$261.502 million and US$294.640 million for weak and strong downstream governance. Second, we estimate the economic costs for downstream if weak governance instead of strong governance determines the consequences of disagreement in the negotiations with upstream for joint management. These estimates for the economic costs of weak downstream governance are US$22 million and US$44 million under cooperation and non-cooperation. Therefore, downstream would be better off if first strengthening its governance before entering the negotiations with upstream. Third, bargaining power determines the distribution of the welfare gains from cooperation. More bargaining power for upstream (e.g., 0.75) increases this region's welfare by US$71.5 million when there are no international transfers (from US$459.150 to 530.687 million), and by US$96.5 million with such transfers (from US$509.152 to 605.687 million).

The gains in economic values under cooperation depend on the transfer received and indirect effects of joint management, which depend on bargaining power and the international budget. The composition of direct and indirect effects in economic values under unequal bargaining power and the amount of exogenous budget are reported in Table 11.7. Under equal bargaining power, the gain in economic value is split equally. In particular, the budget is split equally on top of the equal split of the indirect effects, which are US$121 million and US$143 million for each region for weak and strong governance, respectively, and independent of the international budget. While under unequal bargaining power ($a = 0.75$ and $b = 100$), upstream gets a higher share (a) of both, namely US$75 million of the budget of US$100 million and US$181 million out of US$242 million of indirect benefits, respectively (i.e., US$256.467 million for upstream out of total US$341.956 million).

We also demonstrated that the MRC would gain from strong governance in two ways: It improves efficiency without an agreement with upstream China,

Table 11.7 Economic values under cooperation under different scenarios (million US$)

		Effect	Upstream	Downstream	Total
$a=0.5$	$b=0$	Transfer	0	0	—
		Indirect	120.978	120.978	—
		Total	120.978	120.978	241.956
$a=0.75$	$b=0$	Transfer	0	0	—
		Indirect	181.467	60.489	—
		Total	181.467	60.489	241.956
$a=0.5$	$b=100$	Transfer	50	50	100
		Indirect	120.978	120.978	—
		Total	170.978	170.978	341.956
$a=0.75$	$b=100$	Transfer	75	25	100
		Indirect	181.467	60.489	—
		Total	256.467	85.489	341.956

and if strong governance is achieved before downstream starts negotiations with upstream, it negotiates a more favorable distribution of the joint welfare gains (including transfer and indirect gains). Hence, in what follows, we report and discuss the results on dam capacity and water balances under cooperation for the scenario of $\alpha = 0.75$, b = 100 and strong downstream governance. Table 11.8 reports the expansion of dam capacity under the non-cooperative and cooperative situation. Both regions will increase their dam capacity (from 980 to $2,530.8\,km^3$ for upstream and from 702.9 to $747.8\,km^3$ for downstream), and more dams will be built upstream. The main reason is that, in our simple modeling of water balances, upstream dams prevent flooding for both upstream and downstream. Also, water stored for upstream in the wet season can be used for either hydropower generation, from which the return flow runs to downstream where it can still be used for both consumptive and non-consumptive use, or consumptive use by industry and households or irrigation in the dry season. Therefore, it is cost efficient to store more water upstream, and downstream has less reason to build more dams for flood prevention, but only for hydropower generation and the consumptive use of industry and households.

The water balances for both non-cooperation and cooperation are shown in Table 11.3. Without cooperation, $1,552\,km^3$ of water flows to downstream, which may cause downstream flooding in the wet season. In the dry season, however, no water flows to downstream result in drought conditions and increase sea water intrusion. This does not count for the river flow to the estuary for which the continuous release from Lake Tonle Sap maintains a considerable flow. Under cooperation, upstream will decrease the water flow to downstream in the wet season tremendously to $2.8\,km^3$, and increase the water flow to downstream in the dry season to $657.8\,km^3$ through storing water, which mitigates flooding in the wet season and water scarcity in the dry season for downstream. Therefore, the consumptive use increases under cooperation. The storage of water by upstream increases from 649.2 to $2,007.2\,km^3$ (i.e., by three times). Consequently, the river flow increases in the dry season. This increase does not cause flood damages. And it mitigates water scarcity in the dry season.

Under cooperation, the consumptive use by industry and households and the hydropower generation downstream in the dry season increase because the increased inflow from upstream in this season increases water availability. Water storage is costly not only in terms of dam capacity, but also in terms of operating

Table 11.8 Dam capacity when $\alpha = 0.75$ and b = 100 (km^3)

Dam capacity	Upstream		Downstream	
	Non-cooperation	Cooperation	Non-cooperation	Cooperation
Existing	4.5	4.5	494.3	494.3
Expansion	975.5	2,526.3	208.6	253.5
Total	980.0	2,530.8	702.9	747.8

costs. For these reasons, the increased river flow is used to generate hydropower. The flooding is reduced because less than half of the water flows out to the estuary (from 2,523 to 1,219 km^3). The reduced river flow coming from upstream mitigates flood damages and reduces the need for storing water under joint river basin management.

11.4 Policy implications

Transboundary water resources are often a cause for conflicts among riparian states and negotiations over water among several sovereign nations are typically difficult. Smaller and weaker countries are suffering most because they have neither the political clout nor the economic strength to achieve their goals (Kirmani and Le Moigne 1997). Negotiations on the allocation of a water resource (or the benefits from using it) are more difficult when one does not know in advance how much water supply or demand will be generated under future conditions (e.g., population growth, economic activities, and climate change), such as in the case of the Mekong River. Therefore, the first policy measure is to establish a legal framework including procedures for the MRC. Improved sharing and dissemination of official data could be a first, small but essential step in achieving cooperation. Furthermore, efficient river basin management requires the cooperation of all countries in the MRB, including China. The policy implication from this analysis is the joint management approach to the efficient use of the Mekong River. It is important to strengthen the cooperation of all nations, rather than only the local MRC in the lower Mekong. A wider MRC including China and Myanmar would avoid conflict between upstream and downstream. If there is a wider and stronger MRC including China, the welfare gains are larger. This implies that the future development of MRC should include all the nations along the river for common development and opportunities. Hence, cooperation should start with a common perception of the status quo, including a mutual acceptance of aspects like the presence of claims to water, perceived property rights, and official water use data (Ansink 2009). Consequently, the negotiation process on the specifications of a water allocation agreement or on a jointly supported principle for water sharing can begin.

11.5 Concluding remarks

Applying an axiomatic bargaining approach in the form of the asymmetric Nash bargaining solution to the MRB, this chapter examines the welfare improvements of joint river management and the strengthening of the MRC. Our numerical analysis indicates that the gains from cooperation are significant and that China and the MRC have incentives for joint river basin management because there are welfare improvements to be achieved in both regions from cooperation. Such cooperation is a win-win situation.

Our numerical analysis shows that the welfare gains from strengthening the MRC are substantial. Hence, the MRC should obtain a solid legal framework with strong procedural elements that can implement river basin management. The results also show that China can expand its dam capacity without the need for cooperation with downstream countries. Strengthening the downstream governance will increase the bargaining position of downstream countries by improving the downstream disagreement or fall-back outcome and thus achieve higher benefits in cooperation.

We also show that an exogenous budget (i.e., international grant) provides stronger incentives for cooperation in the MRB because it increases the gains from cooperation by internalizing upstream–downstream externalities. This is achieved by the indirect effects of the transfer. However, our numerical results show that if bargaining power distorts the distribution of the external funds, the welfare gains would also be distorted because the welfare will mostly accrue to the stronger region. In this case, we may need international agreements with respect to the distribution of the exogenous funds.

All the simulations of our model show that the joint management of the Mekong River is efficient. Therefore, the policy implication is to find ways to achieve joint management. This can begin with assistance to foster common perceptions, which should include the sharing of official data on water resources. Gradually, the MRC should be expanded to include all the nations along the river for common development. Improved sharing and dissemination of official data could be the first, vital step in achieving cooperation. Our methodology developed in this study can contribute to a better understanding of the joint management issue in the MRB, as long as more recent and better data become available.

Some of the usual caveats apply to our analysis. We use the 1995 data for our numerical analysis due to data limitations, although the current situation has changed greatly since that time. This obviously raises questions about accuracy of the model results and the interpretation of the quantitative results. Besides, that, water traveling 4,200 km along the MR takes time, and delays are not captured in our simple framework. Also the distinction between the main course of the river and tributaries and the natural storage capacity of Tonle Sap, which maintains a positive flow to the estuary in the dry season, are not modeled. Delays and other changes to our model may partly reduce the positive effects of water storage by upstream in the wet season, as do natural bounds that limit the maximal physically feasible dam capacity. These issues are left for future research. Next, the spatial and temporal scale of our numerical model needs further improvement. Since the four member countries forming the MRC are lumped together, it would be preferable to disaggregate these countries in order to further investigate conditions productive of unanimity. For that reason, we regard our analysis as the first step in developing models that provide some insights into the joint management opportunities in the MRB. For future analysis, we need to consider expansion of the membership of the MRB management. The MRC is not a solid organization yet, which might give more insights into the effectiveness of management of the local MRC or the joint management of all countries along the river.

Notes

1 The "Agreement on the Cooperation for the Sustainable Development of the Mekong River Basin" was signed by four countries in 1995. Myanmar is not party to the 1995 agreement (roughly 2 percent of the Mekong River drains from the portion of the basin that resides in Myanmar).
2 The upstream region of the MRB is mainly situated in Yunnan Province of China.
3 Weak regional governance is defined as a governance structure in which each individual maximizes his own profit without internalizing any externalities within the region due to lack of a regional authority, while strong governance means regional welfare will be optimized through central planning such that externalities are internalized within the region.
4 From a technical point of view, we demonstrate two different ways of modeling the regions. In essence, any combination of weak and strong governance can be modeled, such as both weak, both strong, or upstream being weak and downstream strong. The case of upstream being strong and downstream being weak is the case considered in this chapter.
5 GAMS refers to General Algebraic Mathematical System. It is used for solving constrained optimization problems. See Rosenthal (2007) for details.

References

Ambec, S., and Ehlers, L. (2008) "Sharing a river among satiable agents," *Games and Economic Behavior*, 64: 35–50.

Ansink, E. (2009) "Game-theoretic models of water allocation in transboundary river basins," Ph.D. thesis, Wageningen University.

Bearden, B.L. (2010) "The legal regime of the Mekong River: A look back and some proposals for the way ahead," *Water Policy*, 12(6): 798–821.

Binmore, K., Rubinstein, A., and Wolinsky, A. (1986) "The Nash bargaining solution in economic modelling," *Rand Journal of Economics*, 17: 176–188.

Campbell, I. (2009). *The Mekong: Biophysical Environment of an International River Basin*. London: Elsevier.

Dinar, A., Ratner, A., and Yaron, D. (1992) "Evaluating cooperative game theory in water resources," *Theory and Decision*, 32: 1–20.

Dinar, S. and Dinar, A. (2003) "Recent developments in the literature on conflict and cooperation in international shared water," *Natural Resources Journal*, 43: 1217–1287.

Haddad, M.S. (2011) "Capacity choice and water management in hydroelectricity systems," *Energy Economics*, 33: 168–177.

Houba, H. (2007) "Alternating offers in economic environments," *Economics Letters*, 96: 316–324.

Houba, H. (2008) "Computing alternating offers and water prices in bilateral river basin management," *International Game Theory Review*, 10: 257–278.

Houba, H., Pham Do, K.H., and Zhu, X. (2013) "Saving a river: a joint management approach to the Mekong River Basin," *Environment and Development Economics*, 18, available on CJO 2012 doi:10.1017/S1355770X12000435.

Kalai, E. (1977) "Nonsymmetric Nash solutions and replication of 2-person bargaining," *International Journal of Game Theory*, 6: 129–133.

Kirmani, S. and Le Moigne, G. (1997) "Fostering riparian cooperation in international river basins: The World Bank at its best in development diplomacy," *World Bank Technical Paper*, No. 335.

Madani, K. (2010) "Game theory and water resources," *Journal of Hydrology*, 381: 225–238.

MRC (2005) "Overview of the hydrology of the Mekong Basin," Executive Summary, Mekong River Commission, Phnom Penh.

Nash, J. (1950) "The bargaining problem," *Econometrica*, 18: 155–162.

Osborne, M. (2010) "The Mekong River under threat," *The Asia-Pacific Journal*, January 11.

Phillips, D.J.H., Daoudy, M., Öjendal, J., Turton, A., and McCaffrey, S. (2006) "Transboundary water cooperation as a tool for conflict prevention and for broader benefit-sharing," Ministry for Foreign Affairs, Stockholm, Sweden.

Ringler, C. (2001) "Optimal water allocation in the Mekong River Basin," *ZEF-Discussion Papers on Development Policy*, No. 38.

Ringler, C., von Braun, J., and Rosegrant, M.K. (2004) "Water policy analysis for the Mekong River Basin," *Water International*, 29: 30–42.

Rosenthal, R. (2007) *GAMS: A User's Guide*. Washington, DC: GAMS Development Corporation.

Rubinstein, A. (1982) "Perfect equilibrium in a bargaining model," *Econometrica*, 50: 97–109.

12 Models of repression and revolt in autocracies

A specific point of view on the Arab Spring[1]

Mario Gilli

12.1 Introduction

The aim of this chapter is to provide a specific point of view on the interpretation of the protests that have characterized the Arab countries from December 2010 until now. This is not an empirical chapter, although it will consider some straight descriptive data to corroborate the arguments, nor is it a highly abstract theoretical chapter. The chapter provides a first understanding of some of the reasons behind the Arab Spring, offering a specific point of view through a simple argumentation explained by means of a sketchy basic model to be used as a starting point for a more complex and deep analysis, both theoretical and empirical. The chapter will also demonstrate that the results of the analysis are compatible with some basic stylized facts about the Arab Spring and, in particular, it provides a relevant and not obvious point of view. The value of this chapter is in emphasizing aspects that in popular and media discussions are often neglected, while they are crucial explanatory variables: the country's wealth and the selectorate's size.

A quite well-established body of evidence indicates that objective measures of social grievance, such as economic inequality or lack of democracy, have no systematic effect on the risk of revolts or even on civil wars.[2] On the other hand, the popular perception, reflected by media reports, is that social conflicts such as demonstrations or rebellions are motivated by genuine and extreme personal, social, and political complaints. Of course, it is perfectly possible that popular perceptions are partially shaped by the propaganda discourses that social conflicts themselves generate. Social conflicts themselves often produce atrocities that in turn fuel grievances. But this chapter shows that this popular view on conflicts cannot be taken at face value and should be significantly qualified. It will be argued that the Arab Spring is significant from this point of view, too. A model will be proposed in which revolt and acquiescence are motivated by the expected gain within an autocratic context that determines the distribution of national wealth. In other words, the chapter argues that the motivating force for a revolt is an attempt at changing the distribution of a country's wealth, which should be big enough to motivate citizens to face the serious risks connected to protests. The wealth distribution in turn depends on the relative size of enfranchised people (the selectorate). Moreover, it is intuitive that the likelihood of success plays a very crucial motivating reason for protesters, and it will be analyzed how this probability endogenously depends on the players' behavior.

Empirical evidence also shows, and this is particularly clear in the case of the Arab Spring, that a successful protest is one that escalates through a cascade of participation, drawing in increasingly motivated supporters. Note that, in the case of the Arab protests, besides the temporal dimension, the geographical space has been crucial, too.

Finally, in the Arab Spring, we are also facing significantly different outcomes of these protest movements: from the democratization of Tunisia to the dramatic removal of the incumbent leader and subsequent confrontation between the Army and the Tahrir Square movement in Egypt, and from the civil war in Libya and Syria to the moderate reforms in Morocco, Jordan, and Algeria.

Of course, the basic intuitive model of this chapter has many obvious limitations. For example, it does not distinguish among different sources of a country's wealth, even if it is well known that it matters significantly. In particular, it has been shown that a powerful risk factor is to have a substantial share of gross national income (GNI) coming from primary commodities, such as oil.[3] Moreover, while it has a simple dynamic structure that offers the opportunity of mimicking, in a very simple way, a cascade of activism, it does not take into consideration the geographical dimension, which is clearly very important. Finally and more crucially, the model does consider just two players, the disenfranchised (the citizens) and the enfranchised part of the population (the selectorate), while a more detailed analysis should take into account at least two other actors – the incumbent leader and the foreign countries.[4]

This notwithstanding, the ideas presented in this chapter will cast some light on these aspects, of course from a specific point of view. This means that including another totally different approach might complement this one in providing a more comprehensive and deep interpretation of these phenomena.

The approach in this chapter builds on Acemoglu and Robinson's 2006 seminal work on democracies and dictatorships. The starting point of their work is that the crucial distinction between democracies and autocracies is the different political representation. The first political regime looks after the interests of the majority, hence it is characterized by a greater tendency to redistribute income. In contrast, autocracies give power to a subset of the population, the selectorate, and consequently opt for fewer redistributive policies. Thus, Acemoglu and Robinson (2006) model politics essentially as a conflict over distributional policies, in which the outcome depends on who holds the political power, namely the citizens in democracies, and the selectorate in autocracies. However, their models cannot be directly applied to the Arab Spring events, since they neglect to include the role of private information in generating the informational cascades that characterize successful revolts. Hence, this chapter uses a different modeling approach, proposing a sequential game with asymmetric information, where on one hand the government choices may signal the true state of nature, and on the other hand the citizens' choices are a way to learn the true state of nature. From this point of view, the model is similar to Kuran (1989) or Lehmann (1994). The Kuran and Lehmann models are very different, but share the idea that the dynamics of protest can be successful only if it induces an increasing participation, starting from the most ardent to the less enthusiastic supporters, to reduce the personal risk of punishment. Moreover, the model in this chapter connects the dynamics of protests with the political agency models of Besley (2006) and Maskin and Tirole (2004), particularly when applied to autocracies as in Padro i Miguel (2006), Besley and Kudamatsu (2008), and Gilli and Li (2011a, 2011b), which are all based on the role of asymmetric information. More generally, on the use of games with asymmetric information in conflict theory, see Banks (1994) and Blattman and Miguel (2010).

The main results of the chapter are that the political scenarios expected to prevail in equilibrium depend on the country's wealth and on the selectorate size. In particular, when the country is poor or has intermediate wealth but the regime is so strong to credibly commit to repression, the citizens will not protest, hence the autocracy will carry on. On the other hand, when the country's wealth is intermediate, the citizens will protest and the selectorate will appease, leading to reforms within the regime. Finally, the citizens will revolt and democracy might be achieved if the country's wealth is big enough, or if the selectorate is big enough and the country's wealth is intermediate. It will be argued that these results are roughly consistent with the available descriptive evidence on the Arab Spring, and that they allow a significant insight into these events once the notions of selectorate and of country wealth are correctly interpreted.

The chapter is organized as follows. Section 12.2 presents some stylized facts about the Arab Spring. Section 12.3 presents an illustration of the model of protest, revolt, and repression in autocracies and discusses assumptions and limitations. Section 12.4 illustrates the main results, and section 12.5 concludes. All the technical details are in the Appendix.

12.2 Some relevant facts about the Arab Spring

The series of protests and demonstrations across the Middle East and North Africa, known as the Arab Spring, was sparked by the first manifestations that occurred in Tunisia on 18 December 2010, following Mohamed Bouazizi's self-immolation in protest of police corruption and ill treatment. The increasing wave of protests led to the government being overthrown on 14 January 2011, and so the success of the Tunisian movement induced an even more dramatic wave of demonstrations through all the other Arab countries. The protests have also triggered similar unrest outside the region – for example, in China and, more recently, in Russia.

As of November 2011, rulers have been overthrown in four countries: Tunisia, Egypt, Libya, and Yemen, while revolts are still under way in Syria and partially in Yemen, notwithstanding the change in the leader, while several prime ministers (Algeria, Bahrain, Iraq, Jordan, Kuwait, Morocco, Oman, and Saudi Arabia) either announced their intentions to step down at the end of their

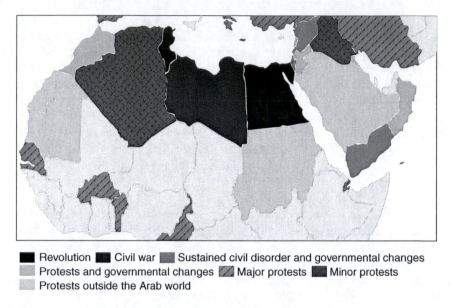

Revolution ■ Civil war ■ Sustained civil disorder and governmental changes
Protests and governmental changes ⧗ Major protests ■ Minor protests
Protests outside the Arab world

Figure 12.1 A map of the 2011 situation in Arab countries.

current terms and/or deliberated significant reforms. Figure 12.1 shows the geo-graphical extension of the revolts that are characterizing the Arab Spring, while Table 12.1 sums up in a more detailed way the dynamic and the variegated set of political outcomes in the different Arab countries. Both are taken from Italian geopolitical magazine *Limes* (2011).

It is generally argued that numerous factors have led to these protests, includ-ing issues such as the countries being autocracies, human rights violations, gov-ernment corruption, economic decline, unemployment, extreme poverty, and a number of demographic structural factors, such as a large percentage of educated but dissatisfied youth within the population. Increasing food prices and global famine rates has also been indicated as a significant factor. It is interesting to note that these motivating factors on one hand are not specific to Arab countries and also significantly differ among these countries. The unique common ele-ments among all Northern African and Persian Gulf countries, apart from the Muslim faith, have been the concentration of wealth in the hands of autocrats in power for decades, insufficient transparency of its redistribution, and corruption. Moreover, note that in recent decades rising living standards and literacy rates, as well as the increased availability of higher education, have resulted in an improved human development index in the affected countries. Many of the Internet-savvy youth of these countries have, increasingly over the years, been viewing autocrats and their privileges as anachronisms. Hence the tension between rising aspirations and lack of opportunities may well have been a

Table 12.1 A view of the 2011 situation in the Arab countries

Country	Date started	Status of protests	Outcome	Death toll	Outcome
Tunisia	18 December 2010	Revolution on 14 January 2011	• Ousting of President Ben Ali and Prime Minister Ghannouchi • Dissolution of the political police • Dissolution of the RCD, the former ruling party of Tunisia and liquidation of its assets • Release of political prisoners • Elections to a Constituent Assembly on 23 October 2011	223	Revolution
Algeria	28 December 2010	Protests subdued since March 2011			
	12 January 2011	Subdued since April 2011	• Lifting of the 19-year-old state of emergency	8	Major protests
Lebanon		Limited		0	Protests and governmental changes
Jordan	14 January 2011	Ongoing	• King Abdullah II dismisses Prime Minister Rifai and his cabinet	1	Protests and governmental changes
Mauritania	17 January 2011	Subdued since May 2011		1	Protests
Sudan	17 January 2011	Subdued since April 2011	• President Bashir announces he will not seek another term in 2015	1	Protests
Oman	17 January 2011	Ended May 2011	• Economic concessions by Sultan Qaboos • Dismissal of ministers • Granting of lawmaking powers to Oman's elected legislature	2–6	Protests and governmental changes
Saudi Arabia	21 January 2011	Subdued since June 2011	• Economic concessions by King Abdullah • Male-only municipal elections to be held 22 September 2011	2	Protests
Egypt	25 January 2011	Revolution on 11 February 2011 Protests ongoing	• Ousting of President Mubarak and Prime Ministers Nazif and Shafik • Assumption of power by the Armed Forces • Suspension of the Constitution • Dissolution of the parliament • Disbanding of State Security Investigations Service • Dissolution of the NDP, the former ruling party of Egypt and transfer of its assets to the state • Prosecution of Mubarak, his family, and his former ministers	846	Revolution

continued

Table 12.1 Continued

Country	Date started	Status of protests	Outcome	Death toll	Outcome
Yemen	3 February 2011	Ongoing	• Resignation of MPs from the ruling party • On 23 November, President Saleh signed a power-transfer agreement brokered by the Gulf Cooperation Council in Riyadh, which will end his 33-year reign	1,016–1,203	Sustained civil disorder and governmental changes
Iraq	10 February 2011	Ongoing	• Prime Minister Maliki announces that he will not run for a third term • Resignation of provincial governors and local authorities	28+	Major protests
Bahrain	14 February 2011	Ongoing	• Economic concessions by King Hamad • Release of political prisoners • Dismissal of ministers	36	Sustained civil disorder and governmental changes
Libya	17 February 2011	Government overthrown on 23 August 2011 Intervention ended on 31 October 2011	• Overthrow of Muammar Gaddafi • Gaddafi killed by NTC forces on 20 October	30,000	Ongoing civil war
Kuwait	18 February 2011	Ended 31 March 2011	• Resignation of cabinet • Resignation of the government	0	Protests and governmental changes
Morocco	20 February 2011	Limited after 1 July 2011	• Political concessions by King Mohammed VI • Referendum on constitutional reforms • Respect to civil rights and an end to corruption	1	Protests and governmental changes
Western Sahara	26 February 2011	Subdued since May 2011		0	Protests
Syria	15 March 2011	Ongoing	• Release of some political prisoners • End of emergency law • Dismissal of provincial governors • Military action in Hama, Daraa, and other areas • Resignations from parliament • Resignations from the government • Large defections from the Syrian army and clashes between soldiers and defectors	2,463–2,654	Sustained civil disorder and governmental changes
Israeli borders	15 May 2011	Ended 5 June 2011		30–40	Major projects
Total death toll:	32,052–37,751+ International estimate				

Table 12.2 The Human Development Index in Arab countries, compared to best and worst countries

HDI rank		HDI	Life exp. at birth	Mean years of schooling	Expected years of schooling	GNI per capita
1	Norway	0.938	81.0	12.6	17.3	58.810
2	Australia	0.937	81.9	12.0	20.5	38.692
3	New Zealand	0.907	80.6	12.5	19.7	25.438
4	United States	0.902	79.6	12.4	15.7	47.094
32	United Arab Emirates	0.815	77.7	9.2	11.5	58.006
38	Qatar	0.803	76.0	7.3	12.7	79.426
39	Bahrain	0.801	76.0	9.4	14.3	26.664
47	Kuwait	0.771	77.9	6.1	12.5	55.719
53	Libyan Arab Jamahiriya	0.755	74.5	7.3	16.5	17.068
55	Saudi Arabia	0.752	73.3	7.8	13.5	24.726
81	Tunisia	0.683	74.3	6.5	14.5	7.979
82	Jordan	0.681	73.1	8.6	13.1	5.956
84	Algeria	0.677	72.9	7.2	12.8	8.320
101	Egypt	0.620	70.5	6.5	11.0	5.889
111	Syrian Arab Republic	0.589	74.6	4.9	10.5	4.760
114	Morocco	0.567	71.8	4.4	10.5	4.628
133	Yemen	0.439	63.9	2.5	8.6	2.387
166	Burundi	0.282	51.4	2.7	9.6	402
167	Niger	0.261	52.5	1.4	4.3	675
168	Congo (Demographic Republic of)	0.239	48.0	3.8	7.8	291
169	Zimbabwe	0.140	47.0	7.2	9.2	176

contributing factor in all of the protests. As will be argued, this is one of the interpretations that follows from the simple model in this chapter.

Table 12.2 reports the Human Development Index (HDI) together with the Gross National Income (GNI) per capita[5] for 2010 for the Arab countries. Compared with the first and last four countries according to the HDI, clearly the Arab countries are at an intermediate level of both HDI and GNI, although there are significant differences.

Similarly, Table 12.3 was constructed from the Polity IV[6] and the World Bank data together with a personal reconstruction of the selectorate size – based on the qualitative information provided by the Polity IV Project and by the World Bank data – and provides further useful information for understanding similarities within and between Arab countries.

12.3 The model

A very simple, tentative model of protest, repression, and revolutions in autocracies is presented, constructed as an incomplete information game with a critical role for private information and of sequential choices by the political actors.

Table 12.3 Political characteristics of the Arab countries

	Fragility index	Security effectiveness	Security legitimacy	Political effectiveness	Political legitimacy	Size selectorate	Regime type	Popul. 2010	GDP 2010	GNI Atlas	GNI PPP
Iraq	19	Low	Moderate	Low	Moderate	Intermediate	—	32,030,823	82.150	2.340	3.350
Algeria	16	Moderate	Low	Intermediate	Low	Intermediate	AUT	35,468,208	159.426	4.450	8.120
Yemen	16	Intermediate	Moderate	Intermediate	Low	Small	AUT	24,052,514	26.365	1.070	2.350
Egypt	13	High	Moderate	Low	Low	Intermediate	AUT	81,121,077	218.912	2.440	6.160
Lebanon	10	Moderate	Low	Intermediate	Moderate	Intermediate	DEM	4,227,597	39.155	9.080	14.260
Saudi Arabia	10	Intermediate	Low	Intermediate	Low	Big	AUT	27,448,086	434.666	16.190	22.540
Syria	9	High	Intermediate	High	Low	Intermediate	AUT	20,446,609	59.103	2.790	5.150
Libya	7	High	Intermediate	Intermediate	Intermediate	Small	AUT	6,461,454	62.360	12.320	16.740
Tunisia	7	High	Intermediate	Intermediate	Low	Intermediate	AUT	10,549,100	44.291	4.060	8.130
Jordan	6	High	Intermediate	High	Low	Small	AUT	6,047,000	27.574	4.390	5.810
Morocco	6	High	Intermediate	High	High	Small	AUT	31,951,412	91.196	2.900	4.620
Qatar	6	High	High	Low	High	Big	AUT	1,758,793	98.313	—	—
Oman	5	High	High	Low	High	Big	AUT	2,782,435	46.866	18.260	24.960
Bahrain	4	High	High	High	Intermediate	Big	AUT	1,261,835	20.595	18.730	24.710
United Arab Emirates	3	High	High	High	High	Big	AUT	7,511,690	230.252	—	—
Kuwait	3	High	High	High	High	Big	AUT	2,736,732	109.463	—	—

The starting point is the Bueno de Mesquita *et al.* (2003) approach that models autocracies as a context of strategic interaction between two key players, the Citizens, *C*, and the selectorate, *S*, (i.e., the disenfranchised and the enfranchised part of the population). The starting point is thus the existing literature on political economics of autocracy,[7] suggesting that the real power in non-democratic regimes comes from the selectorate (i.e., from those citizens that in a given political regime have the actual possibility to depose a leader). This expression is adopted from British parliamentary politics to define the group within a political party that has the effective power to choose leaders. In particular, the model follows Bueno de Mesquita *et al.* (2003), identifying a country selectorate with the set of citizens that have a say in choosing the leader and with a prospect of gaining access to special privileges. The idea of distilling the infinite variety of real-world political institutions according to these two critical dimensions, the citizens and the selectorate, is clearly a major simplification, but it allows a deep insight to be gained into the Arab Spring, although at the cost of sacrificing details and specific local characteristics. In particular, note that one of the central underlying features of the Middle East (i.e., the massive youth bulge that have strong aspirations of inclusion) is implicitly included in this contrast between enfranchised and disenfranchised people. On the other hand, questions such as separation of powers, checks and balances, implementations of policy choices, and similar topics lie outside this model. Finally, I also abstract from individual heterogeneity within each group, the selectorate and the citizens: The idea is that the people in each group share significant interests that prevail on individual specific characteristics. This allows the chapter to focus on what I believe is the crucial root of political struggle, the allocation of existing resources, both tangible and intangible. The main novelty of this chapter's model is then the key role played by the selectorate's private information on the likelihood of success of the citizens' revolt.

Let us consider the more specific assumptions needed to build a manageable model and to find closed-form solutions to connect with the data previously reported. Let the country population be normalized to 1, and let $\phi \in [0, 1]$ be the size of the selectorate. The rest of the people who do not have the power to choose leaders and are disenfranchised are the citizens and their size is $1 - \phi$. The strategic situation is characterized by two possible states of nature $\omega \in \{H, L\}$: high or low likelihood of getting democracy through revolt. In particular, the true state of nature is assumed to be private information and access to private inside information on the global situation. On the other hand, the citizens can exert costly effort in their protests, inducing a possible reply associated with a costly effort on the part of the selectorate in repressing the citizens' protest, which however might signal the selectorate's private information.

To simplify the model, we assume that the game is finite. Hence the citizens have three possible actions:

$e_C = 0$ (i.e., no protest);
$e_C = 1$ (i.e., protest);
$e_C = 3$ (i.e., revolt, which is assumed to be possible only after protesting).

Similarly, there are two possible reactions of selectorate to the citizens' protest:

$e_S = 0$ (i.e., appeasement after protest);
$e_S = 2$ (i.e., repression after protest).

The timing of the game is as follows:

1   The citizens, without knowing the true state of the world, choose whether or not to protest;
2   After observing the state of the world and the citizens' previous choice, the selectorate decides whether to appease or to repress;
3   After observing the selectorate's choice, the citizens decide whether or not to revolt.

There are three possible political regimes as possible outcomes of these choices: Autocracy (A), Reforms within the existing regime (R), and Democracy (D). These outcomes depend on the players' actions: To get democracy with a positive probability, the citizens should revolt, while if after protest there is appeasement by the selectorate and no revolt by the citizens, then there are reforms within the regime; in all other situations the autocratic regime carries on.

The generic scheme of the model is represented in Figure 12.2, while in the Appendix there is the fully detailed game and the consequent analysis.

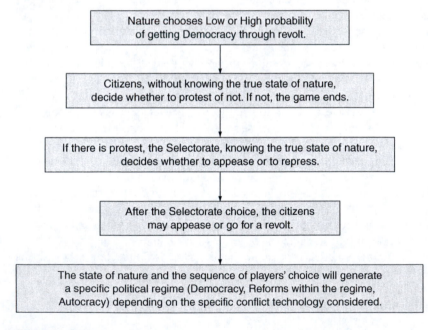

Figure 12.2 The structure of the game.

Table 12.4 The notation of the paper

Symbol	Definition
Players	
C	Citizens
S	Selectorate
Exogenous variables	
$\omega \in \{H, L\}$	State of nature, i.e., likelihood of getting democracy
X	Country wealth
$\phi \in [0, 1]$	Selectorate size
$TC(E_i, E_j)$	Total cost for player i of exerting total effort E_i when the opponent is exerting E_j
$\mathbf{Pr}\{PR\vert E_C, E_S, \omega\}$	Probability of getting a political regime $PR \in \{D, A, R\}$ as a function of players' choices E_C, E_S and of the true state of nature ω
$U^C(PR, E_C, E_S)$	Utility function of the Citizens
$U^S(PR, E_C, E_S)$	Utility function of the Selectorate
Endogenous variables	
$e_C \in \{0, 1, 3\}$	Citizens' behavior: no protest, protest, and revolt
$e_S \in \{0, 2\}$	Selectorate's behavior: appeasement and repression
$PR \in \{D, A, R\}$	The political regime that results from players' choices, state of nature, and the technology

As standard in this literature,[8] the political regime matters for the distribution pro quota of the national wealth X to the citizens and to the selectorate. Finally to get closed-form results, some further simplifications are needed, which are reported in the Appendix.

The symbols used in this chapter are summarized in Table 12.4.

12.4 Main results

The analysis is pursued using the notion of pure strategy Sequential Equilibrium (hence SE) as a solution concept. As mentioned earlier, the detailed calculations are reported in the Appendix. The results and comment on them are considered here. As usual in games with asymmetric information, there are many Sequential Equilibria. In particular, this game has no separating equilibria, but several pure strategy pooling equilibria, depending on the values of the parameters:

the country wealth, X,
the selectorate size ϕ, and
the marginal cost of the players' joint cumulative effort γ and, as usual, on the out-of-equilibrium beliefs.

The following proposition will just report the interpretation of the formal results that are developed in full detail in the Appendix.

12.4.1 Proposition

Denote by $\mu[0] \in [0, 1]$ and $\mu[2] \in [0, 1]$ the out-of-equilibrium beliefs after respectively the selectorate's choice $e_S = 0$ and $e_S = 2$, then

when $X \in \left[2(1-\phi)\gamma, \dfrac{9(1-\phi)\gamma}{2-\mu[2]} \right]$ the political regime outcome is Reform within

the existing regime;

when $X \le 2(1-\varphi)\gamma$ the political regime outcome is Reform within the regime;

when $X \in \left[\dfrac{9(1-\phi)\gamma}{2-\mu[2]}, \min\{12(1-\phi)\gamma, 30\phi\gamma\} \right]$ the political regime outcome is

Reform within the existing regime;

when $X \in [12(1-\varphi)\gamma, 6\varphi\gamma]$ the political regime outcome is Democracy with probability 3/4 and Autocracy with probability 1/4;

when $X \ge \max\left\{ 12(1-\phi)\gamma, 12\phi\gamma, \dfrac{6(1-\phi)\gamma}{1-\mu[0]} \right\}$ the political regime outcome is

Democracy with probability 1/2 and Autocracy with probability 1/2;

when $X \in \left[\max\left\{ 12\phi\gamma, \dfrac{6(1-\phi)\gamma}{1-\mu[0]} \right\}, 12(1-\phi)\gamma, \right]$ the political regime outcome is

Autocracy.

12.4.2 Proof: See the appendix

Remark

The characterization of the set of pure strategy Sequential Equilibria provided by this proposition shows that in equilibrium we might get the following situations:

1   No protest if the country is poor or even has a moderate wealth, but the regime is powerful enough to credibly threat a repression;
2   Protest, appeasement by the regime, and no revolt if the national wealth is intermediate;
3   Protest, appeasement by the regime, and revolt if the national wealth is intermediate and the selectorate is big enough;
4   Protest, repression by the regime, and revolt if the national wealth is big enough.

12.5 Policy implications

The previous proposition helps relate two important variables, the national wealth and the selectorate size, to the different ways used by the Arab countries in approaching the requests of transforming autocracies into democracies. In particular, the country's wealth plays a role different from what is often thought:

Being poor is not conducive to revolt or protest, while an intermediate or a big national wealth is necessary and sometimes even sufficient to propel massive revolts, which of course might be unsuccessful. A quick look at the GNI of the Arab countries compared to the diversity in countries' demonstrations does not falsify these statements: Libya and Tunisia are the richest countries of North Africa, while Egypt and Syria have intermediate GNI but the selectorate substantially coincides with the army, which means that it is big with respect to country population. Similarly Oman, Bahrain, and Kuwait are rich countries where massive protests have induced changes and reforms within the existing regime. Other Arab countries where there have been no revolts but simply protests, such as Morocco, Algeria, and Jordan, are instead significantly poorer countries. More difficult to interpret and probably outside the domain of this model are the massive protests and revolts in Yemen. Of course this analysis does not consider a crucial dimension of the national wealth (i.e., its distribution: clearly GNI per capita is a biased measure, since it is not taking into account the skew of the GNI distribution). This is an important aspect that should be considered in further analysis.

Of course, this is not an empirical test of the model or of the results, but is a simple impressionistic first look at the data vis-à-vis the theoretical prediction of the model.

12.6 Conclusions

Obviously, this model is a simplistic way of organizing systematic reflections on protest and repression in autocratic systems. It is clearly far too simple to consider important aspects of real events of the Arab Spring, such as the role of corruption and of the demographic structure of these countries, or the composition of GDP or the income distribution. However, even with its naive structure, the model includes two critical elements for explaining the recent events in these countries (i.e., the division between insiders that get the patronage from the regime with their vested interest – the selectorate – and the outsiders who get no benefit from the regime – the citizens). These elements have often been overlooked by the public and scientific discussion on these events. Further, the simplifying assumptions of a finite set of actions and state of nature, together with specific technological and institutional functions, allow finding closed-form solutions for the set of Sequential Equilibria to admit a simple qualitative comparison between real data and theoretical results.

Future work on this line of research should consider more complex models with a continuum of possible agents' choices, including a check for robustness of the technological and institutional details (e.g., considering different specifications for the success probability and the cost functions). Moreover, I believe it might be important to include at least a third player (i.e., the incumbent leader, as in Gilli and Li 2011b).[9] Finally, an empirical test of the model would be important. This model provides an important and relevant starting point in understanding the role of two important parameters – the national income and the size of the selectorate. In particular, the model shows why the revolts are more likely in countries with a significant income and thus explains why the common argument about poverty and desperation as critical reasons to revolt is deeply wrong, because without a cake to divide, there is no motive to sustain a significant cost to get it. The model also explains why the Arab revolts have been so relevant in some of the most developed North African countries.

12.7 Appendix

The game form representing the model is illustrated in Figure 12.1A:

As standard in the literature,[10] the political regime matters for the distribution pro quota of the national wealth X to the citizens and to the selectorate. To simplify, let us assume that when there is an autocracy the citizens get nothing[11] and X is divided among the members of the selectorate. Similarly, in democracy the selectorate get nothing[12] while X is divided among the citizens. Finally, when there are reforms within the regime, X is equitably divided among the citizens and the selectorate. To conclude, in order to get closed-form results, some further simplification is used: Let us define each player's total effort $E_i = \sum e_i$ for $i \in \{C, S\}$. Then the costs of players' efforts are supposed to be the same for both agents and linear in the total joint effort; in particular, the effort total cost function $TC(.)$ is defined as follows: $TC(E_C + E_S) = \gamma (E_C + E_S)$. Let us denote by $\Pr\{PR | E_C, E_S, \omega\}$ the probability of getting a specific political regime $PR \in \{D, A, R\}$ as functions of players' choices E_C, E_S, and of the true state of nature ω; in particular, the following specific conflict technologies are assumed:

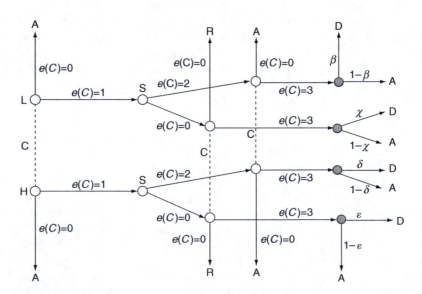

Figure 12.1A The game form representing the model.

$$\Pr\{D \mid E_C, E_S\} = \begin{cases} \alpha(\omega)\dfrac{E_C}{4+E_S} & \text{if } E_C = 4 \\ 0 & \text{otherwise} \end{cases} \quad \text{where } \alpha(\omega) = \begin{cases} 1 & \text{if } \omega = H \\ 0.5 & \text{if } \omega = L \end{cases}$$

$$\Pr\{R \mid E_C, E_S\} = \begin{cases} 1 & \text{if } E_C = 1 \text{ and } E_S = 0 \\ 0 & \text{otherwise} \end{cases};$$

$$\Pr\{A \mid E_C, E_S\} = 1 - \Pr\{R \mid E_C, E_S\} - \Pr\{D \mid E_C, E_S\}.$$

Finally, to close the model and to simplify the calculus of closed-form equilibria, assume that the prior probability of $\omega = H$ is 0.5.

Figure 12.2A depicts the specific game that represents the model after the calculations of the final expected payoffs, using the technology previously illustrated.

The game is solved using Sequential Equilibrium (SE) as a solution concept instead of the more common Perfect Bayesian Equilibrium, as usually done in the political agency approach to political economics. This game has a more complex sequential structure with possibly two subsequent out-of-equilibrium information sets. In this case, the concept of consistency implied by the notion of Sequential Equilibrium requires agreement on the out-of-equilibrium beliefs in these information sets, which restrict the set of possible equilibria in a convincing way.

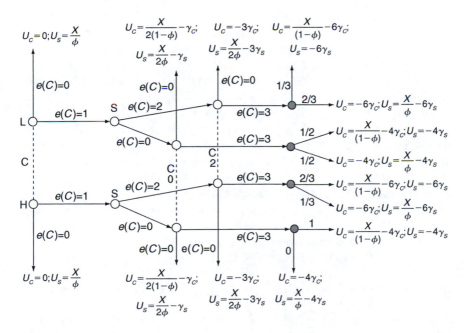

Figure 12.2A The extensive form game.

To solve the game, let us first consider the possible strategy profiles of the informed player (the selectorate), hence deriving the consequent citizens' beliefs, denoted by $\mu[2]:=\Pr\{\omega=L\,|\,e_S=2,\,e_C=1\}$ and by $\mu[0]:=\Pr\{\omega=H\,|\,e_S=0,\,e_C=1\}$.

Note that by Bayes' rule

$$= \frac{\Pr\{\omega=L\,|\,e_S=2/0,e_C=1\} = \Pr\{\omega=L\}\times\pi_S(e=2/0\,|\,L)\times\pi_C(e=1)}{\Pr\{\omega=L\}\times\pi_S(e=2/0\,|\,L)\times\pi_C(e=1)+\Pr\{\omega=H\}\times\pi_S(e=2/0\,|\,H)\times\pi_C(e=1)}$$

However, since consistency implies $\pi_C\,(e=1)>0$, it is possible to write the citizens' beliefs as

$$\frac{\Pr\{\omega=L\}\times\pi_S(e=2/0\,|\,L)}{\Pr\{\omega=L\}\times\pi_S(e=2/0\,|\,L)+\Pr\{\omega=H\}\times\pi_S(e=2/0\,|\,H)} = \mu[2/0]$$

hence these beliefs do not depend on the first move by the citizens but only on the selectorate's choice, as we should expect, since the citizens are uninformed and thus their choice cannot provide any information on the true state of nature.

Suppose the selectorate chooses $e_S(L)=2$ and $e_S(H)=0$. Then $\mu[2]=1$ and $\mu[0]=0$, which would imply $e_C[2]=0$ if and only if $X\leq 9(1-\phi)\gamma$ and $e_C[0]=0$ if and only if $X\leq 6(1-\phi)\gamma$. Suppose $X\leq 6(1-\phi)\gamma$, then the selectorate in $\omega=L$ has an incentive to deviate to $e_S(L)=0$ and these actions are not part of a SE. Hence suppose $X\in[6(1-\phi)\gamma,\ 9(1-\phi)\gamma]$, which would imply $e_C[2]=0$ and $e_C[0]=3$. Then the selectorate in $\omega=H$ has an incentive to deviate to $e_S(H)=2$, hence these actions are not part of a SE. Finally, suppose $X\in 9(1-\phi)\gamma$, which would imply $e_C[2]=3$ and $e_C[0]=3$. Then the selectorate in $\omega=L$ has no incentive to deviate to $e_S(L)=0$ if and only if $X\leq 12\phi\gamma$; similarly the selectorate in $\omega=H$ has no incentive to deviate to $e_S(H)=0$ if and only if $X\leq 6\phi\gamma$; hence at least in one of the two information sets the selectorate will have an incentive to deviate and these actions are not part of a SE. To conclude, there is no SE where $e_S(L)=2$ and $e_S(H)=0$.

Suppose the selectorate chooses $e_S(L)=0$ and $e_S(H)=2$. Then $\mu[2]=0$ and $\mu[0]=1$, which would imply $e_C[0]=0$ for any X, ϕ, and γ, and $e_C[2]=3$ if and only if $X\in 4.5(1-\phi)\gamma$. Suppose $X\in 4.5(1-\phi)\gamma$, then the selectorate in $\omega=H$ has an incentive to deviate to $e_S(H)=0$ and thus these actions are not part of a SE. Hence suppose $X\leq 4.5(1-\phi)\gamma$, which would imply $e_C[2]=0$ and $e_C[0]=0$. Then again the selectorate in $\omega=H$ has an incentive to deviate to $e_S(H)=0$ and these actions are not part of a SE. To conclude, there is no SE where $e_S(L)=0$ and $e_S(H)=2$.

Suppose the selectorate chooses $e_S(L)=e_S(H)=0$. Then $\mu[2]\in[0,\ 1]$ and $\mu[0]=0.5$, which would imply $e_C[0]=0$ if and only if $X\leq 12(1-\phi)\gamma$ and $e_C[0]=0$

if and only if $X\leq\dfrac{9(1-\phi)\gamma}{2-\mu[2]}$. Clearly, the second condition is more restrictive

than the first for any $\mu[2]\in[0,1]$. Suppose $X\leq\dfrac{9(1-\phi)\gamma}{2-\mu[2]}$, then the selectorate has no incentive to deviate and we can consider the citizens' choice at the beginning of the game: The citizens will choose $e_C=1$ if and only if $X \in 2(1-\phi)\gamma$, hence we have a SE with $e_C=1$, $e_S[L]=e_S[H]=0$, $e_C[0]=e_C[2]=0$ if and only if

$$X \in \left[2(1-\phi)\gamma, \frac{9(1-\phi)\gamma}{2-\mu[2]} \right]$$ where $\mu[2] \in [0, 1]$ and a second SE with $e_C=0$,

$e_S[L]=e_S[H]=0$, $e_C[0]=e_C[2]=0$ if and only if $X \leq 2(1-\phi)\gamma$. Suppose now that

$$X \in \left[\frac{9(1-\phi)\gamma}{2-\mu[2]}, 12(1-\phi)\gamma \right]$$, which would imply $e_C[0]=0$ and $e_C[2]=3$. Then the

selectorate in $\omega=H$ has no incentive to deviate and in $\omega=L$ would not deviate if and only if $X \leq 30\phi\gamma$. Now consider the citizens' choice at the beginning of the game: The citizens will choose $e_C=1$ if and only if $X \geq 2(1-\phi)\gamma$, which is implied

by $X \geq \dfrac{9(1-\phi)\gamma}{2-\mu[2]}$, hence we have a SE with $e_C=1$, $eS[L]=e_S[H]=0$, $e_C[0]=0$,

$e_C[2]=3$ if and only if $X \in \left[\dfrac{9(1-\phi)\gamma}{2-\mu[2]}, \min\{12(1-\phi)\gamma, 30\phi\gamma\} \right]$ where $\mu[2] \in [0, 1]$.

Finally, suppose that $X \geq 12(1-\phi)\gamma$, which would imply $e_C[0]=3$ and $e_C[2]=3$. Then the selectorate in $\omega=H$ has no incentive to deviate if and only if $X \leq 6\phi\gamma$ and in $\omega=L$ would not deviate if and only if $X \leq 12\phi\gamma$. Now consider the citizens' choice at the beginning of the game: The citizens will choose $e_C=1$ if and only if

$$X \geq \frac{16}{3}(1-\phi)\gamma,$$ which is implied by $X \geq 12(1-\phi)\gamma$, hence we have a SE with

$e_C=1$, $e_S[L]=e_S[H]=0$, $e_C[0]=e_C[2]=3$ if and only if $X \in [12(1-\phi)\gamma, 6\phi\gamma]$ which

is nonempty if and only if $\phi \in \left[\dfrac{2}{3}, 1 \right]$.

Suppose the selectorate chooses $e_S(L)=e_S(H)=2$. Then $\mu[0] \in [0, 1]$ and $\mu[2]=0.5$, which would imply $e_C[2]=3$ if and only if $X \geq 6(1-\phi)\gamma$ and $e_C[0]=3$ if

and only if $X \geq \dfrac{6(1-\phi)\gamma}{1-\mu[0]}$. Clearly the second condition is more restrictive than

the first for any $\mu[0] \in [0, 1]$. Suppose $X \geq \dfrac{6(1-\phi)\gamma}{1-\mu[0]}$ so that the citizens will

always choose $e_C=3$, then the selectorate has no incentive to deviate in $\omega=L$ if and only if $X \geq 12\phi\gamma$ and in $\omega=H$ if and only if $X \geq 6\phi\gamma$, hence suppose $X \geq 12\phi\gamma$. Now consider the citizens' choice at the beginning of the game: The citizens will choose $e_C=1$ if and only if $X \geq 12(1-\phi)\gamma$, hence there is a SE with $e_C=1$, $e_S[L]=e_S[H]=2$, $e_C[0]=e_C[2]=3$ if and

only if $X \geq \max\left\{ 12(1-\phi)\gamma, 12\phi\gamma, \dfrac{6(1-\phi)\gamma}{1-\mu[0]} \right\}$ where $\mu[0] \in [0, 1]$ and a second

SE with $e_C=0$, $e_S[L]=e_S[H]=2$, $e_C[0]=e_C[2]=3$ if and only if

$$X \in \left[\max\left\{ 12\phi\gamma, \frac{6(1-\phi)\gamma}{1-\mu[0]} \right\}, 12(1-\phi)\gamma \right]$$ where $\mu[0] \in [0, 1]$: Clearly this interval might be empty depending on the values of ϕ, in particular $\phi \in \left[\frac{1}{3}, \frac{1}{2} \right]$ guarantees its nonemptiness. Then, suppose that $X \in \left[12(1-\phi)\gamma, \frac{6(1-\phi)\gamma}{1-\mu[0]} \right]$, which would imply $e_C[0]=0$ and $e_C[2]=3$. However, then the selectorate in $\omega=H$ has an incentive to deviate and thus there is no SE for this range of X values. Finally, suppose that $X \leq 6(1-\phi)\gamma$, which would imply $e_C[0]=e_C[2]=0$. Then the selectorate in $\omega=L$ has an incentive to deviate and thus there is no SE for this range of X values.

Consequently, we can state the following result.

12.7.1 Proposition

The model proposed has no Separating Sequential Equilibrium, but several pure strategy Pooling Sequential Equilibria, depending on the values of the country wealth, X, the selectorate size, ϕ, the marginal cost of the players' joint cumulative effort, γ, and on out-of-equilibrium beliefs. In particular, let us denote by $\mu[0] \in [0, 1]$ and $\mu[2] \in [0, 1]$ the out-of-equilibrium beliefs after, respectively, the selectorate's choice $e_S=0$ and $e_S=2$, then

when $X \in \left[2(1-\phi)\gamma, \frac{9(1-\phi)\gamma}{2-\mu[2]} \right]$ there is a pure strategy Pooling Sequential

Equilibrium with $e_C=1$, $e_S[L]=e_S[H]=0$, $e_C[0]=e_C[2]=0$, hence the political regime outcome is reform within the existing regime;
when $X \leq 2(1-\phi)\gamma$ there is a pure strategy Pooling Sequential Equilibrium with $e_C=0$, $e_S[L]=e_S[H]=0$, $e_C[0]=e_C[2]=0$, hence the political regime outcome is reform within the existing regime;

when $X \in \left[\frac{9(1-\phi)\gamma}{2-\mu[2]}, \min\{12(1-\phi)\gamma, 30\phi\gamma\} \right]$ there is a pure strategy Pooling

Sequential Equilibrium with $e_C=1$, $e_S[L]=e_S[H]=0$, $e_C[0]=0$, $e_C[2]=3$, hence the political regime outcome is reform within the existing regime;
when $X \in [12(1-\phi)\gamma, 6\phi\gamma]$ there is a pure strategy Pooling Sequential Equilibrium with $e_C=1$, $e_S[L]=e_S[H]=0$, $e_C[0]=e_C[2]=3$, hence the political regime outcome is democracy with probability 3/4, and autocracy with probability 1/4;

when $X \geq \max\left\{ 12(1-\phi)\gamma, 12\phi\gamma, \frac{6(1-\phi)\gamma}{1-\mu[0]} \right\}$ there is a pure strategy Pooling

Sequential Equilibrium with $e_C=1$, $e_S[L]=e_S[H]=2$, $e_C[0]=e_C[2]=3$, hence the political regime outcome is democracy with probability 1/2, and autocracy with probability 1/2;

when $X \in \left[\max\left\{ 12\phi\gamma, \dfrac{6(1-\phi)\gamma}{1-\mu[0]} \right\}, 12(1-\phi)\gamma \right]$ there is a pure strategy Pooling

Sequential Equilibrium with $e_C=0$, $e_S[L]=e_S[H]=2$, $e_C[0]=e_C[2]=3$, hence the political regime outcome is autocracy.

Notes

1 I am indebted to Ariel Dinar, Li Yuan, Roberta Garruccio, Enzo Dia, Giulio Mellinato, and Paolo Tedeschi for valuable insights, as well as the seminars participants at the University of Milano-Bicocca, Humboldt Universitat zu Berlin and SED 2011. The financial support from the Center in Interdisciplinary Studies in Economics, Psychology and Social Sciences (CISEPS) is gratefully acknowledged.
2 See for example Collier (2007).
3 Collier (2007).
4 For example, Gilli and Li (2011b) consider the role of the incumbent leader in an autocratic regime, while, to the best of the author's knowledge, there is no paper on revolts considering foreign powers too.
5 See http://hdr.undp.org/en/statistics/.
6 The Polity Project is a research program aimed to code the authority characteristics of states in the world system for purposes of comparative, quantitative analysis. The Polity Project is the most widely used data resource for studying regime change and the effects of regime authority. The Polity IV Project carries data collection and analysis through 2010 and is under the direction of Dr. Monty G. Marshall and supported by the Political Instability Task Force, Societal-Systems Research, and Center for Systemic Peace.
7 See, for example, Bueno de Mesquita *et al.* (2003), Besley and Kudamatsu (2008), and Gilli and Li (2011a, 2011b).
8 See, for example, Acemoglu and Robinson (2006), and Gilli and Li (2011a, 2011b).
9 Think, for example, about the actual situation in Egypt: The selectorate might try to remove the leader just to appease the citizens without really changing the political regime.
10 See, for example, Acemoglu and Robinson (2006), and Gilli and Li (2011a, 2001b).
11 Of course, this is just a normalization assumption.
12 Again, this is just a normalization assumption.

References

Acemoglu, D. and Robinson J. (2006) *Economic Origins of Dictatorship and Democracy*. Cambridge: Cambridge University Press.

Banks, J. (1994) *Signaling Games in Political Science*. London: Routledge.

Besley, T. (2006) *Principled Agents? The Political Economy of Good Government*. Oxford: Oxford University Press.

Besley, T. and Kudamatsu, M. (2008) "Making autocracy work," in E. Helpman (ed.), *Institutions and Economic Performance* (pp. 452–510), Cambridge, MA: Harvard University Press.

Blattman, C. and Miguel, E. (2010) "Civil wars," *Journal of Economic Literature*, 48: 3–57.

Bueno de Mesquita, B., Smith, J., Siverson, R., and Morrow A. (2003) *The Logic of Political Survival*. Cambridge, MA: The MIT Press.

Collier, P. (2007) "Economic causes of civil conflict and their implications for policy," in C.A. Crocker, F.O. Hampson, and P. Aall (eds), *Leashing the Dogs of War: Conflict Management in a Divided World* (pp. 197–218), Washington: United States Institute for Peace Press.

Gilli, M. and Li, Y. (2011a) "A model of Chinese central government: The role of reciprocal accountability," University of Milano-Bicocca Working Paper 9–2011.

Gilli, M. and Li, Y. (2011b) "Accountability in one-party government: The role of revolution threat," University of Milano-Bicocca Working Paper 12–2011.

Kuran, T. (1989) "Sparks and prairie fires: A theory of unanticipated political revolution," *Public Choice*, 61: 41–74.

Lehmann, S. (1994) "Information aggregation through costly political action," *American Economic Review*, 84: 518–530.

Limes (2011) Italian journal of geopolitical science, Roma: Edizioni l'Espresso.

Marshall, M.V. (Dir.) (2010) Polity IV Project, Online. Available at: www.systemicpeace.org/polity/polity4.htm.

Maskin, E. and Tirole, J. (2004) "The politician and the judge: Accountability in government," *American Economic Review*, 94: 1034–1054.

Padro i Miquel, G. (2006) "The control of politicians in divided societies: The politics of fear," *NBER Working Paper*, No. 12573.

World Bank (2011) "Fragility and conflict," Online. Available at: http://web.worldbank.org/WBSITE/EXTERNAL/PROJECTS/STRATEGIES/EXTLICUS/0,,menuPK:511784~pagePK:64171540~piPK:64171528~theSitePK:511778,00.html.

13 Optimal tariffs on exhaustible resources

The case of quantity-setting

Kenji Fujiwara and Ngo Van Long

13.1 Introduction

The world markets for gas and oil consist mainly of a small number of large sellers and buyers. For instance, the U.S. Energy Information Administration reports that the major energy exporters are concentrated in the Middle East and Russia, whereas the United States, Japan, and China have a substantial share in the imports.[1] These data suggest that bilateral monopoly roughly prevails in the oil market in which both parties exercise market power. What are the implications of market power for the welfare of importing and exporting countries, and the world?

On the one hand, the exporting country has an incentive to control a quantity exported to make a rent from the resource as large as possible. The importing country, on the other hand, seeks to capture such a rent by imposing an import tariff. Hence, the above situation is best modeled as a bilateral monopoly game in which both parties have market power.

There is a large body of literature that attempts to answer this question by using a dynamic game. Newbery (1976) and Kemp and Long (1980) were among the earliest contributors, showing that if the importing country, acting as a leader in a leader–follower game, chooses an optimal time path of the optimal tariff rate, it will later have an incentive to deviate from such a path. This is in line with the general result of time inconsistency of open-loop Stackelberg equilibrium.[2] In order to overcome this difficulty, Karp and Newbery (1991, 1992) considered the Nash equilibrium model in which importing countries play a dynamic game without pre-commitment: They determine the tariff rate in each period, taking into account the concurrent level of the resource stock. Karp and Newbery (1991) compared two situations: one in which the importing countries move first in each period, and the other in which the competitive exporters choose their outputs before the importing countries set their tariff rates. They numerically demonstrated that being the first-mover can be disadvantageous. In a related paper, Karp and Newbery (1992) made a welfare comparison between free trade and the Markov perfect Nash equilibrium.

While Karp and Newbery (1991, 1992) assumed perfect competition among suppliers, Wirl (1994) considered the bilateral monopoly case, in which both the importing and the exporting countries have market power. He focused on feed-back Nash equilibrium. His novel result is that, in the Nash equilibrium, the time path of resource extraction is more conservative than the globally efficient one, in which the remaining stock is converging to the efficient steady state level.[3] His model has been extended in several ways. Maintaining the assumption of Nash behavior, Chou and Long (2009) extended the model to accommodate many importers and compared welfare between free trade and the Nash equilibrium. Tahvonen (1996) and Rubio and Escriche (2001) turned attention to a type of Stackelberg game, in which the leader is defined as the player that can make the first move in each period. Both papers show that outcome of the Nash equilibrium is identical to that of the Stackelberg equilibrium, in which the exporting country leads.[4]

Our chapter contributes to this bilateral monopoly literature, although our model and its purpose are quite different. First, we consider the case in which the exporter chooses quantity; whereas all of the above papers assume price-setting behavior. Given the fact that recent price fluctuations of oil are partially caused by quantity controlled by the resource-rich countries, our quantity-setting formulation seems more plausible. Second, we compare the welfare of each country and the world in the Nash equilibrium and in the two Stackelberg equilibria, in which the leadership role is taken by the importer and the exporter, respectively. Third and most importantly, we derive feedback from Stackelberg equilibria which are conceptually different from Tahvonen (1996) and Rubio and Escriche (2001). Roughly speaking, they assume that the leader moves first in each period, but does not necessarily try to improve upon its Nash equilibrium payoff stream. Such a solution may be called a *stagewise Stackelberg equilibrium*. In contrast, we suppose that the leader determines a Markovian rule for the entire horizon of the game, taking into account the follower's response to such a rule. Thus we use a solution concept that has been called a *global Stackelberg equilibrium*.[5] With these differences, we establish that (i) as compared to the Nash equilibrium, both the exporting country and the (strategically behaving) importing country are better off if the importing country leads; (ii) the importing country becomes worse off if the exporting country leads; and (iii) the world welfare is highest under the importing country's leadership and lowest under the exporting country's leadership. Therefore, an important implication derived from our findings is that the importing country should have a leadership over the exporting country.

These findings are in sharp contrast to the results of Tahvonen (1996) and Rubio and Escriche (2001) in that the exporting country's welfare under its leadership is the same as in the Nash equilibrium. They are also in sharp contrast to the price-setting model of Fujiwara and Long (2011), in which the world welfare is highest in the Nash equilibrium.[6]

This chapter is organized as follows. Section 13.2 presents a static version of our model to better motivate our purpose. Section 13.3 turns the model into a dynamic game. Section 13.4 numerically compares the equilibrium strategies and welfare levels in three different equilibria situations, providing some policy implications. Section 13.5 concludes.

13.2 A static game

Before considering a dynamic game, this section briefly looks at a static model, which allows us to find the equilibria and the associated welfare visually. There are three countries labeled Home, Foreign, and ROW (the rest of the world). Foreign monopolistically exports a quantity y of a good y to Home and ROW.[7] The utility function of the two importing countries is specified by

$$u^H = aq_1^H - \frac{\left(q_1^H\right)^2}{2b} + q_2^H$$

$$u^{ROW} = aq_1^{ROW} - \frac{\left(q_1^{ROW}\right)^2}{2(1-b)} + q_2^{ROW}, \quad a > 0, \tag{1}$$

where u^i and q_j^i, i=1, 2, j=H, ROW are utility of country i and consumption of the imported good q_1^j (Good 1) and numeraire good q_2^j>, respectively. The parameter $b \in (0, 1)$ represents the share of the Home demand in the world demand if there is no tariff. Assuming that the Home government imposes a specific tariff on the import of Good 1 and that ROW observes laissez-faire, utility maximization under the budget constraint yields the demand functions:

$$q_1^H = b(a-p-\tau), \quad q_1^{ROW} = (1-b)(a-p), \tag{2}$$

where p is the world price of Good 1 and τ is the tariff imposed by Home.[8] Letting y be the total supply of the Foreign country, the market-clearing condition is

$$b(a-p-\tau)+(1-b)(a-p)=a-p-b\tau = y,$$

from which the inverse demand function is defined by $p=a-y-b\tau$. Substituting this into (2) and (1), and considering that Home's welfare W consists of consumer surplus and tariff revenue, we obtain

$$W = \frac{b\left[y^2 + 2b\tau y - \left(1-b^2\right)\tau^2\right]}{2}. \tag{3}$$

On the other hand, the profit of Foreign is

$$\pi = (a-b\tau-y)y. \tag{4}$$

Since the static game contains no state variable, optimization decisions are simple. Home chooses τ to maximize (3), and Foreign chooses y to maximize (4). Then, the first-order conditions are

$$\frac{\partial W}{\partial \tau} = \frac{b}{2}\left[-2(1-b^2)\tau + 2by\right] = b\left[-(1-b^2)\tau + by\right] = 0 \tag{5}$$

$$\frac{\partial \pi}{\partial y} = a - b\tau - 2y = 0. \tag{6}$$

In the rest of this section, we explain how the equilibria and the associated welfare are determined, using Figures 13.1 and 13.2. In the figures, the upward-sloping line is a reaction curve of Home, which illustrates Eq. (5). Similarly, the downward-sloping line is a reaction curve of Foreign, which comes from Eq. (6). The Nash equilibrium is thus determined by the intersection of these two reaction curves at point N. The corresponding welfare of each country is measured by an iso-welfare curve.

If Home is a leader, the Stackelberg equilibrium is determined by a point at which the iso-welfare curve of Home (the leader) is tangent to the reaction curve of Foreign (the follower). Such a point is given by H in Figure 13.1. In the figure, the U-shaped locus represents an iso-welfare curve of Home, and welfare of Home becomes higher as its iso-welfare curve shifts above. Similarly, a side-ways U-shaped locus represents an iso-welfare curve of Foreign, and welfare of Foreign becomes higher as its iso-welfare curve shifts left.[9] Figure 13.1 reveals that in the Stackelberg equilibrium, at point H, welfare of Foreign as well as Home is higher than the Nash level. This is because the iso-welfare curve of Home shifts above and that of Foreign shifts to the left by moving from the Nash equilibrium (point N) to the Stackelberg equilibrium (point H).

If, in contrast, Foreign is a leader, the Stackelberg equilibrium is obtained by F in Figure 13.2, at which the iso-welfare curve of Foreign (the leader) is tangent to the reaction curve of Home (the follower). By moving from the Nash equilibrium (point N) to the Stackelberg equilibrium (point F), the iso-welfare curve of Home shifts down and that of Foreign shifts to the left. Therefore, Foreign's welfare improves but Home's welfare deteriorates as compared to the Nash equilibrium.

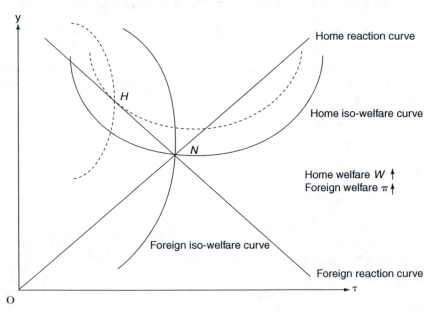

Figure 13.1 Stackelberg equilibrium with Home's leadership.

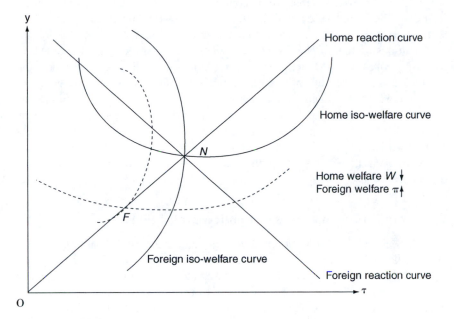

Figure 13.2 Stackelberg equilibrium with Foreign's leadership.

Are these results robust in a dynamic game? The next section extends the present model to incorporate a stock variable whose evolution is affected by the strategies of each player.

13.3 A dynamic game

We assume now that the production of Good 1 originates from the extraction of an exhaustible resource $S(t)$.[10] Due to geological factors, it is commonly observed that marginal extraction cost increases as the remaining stock of resource decreases. We suppose that the marginal production cost is proportional to the remaining resource stock S so that marginal production cost is cS, where $c>0$ is a parameter of costliness. And both players choose their time path of tariffs and outputs. Then, our dynamic game model is formulated as

$$\max_{\tau} \int_{0}^{\lessgtr} e^{-rt} \frac{b\left[y^2 + 2b\tau y - \left(1-b^2\right)\tau^2\right]}{2} dt$$

$$\max_{y} \int_{0}^{\lessgtr} e^{-rt} \left(a - b\tau - cS - y\right) y\, dt$$

s.t. $\dot{S} = y$, $y(0)$: given, $\lim_{t\to\infty} S(t) \le \dfrac{a}{c}$, where r>0 is a discount rate that is common for both players. This is a severe restriction, but we assume it in order to obtain transparent results.

In a dynamic game, we can define two strategy concepts, depending on the information structure of players.[11] One is an open-loop strategy and the other is a feedback (Markovian) strategy. The former strategy requires players to precommit their actions over the entire horizon, while the latter does not impose such a requirement. In this chapter, we focus on the stationary Markovian strategy according to which players' action at time t depends only on the state variable at time t. Therefore, the equilibria to be considered are a feedback Nash equilibrium, in which players choose their strategies simultaneously; and two feedback Stackelberg equilibria, in which the leader chooses its Markovian strategy before the follower does.

13.4 Equilibrium outcomes and policy implications

This section seeks the equilibrium strategies in the Nash equilibrium, the Stackelberg equilibrium with Home's leadership, and in the Stackelberg equilibrium with Foreign's leadership, as well as the associated welfare in the dynamic game model formulated in the previous section. However, the derivation of the equilibrium strategies is so cumbersome that we only list the final outcomes.[12]

Tables 13.1 and 13.2 report a comparison among the equilibrium strategies under the assumption that both the tariff strategy of Home and the output strategy of Foreign are a linear function of the current resource stock. Without loss of generality, we assume that $\tau = \alpha S + \beta$ and that $y = \alpha^* S + \beta^*$, where α and α^* denote a choice variable that represents how each country's strategy varies with the current resource stock, while β and β^* denote a choice variable that is independent of the stock level over time. Home chooses α and β to maximize the discounted stream of its welfare, and Foreign chooses α^* and β^* in the same way.

Since Foreign is a monopoly, like OPEC in the petroleum market, it produces less than the socially optimal level to make a rent (profit) as large as possible. This behavior is mitigated if Home imposes a lower tariff because a lower tariff makes the production less costly. When Home is a leader, it chooses a lower initial tariff than in the Nash equilibrium. This is because the Home government is motivated to counter the tendency of Foreign to be conservationist.[13] In response to this strategy of Home, Foreign naturally increases production. If, on the other hand, Foreign is a leader, it chooses a lower output earlier on to seek a high price and large rent. Observing this strategy choice of Foreign, Home retaliates by lowering

Table 13.1 Strategy of Home country

	alpha	alpha*
Nash	−0.227475584	−0.160849528
Home leader	−0.200588442	−0.163091829
Foreign leader	−0.16381011	−0.11583124

Table 13.2 Strategy of Foreign country

	beta	*beta**
Nash	0.227475584a	0.160849528a
Home leader	0.200588442a	0.163091829a
Foreign leader	0.163810111a	0.11583124a

a tariff for shifting the Foreign rent. These findings are well consistent with the outcomes in static games (see once again Figures 13.1 and 13.2).

Table 13.3 summarizes the welfare comparisons among equilibria. Not surprisingly, the leader improves its welfare as compared to the Nash equilibrium, which comes from the definition of the Stackelberg equilibria. In contrast, the effect on the follower's welfare is different between the two Stackelberg equilibria. If Home leads, welfare of Foreign as well as Home improves – that is, Home's leadership entails a Pareto improvement from the Nash equilibrium. However, if Foreign leads, Home (the follower) becomes worse off than in the Nash equilibrium. These welfare changes are also confirmed in Figures 13.1 and 13.2 in which static games are assumed.

In Figure 13.1, where Home is a leader, the associated Stackelberg equilibrium raises welfare of both countries as compared to the Nash level. The same survives in a dynamic game, as the second row of Table 13.1 tells. In Figure 13.2, in which Foreign is a leader, welfare of Home is smaller than the Nash level, whereas Foreign is better off than in the Nash equilibrium. The third row allows us to find the same qualitative result in a dynamic game context.

The third column in Table 13.3 shows the welfare levels of ROW. It reveals that the presence of leaderships has a detrimental effect on ROW and that its welfare is lowest when Foreign is a leader.[14] The last column provides the welfare of the world, defined as the sum of the three countries' welfare. We can easily see that the world welfare is highest when Home is a leader. This is because, as mentioned above, this case yields a Pareto improvement from the Nash equilibrium. On the other hand, when Foreign is a leader, the world welfare is lowest. The reason is that Foreign chooses a much smaller output than in the Nash case, which reduces consumer surplus of the two importing countries. As a result, the absolute value of the fall in welfare of Home and ROW exceeds the welfare gain of Foreign, which leads to the lowest welfare of the world.

A major policy implication of the model is that, if both countries have market powers and the resource-exporting country uses quantity-setting strategies, it

Table 13.3 Welfare comparisons

	Home	*Foreign*	*ROW*	*World*
Nash	$0.043383237a^2$	$0.258725708a^2$	$0.015155801a^2$	$0.317264746a^2$
Home leader	$0.043757137a^2$	$0.265989447a^2$	$0.013616879a^2$	$0.323363463a^2$
Foreign leader	$0.028604876a^2$	$0.268337521a^2$	$0.007859424a^2$	$0.304801821a^2$

would be in their interest to agree on the order of moves. In fact, this gives priority of moves to the importing country, as opposed to making their moves simultaneously. Not only is world welfare higher, but also, after appropriate side payments, all players are made better off.

13.5 Conclusions

We have explored feedback Stackelberg equilibria in a two-country (strategic) dynamic game model of an exhaustible resource. Unlike the existing literature that employs a stagewise Stackelberg solution, we have paid attention to the global Stackelberg solution, since the latter concept is more appropriate to model a world resource market in which both the exporter and the importer seek to capture the rent by precommitting. Despite the above contributions, we have left much unexplored. In particular, we have restricted attention to linear strategies. However, Shimomura and Xie (2008) have provided an example of *renewable* resource exploitation in which there exist nonlinear feedback strategies that are superior to linear strategies.[15] In addition, in order to obtain clear results, we have imposed the restriction that both countries share the same discount rate. In reality, it is likely that countries have different discount rates. Tackling these problems in the context of exhaustible resource markets is part of our future research agenda.

Notes

1 The latest data are available at www.eia.gov.
2 The time consistency issue is further studied by Karp (1984), who assumes that production cost depends on the resource stock. Newbery (1981) does not deal with the optimal tariff issues, but points to another type of time inconsistency when a cartel is the open-loop Stackelberg leader and a fringe of competitive producers acts as the followers.
3 In the steady state, a positive resource stock remains in the ground even though extraction is costless. This is because a Pigouvian tax that corrects stock-pollution externalities chokes off the demand.
4 While Wirl (1994) assumes costless extraction, Tahvonen postulates a quadratic extraction cost function, and the other two papers assume a stock-dependent cost.
5 This concept is discussed in Dockner *et al.* (2000), Basar and Olsder (1995), Mehlmann (1988), and Long (2010).
6 Fujiwara and Long (2011) assume that the exporting country chooses prices, as in the cited papers.
7 The good is not consumed in Foreign, and the market of Home and ROW is assumed to be integrated and hence the Foreign firm does not supply to each country separately.
8 Throughout this chapter, we assume that τ is a specific (per-unit) tariff rather than an ad valorem one.
9 See, for instance, Varian (1992, p. 296) for a graphical representation of payoffs in a reaction curve diagram.
10 In the subsequent arguments, the time argument t is sometimes suppressed as long as no confusion arises.
11 See Dockner *et al.* (2000), Long (2010), and Benchekroun and Long (2011) for more details.

12 The results in this section are all based on Fujiwara and Long (2012). See also the companion paper, Fujiwara and Long (2011).
13 Recall Solow's (1974) famous remark that the resource monopolist is the conservationist's best friend.
14 The calculation of welfare of ROW is omitted in the static game in section 13.2 because it involves a messy task. It is available from the authors upon request.
15 For further issues relating to Stackelberg leadership with a renewable resource, see Long and Sorger (2010).

References

Basar, T. and Olsder, G. (1995) *Dynamic Noncooperative Game Theory*. San Diego: Academic Press.

Benchekroun, H. and Long, N.V. (2011) "Game theory: Static and dynamic games," in A.A. Batabyal and P. Nijkamp (eds), *Research Tools in Natural Resource and Environmental Economics* (pp. 89–140), Singapore: World Scientific Publishing Co.

Chou, S. and Long, N.V. (2009) "Optimal tariff on exhaustible resource in the presence of cartel behavior," *Asia-Pacific Journal of Accounting and Economics*, 16: 239–254.

Dockner, E., Jorgensen, S., Long, N.V., and Sorger, G. (2000) *Differential Games in Economics and Management Science*. Cambridge: Cambridge University Press.

Fujiwara, K. and Long, N.V. (2011) "Welfare implications of leadership in a resource market under bilateral monopoly," *Dynamic Games and Applications*, 1: 479–497.

Fujiwara, K. and Long, N.V. (2012) *Optimal Tariffs on Exhaustible Resources: The Case of Quantity-Setting*, Department of Economics, McGill University.

Karp, L. (1984) "Optimality and consistency in a differential game of non-renewable resources," *Journal of Economics Dynamics and Control*, 8: 73–98.

Karp, L. and Newbery, D. (1991) "Optimal tariffs on exhaustible resources," *Journal of International Economics*, 30: 285–299.

Karp, L. and Newbery, D. (1992) "Dynamically consistent oil import tariffs," *Canadian Journal of Economics*, 25: 1–21.

Kemp, M.C. and Long, N.V. (1980) "Optimal tariffs on exhaustible resources," in M.C. Kemp and N.V. Long (eds), *Exhaustible Resources, Optimality, and Trade* (pp. 183–186), Amsterdam: North Holland.

Long, N.V. (2010) *A Survey of Dynamic Games in Economics*. Singapore: World Scientific Publishing Co.

Long, N.V. and Sorger, G. (2010) "A dynamic principal-agent problem as a feedback Stackelberg differential game," *Central European Journal of Operations Research*, 18: 491–509.

Mehlmann, A. (1988) *Applied Differential Games*. New York: Kluwer Academic Publishers.

Newbery, D. (1976) *A Paradox in Tax Theory: Optimal Tariffs on Exhaustible Resources*, typescript, Cambridge University.

Newbery, D. (1981) "Oil prices, cartels, and dynamic inconsistency," *Economic Journal*, 91: 617–646.

Rubio, S. and Escriche, L. (2001) "Strategic Pigouvian taxation, stock externalities and polluting non-renewable resources," *Journal of Public Economics*, 79: 297–313.

Shimomura, K. and Xie, D. (2008) "Advances on Stackelberg open-loop and feedback strategies," *International Journal of Economic Theory*, 4: 115–133.

Solow, R.M. (1974) "The economics of resources or the resources of economics," *American Economic Review Papers and Proceedings*, 64: 1–14.

Tahvonen, O. (1996) "Trade with polluting non-renewable resources," *Journal of Environmental Economics and Management*, 30: 1–17.

Varian, H.R. (1992) *Microeconomic Analysis*. New York: W.W. Norton & Company.

Wirl, F. (1994) "Pigouvian taxation of energy for flow and stock externalities and strategic, non-competitive energy pricing," *Journal of Environmental Economics and Management*, 26: 1–18.

14 A market-based design for international environmental agreements

Andries Nentjes, Bouwe R. Dijkstra, and Frans P. de Vries

14.1 Introduction

Why should countries contribute voluntarily to the solution of international and global problems? Often such problems are an international public bad, and participation in a common approach to solve or mitigate the problem is like voluntarily contributing to the production of an international public good. A prominent example is climate change. No country can be excluded from enjoying the benefits once the public good has been delivered. Economically speaking, it looks wiser to leave the provision to other countries and reap the benefits of the good without any effort or sacrifice. Every economist knows the refutation of this rhetorical question. When all agents reason like this, the public good will not be provided at all, or at a level far too low relative to the optimum level of provision.

The issue then is how to prevent such an inefficient outcome. Are there incentive mechanisms that could make potential users willing to participate of their own free will in the provision of the public good? Wicksell (1896) made the first attempt to crack the egg on which Samuelson (1954) built and formalized the approach. It assumes that it is feasible to identify the individual marginal benefit functions of all consumers of the public good. The next step is then to aggregate all the individual benefit functions. In the third step, the optimal level of provision is calculated as the point where the aggregated benefit function intersects with the marginal cost function of producing the good. The question that both Wicksell and Samuelson left unsolved was how the potential users can be tempted to reveal their willingness to pay for successive units of the good. This specific problem was identified from the early 1980s onward in the literature on the voluntary or private provision of public goods. Several authors have proposed tax-subsidy schemes and matching schemes as mechanisms that might result in a Pareto-efficient level of provision of the public good (e.g., Guttman 1978, 1987; Andreoni and Bergstrom 1996; Falkinger 1996).

To the best of our knowledge, a solid generalization of all these studies is still lacking and a number of issues remain neglected. In particular, we are critical of the focus on the demand side of the problem, while laying aside its supply. That is, due to the implicit assumption that once the optimal level of public good has been determined, a public authority can produce the good itself or it can "order" the quantity needed from producers that are competing in a perfectly competitive market. What is overlooked here is that there are a lot of public good and common pool problems for which such an authority is lacking and potential users have to design an integrated solution to the problem of how much public good to provide and, moreover, how to allocate the production of the public good among agents consuming the good. Such problems of coordination are most apparent in cases featuring international common scarcity: global climate change and other types of transboundary air pollution, pollution of the oceans, over-exploitation in international fisheries, and preservation of nature in the arctic areas. However, from a game-theoretic point of view, the same problem of how to coordinate action of sovereign countries is at hand when it comes to potential and actual international conflicts: piracy in international waters, rogue states threatening international peace, and armament races. The structure of such problems very much resembles the issue of a group of potential consumers who have the option to produce a public good in a common effort. In the distant past, people in Ireland built ring forts to protect life and property. In the Netherlands inhabitants protected themselves against potential floods by joining hands in erecting dwelling mounds and constructing dykes. A more recent example is the voluntary (or negotiated) environmental agreement between a group of firms and a public authority to control pollution. In such cases, firms will only have benefits from preempting sanctions by the authority when they come up with an acceptable collective pollution abatement proposal. In a similar way, in all aforementioned cases, parties have to conclude a contract specifying each party's contribution to the common good.

Therefore, an inquiry into the incentives for the consumers of the public good to participate in its production is of more than theoretical interest only. And so are the related questions of whether there is an equilibrium solution, what the allocation of production tasks looks like, and whether that allocation is Pareto efficient. Among the many Pareto-efficient solutions exists a trade-off between the size of the surplus and the equality in the distribution of the surplus. A common approach to tackle these questions is to select the Nash Bargaining Solution (NBS) from the Pareto-efficient outcomes. Loosely speaking, the NBS seeks to maximize the collective net benefits from cooperative action while splitting it up in parts of individual net benefits that are as equal as possible (Nash 1950). Nash himself saw the NBS as the solution that (ex ante) would be acceptable to all potential participants and would be recommended by an impartial arbitrator.

The NBS originally only provided the algorithm for calculating the solution meeting the aforementioned properties. It did not provide detail on how the solution could be reached. The (implicit) assumption seems to be that all information on the benefits and costs of individual participants is available to everyone, or at least to the arbitrator or social planner, enabling him to use the algorithm to calculate the solution. Further, the NBS has the property that it is not Pareto-dominated by other outcomes in the feasibility set. To this one can add that, in order to implement an NBS proposed by a planner or arbitrator, either the solution should be acceptable to all, as postulated by Nash, or an authority needs to impose the solution on all. In later work, the NBS has been modeled as the outcome of negotiations between participants in a sequential game. For example, in the spirit of non-cooperative Nash bargaining, Binmore *et al.* (1986) show, in a variation of a bargaining game of alternating offers with a risk of breakdown, the agreements proposed by players converge to the NBS. However, the bargaining game only leads to NBS straightforwardly for two players and information has to be perfect – that is, agents need information not only on their own cost and benefit functions, but also on the other agents' costs and benefits. Up until now, the literature on NBS has no answer to the question of how this general knowledge on individual costs and benefits is generated. The Nash Bargaining Solution has been used widely as the solution to common pool problems in which parties have to agree on the allocation of use; for example, agreements on international emission reduction by Hoel (1991), Helm (2003), and Boom (2006).

Considering the aforementioned questions that remain unanswered in the NBS approach to public good and common pool problems, an alternative and competing approach should be welcomed. A first sketch of a different view was given in Nentjes (1990). The approach, which we shall label the Market Exchange Solution (MES), views the solution as the outcome of an exchange in which agent *A* out of self-interest offers units of the public good in exchange for offers of the public good by agent *B*; and vice versa, *B* offers units of the public good in exchange for units offered by agent *A*. The equilibrium is determined by an exchange rate in which the demands of *A* and *B* for the public good equal its total supply – that is, the sum of the offers by *A* and *B*. The study was inspired by the question of how states involved in reciprocal transboundary pollution can solve the problem of excessive environmental damage when they only have information on their own costs of abatement and on the benefits of a lower national pollution load due to lower emissions by national and foreign sources. Each state offers reduction of its emissions in return for emission reduction of the other states involved in the agreement. The equilibrium is achieved when exchange rates are such that the total supply of emission reductions of all countries is equal to the demand of emission reduction of each country. The model has been more solidly underpinned mathematically by Kryazhimskii *et al.* (2000). More recently, MES has been applied to calculate an alternative allocation of emission reductions for the Second Sulphur Protocol of 1994 (Nentjes and Shibayev 2006) and to analyze the properties and cost efficiency of the allocation of abatement tasks in negotiated environmental agreements (Nentjes and de Vries 2012).

NBS and MES differ diametrically in their underlying views: planning for the common good and fair distribution of net benefits in NBS versus a market mechanism coordinating self-interested agents in MES. The two approaches also make opposing assumptions on information: general knowledge of costs and benefits in NBS versus private information in MES. Considering those differences, one would intuitively expect that the solutions regarding the allocation of production of the public good, as well as the distribution of the net benefits agents derive from the public good, will be quite different under the two approaches. And what could one infer about the total provision of the public good and the efficiency of the two solution concepts? It is our aim to confront NBS with MES and compare their computable solutions in order to find an answer to these questions.

In what follows, we shall apply NBS and MES to an agreement in which each agent implements his commitment to contribute to the public good by producing an amount of the good equal to his commitment. Agents cannot outsource the production to other agents, who can produce the public good at lower cost. Neither are side payments among participants allowed. The typical example is an international environmental agreement in which states commit to make quantified contributions to reducing global pollution and have to deliver those contributions through measures on their own national territory. International emissions trading between countries is not part of the agreement.

The chapter is structured as follows. Section 14.2 analyzes the properties of the benchmark Pareto-efficient allocation of the public good. In sections 14.3 and 14.4, the Nash Bargaining Solution and the Market Equilibrium Solution, respectively, are analyzed. It turns out that NBS as well as MES have a Pareto-efficient outcome; yet we shall see in section 14.5 that they can differ in allocation of production and also in distribution of net benefits (payoffs). Conclusions are presented in section 14.6.

14.2 A benchmark: Pareto efficiency

The production of a public good provides benefits for its group of consumers. There are n agents, $i=1,\ldots, n$, producing as well as consuming a public good Q. Let q_i be the quantity produced by agent i, $C_i=C_i(q_i)$ its strictly convex cost function with $C_i'=(>) \, 0$ for $q_i=(>) \, 0$, $C_i''>0$, and total quantity

$$Q \equiv \sum_{j=1}^{n} q_j \tag{1}$$

$B_i=B_i(Q)$ is agent i's strictly concave benefit function with $B_i'>0$, $B_i''<0$. The benefit function defines the public good property of consumption: There is no rivalry and no exclusion in consumption.

Let us first establish the Pareto-efficient outcome. Pareto efficiency amounts to maximizing (a randomly selected) agent 1's payoff under the condition that everyone else's payoff does not decrease. The maximization problem for Pareto efficiency is:

$$\max_{q_i} \quad B_1(Q)-C_1(q_1)-\sum_{k=2}^{n} \lambda_k \left[\bar{W}_k - B_k(Q)+C_k(q_k) \right]$$

The first order condition for agent i, $i = 1, \ldots, n$ reads:

$$\sum_{j=1}^{n} \lambda_j B'_j(Q) - \lambda_i C'_i(q_i) = 0 \tag{2}$$

with $\lambda_1 = 1$. These conditions can be interpreted as the outcome of weighted welfare maximization, with weight 1 for agent 1's welfare and λ_k for agent k's welfare. There is a continuum of constrained Pareto-efficient outcomes, because Pareto efficiency leaves the welfare weights λ_k and the contributions q_i undetermined. To foster simplicity and transparency, we shall focus on outcomes with just two players. Solving (2) for two agents gives as first-order condition:

$$\frac{B'_1(Q)}{C'_1(q_1)} + \frac{B'_2(Q)}{C'_2(q_1)} = 1 \tag{2a}$$

This will be the benchmark to be used for later purposes.

14.3 The Nash bargaining solution

Coordination internalizes the benefits of other agents in the actions of individual agents, hence creating scope for a Pareto-efficient outcome. The NBS with equal bargaining weights does so by maximizing the product of individual net benefits, thus splitting up the total gain in net benefits between group members:

$$\max_{q_i} \sum_{j=1}^{n} \log\left[B_j(Q) - C_j(q_j) - A_j \right]$$

where A_j is agent j's payoff in the threat point where NBS is rejected. For simplicity and transparency, we assume in this chapter that no one produces anything in the threat point and thus $A_j = 0$ for all agents j. The first-order condition for each participant can then be written as:

$$\sum_{j=1}^{n} \frac{B'_j(Q)}{B_j(Q) - C_j(q_j)} = \frac{C'_i(q_i)}{B_i(Q) - C_i(q_i)} \tag{3}$$

Comparing (3) to (2), we see that the outcome is Pareto efficient with implicit weights $\lambda_j = 1/(B_j - C_j)$. Unless benefit and cost functions are identical, the welfare weights differ per agent.

We now turn to an analysis of the allocation and cost efficiency in NBS, focusing on the case of two players. The first-order conditions are then:

$$\left[\frac{1}{(B_1 - C_1)} \right] B'_1 + \left[\frac{1}{(B_2 - C_2)} \right] B'_2 = \left[\frac{1}{(B_1 - C_1)} \right] C'_1 \tag{3a}$$

$$\left[\frac{1}{(B_1 - C_1)} \right] B'_1 + \left[\frac{1}{(B_2 - C_2)} \right] B'_2 = \left[\frac{1}{(B_2 - C_2)} \right] C'_2 \tag{3b}$$

These can be reduced to:

$$\frac{(B_1 - C_1)}{(B_2 - C_2)} = \frac{C_1'}{C_2'} \tag{4}$$

In the constrained NBS, the payoffs are proportional to marginal cost. To investigate the consequences for the allocation, we follow the procedure of making assumptions on the characteristics of the agents' benefit functions and cost functions, and derive the costs and net benefits that are technically feasible from those combinations of outputs. We subsequently select from the technically feasible outcomes the results that meet the economic condition for the constrained NBS as shown in (4).

Assume benefit and marginal cost functions to be homogeneous and heterogeneous respectively, and fixed costs to be zero. Define C_1' as the lowest marginal cost function for any given q. The technically feasible combinations are then as follows:

1   for $q_1 < q_2$: $C_1' < C_2'$, $C_1 < C_2$, $(B - C_1) > (B - C_2)$
2   for $q_1 = q_2$: $C_1' < C_2'$, $C_1 < C_2$, $(B - C_1) > (B - C_2)$
3   for $q_1 > q_2$:
    a $C_1' < C_2'$, $C_1 \leq$ or $> C_2$, $(B - C_1) \geq$ or $< (B - C_2)$
    b $C_1' = C_2'$, $C_1 \leq$ or $> C_2$, $(B - C_1) \geq$ or $< (B - C_2)$
    c $C_1' > C_2'$, $C_1 > C_2$, $(B - C_1) < (B - C_2)$

Of all combinations for q_1 and q_2 the only outcomes potentially consistent with (4) are options 3a and 3b. In 3a, the result is $q_1 > q_2$ with $C_1' < C_2'$ and for consistency with equation (4), $C_1 > C_2$ to make $(B - C_1) < (B - C_2)$. The low-cost producer will take the largest share in production of the public good. Although his marginal cost remains below the marginal cost of the high-cost producer, his output q_1 is so much higher relative to q_2 that he has the highest total cost and hence the lowest payoff. The total surplus (sum of net benefits) could be increased by reallocating production even more to agent 1 to lower total production costs even further. However, this would increase the inequality in net benefits. Thus, NBS accepts a certain inequality in the distribution if that increases aggregate net benefits; however, up to some limit.

In (3b), the consistent combination is $q_1 > q_2$ with $C_1' = C_2'$, together with $C_1 = C_2$ and consequently $(B - C_1) = (B - C_2)$. When the specific cost functions happen to be such that the combination $C_1' = C_2'$ goes hand in hand with $C_1 = C_2$, production is fully cost efficient. That is, the costs per unit of output are minimized and an equal level of payoffs is realized in this "best of all possible worlds" from the NBS point of view.

However, the above holds for the case of homogeneous benefit functions and heterogeneous cost functions. Let us assume the converse case with homogeneous cost functions but heterogeneous benefit functions. Let us assume that agent 1 faces the highest benefit function for any given Q. The technically feasible combinations are then:

4   for $q_1 < q_2$, the result is $C_1' < C_2$, $C_1 < C_2$,$(B-C_1) > (B-C_2)$
5   for $q_1 = q_2$, the result is $C_1' = C_2'$, $C_1 = C_2$,$(B-C_1) > (B-C_2)$
6   for $q_1 > q_2$, the result is $C_1' > C_2'$, $C_1 > C_2$,$(B-C_1) \leq$ or $> (B-C_2)$

From these technically feasible combinations, the only outcome consistent with equation (4) is option 6; that is $q_1 > q_2$, implying $C_1' > C_2'$ and $C_1 > C_2$, but with output q_1 in excess of q_2 sufficiently small to keep $(B_1 - C_1) > (B_2 - C_2)$. The agent with the highest benefits will take the largest share in the production and consequently will incur the highest cost. However, the costs are low enough to have the highest payoff, thanks to his comparatively high benefits of consuming the public good. More equality in payoffs could be attained by reallocating production from agent 2 to agent 1, but this would reduce cost efficiency and total surplus. The lesson here is that there is a limit to the sacrifice in surplus that is accepted in exchange for sharing the surplus more equally.

14.4 The Market Exchange Solution

In this section, the Market Exchange Solution (MES) will be explained and compared with NBS. Different from NBS, each agent maximizes its private net benefits given information on his own cost and benefit functions only, and acting on the expectation that in return for his production offer q_i the group will offer to produce $p_i q_i$ units of the public good. Subsection 14.4.1 analyzes each agent's decision of how much production effort to offer and of how much public good to demand. In subsection 14.4.2, it is demonstrated that a set of exchange rates exist in which every agent receives the quantity of the public good that it demands in exchange for its supply. Subsection 14.4.3 gives an exposition of how market equilibrium is detected through a process of equilibrium search. In subsection 14.4.4, it is demonstrated that MES is Pareto efficient. The allocation of contributions to the public good is discussed in subsection 14.4.5.

14.4.1 Utility maximization and the exchange rate

The potential consumer of the public good Q, who also participates in the production of the good, acts on the expectation that in exchange for his production offer q_i the coalition of consumers–producers will offer to produce Q_i units of the public good. The exchange rate defined as $p_i = Q_i / q_i$ is an exogenous variable for agent i. Further, the agent has knowledge of his strictly convex cost function $C_i(q_i)$ and his strictly concave benefit function $B_i(Q_i)$. Agent i maximizes the individual net benefit function W_i under the constraint of the exchange rate:

$$\max_{q_i} W_i = B_i(Q_i) - C_i(q_i) \text{ s.t. } Q_i - p_i q_i = 0$$

The first-order conditions for utility maximization are:

$$p_i B_i'(Q_i) = C_i'(q_i) \tag{5}$$

$$Q_i - p_i q_i = 0 \tag{6}$$

Equation (5) shows that raising the price p_i above 1 increases the marginal benefits, since the agent gets more units of the public good per unit produced. This makes him willing to incur higher marginal cost by increasing his supply of the public good. Substituting (6) into (5) and writing q_i as a function of p_i transforms the first-order conditions into a supply function:

$$q_i = q_i(p_i) \quad q_i' > 0, \; q_i'' > 0 \tag{7}$$

where $q_i' > 0$ and $q_i'' > 0$ – that is, the contribution to the public good is increasing in the exchange rate.

14.4.2 Equilibrium

The model views the negotiations between n agents as a market in which agents supply quantities q_i and demand quantities Q_i of the public good. In equilibrium, the exchange rates are such that total supply of all agents meets the demand of every agent. The n supply functions are defined in (7). The agent's supply q_i multiplied with the exchange rate p_i defines his demand (6) for units of the public good. A market equilibrium for the public good can only exist when all agents demand the same quantity and demand equals supply:

$$Q_i = Q \text{ for all } i \tag{8}$$

Total quantity supplied is the sum of individually supplied quantities:

$$Q_j = \sum q_j (j,...,n) \tag{9}$$

With n agents, the model consists of n demand equations (6), n supply equations (7), n conditions for market equilibrium (8), and one definition of total supply (9). From this system of $3n+1$ equations, the $3n+1$ variables p_i, q_i, Q_i, and Q can be solved. In market equilibrium, the vector of individual exchange rates is such that the individual supply offers sum up to a total supply of the public good equal to the quantity demanded by every agent. Based on Nentjes (1990), the advanced mathematical proof is Kryazhimskii *et al.* (2000), who have demonstrated that, with strictly convex cost functions and strictly concave benefit functions, the market equilibrium is unique and Pareto-optimal.

14.4.3 Equilibrium search

A key question now is how the equilibrium solution can be detected. Crucial is that each agent is informed about his exchange rate, which is adjusted when demand and supply do not meet. For that task, an auctioneer can be installed who provides each agent with his "private" exchange rate, registers the quantities supplied and demanded by each agent, and calculates the gap between demand and supply. For instance, assume that all individual contributions to the public good are zero prior to the start of the "auction," and that the auctioneer sets the exchange rate equal to 1 in the first round. This means that, for the contribution of one unit, the agent can expect one unit in return. Note that this is the implicit price of the non-cooperative Nash equilibrium. The price is proposed to each single agent, and each agent informs the auctioneer about the quantity he is willing to contribute at that specific exchange rate. The auctioneer subsequently registers each agent's offer q_i and calculates the agent's demand $Q_i = q_i$. The last action of the auctioneer in round one is to sum up all individual offers, thus identifying total supply $Q = \sum_{i=1}^{n} q_i$ and calculate for each agent his excess demand $Q_i - Q$. At $p_i = 1$ each agent's excess demand, equal to $(q_i - \sum_{j=1}^{n} q_j)$, is negative.

The second round would start with a new set of exchange rates. To identify the rule for price adjustment, one has to substitute (6), (8), and (9) into $(Q_i - Q)$ and differentiate:

$$\frac{d(Q_i - Q)}{dp_i} > 0 \tag{10}$$

A rise in exchange rate will increase a positive excess demand further and decrease demand deficits. To decrease the demand deficits that appeared in the first round, all exchange rates have to be set higher in the second round. Again, the auctioneer registers each agent's contribution offer and the corresponding quantity demanded. Total supply and each agent's positive or negative excess demands are again calculated. Based on this information, the vector of new exchange rates for round three is calculated. Price adjustments can be tuned to the relative size of the gap $(Q_i - Q)/Q$. When a positive excess demand appears for an agent, the price adjustment rule prescribes a lower price in the next round. Price adjustments in consecutive rounds will reduce positive and negative excess demands toward convergence at zero in market equilibrium.

Raising the exchange rate when there is a demand deficit may seem odd because it is in contradiction with the downward price adjustment required to reduce excess supply and clear markets for private goods. Yet it is correct for a public good for a market in which consumers provide the good collectively. Given total supply, the demand deficit can be reduced by increasing demand Q_i more than supply Q. According to (10), this is exactly what an increase of the exchange rate p_i does: Agent i increases output q_i, and since $Q_i = p_i q_i$, supply creates more than its own demand if $p_i > 1$.

14.4.4 Pareto efficiency of the Market Exchange Solution

We will now check whether the Market Exchange Solution is Pareto efficient. Substitution of (6) into (5) yields:

$$\frac{B'_j(Q)}{C'_j(q_j)} = \frac{q_j}{Q} \tag{11}$$

Summing this over j and applying (8) and (9) yields

$$\sum_j \left[\frac{B'_j(Q)}{C'_j(q_j)} \right] = \sum \frac{q_j}{Q} = 1$$

Multiplying both sides by $C'_j(q_j)$ gives

$$\sum \left[\frac{C'_i(q_{iM})}{C'_j(q_{jM})B'_i(Q)} \right] = C'_j(q_{jM}) \tag{12}$$

where q_{iM} is agent i's supply in the MES. Comparing (12) to (2) shows that this is a Pareto-efficient outcome with weights:

$$\lambda_i = \frac{C'_1(q_{1M})}{C'_i(q_{iM})} \tag{13}$$

For the case of two agents, equation (13) reads

$$\lambda_1 = 1 \text{ and } \lambda_2 = (C_1'/C_2')\lambda_1 = C_1'/C_2'$$

Substitution in (2) results in

$$B'_1 + \left(\frac{C'_1}{C'_2} \right) B'_2 = C'_1 \tag{12a}$$

$$B'_1 + \left(\frac{C'_1}{C'_2} \right) B'_2 = \left(\frac{C'_1}{C'_2} \right) C'_2 \tag{12b}$$

Thus, MES is Pareto efficient, with the welfare weights determined by the ratio of marginal costs. The weights differ from the Pareto-efficient NBS, which is a first indication that the allocation of q_i can differ between the two approaches.

14.4.5 Allocation of contributions and production in MES

The individual optimum in market equilibrium expresses the share agent i will contribute to the public good under the MES regime. From (11), it follows for two agents that:

$$\left[\frac{B'_1(Q)}{B'_2(Q)} \right] \left[\frac{q_2}{q_1} \right] = \frac{C'_1(q_1)}{C'_2(q_2)} \tag{14}$$

When two agents have identical benefit functions and agent 1 has a lower marginal cost function compared to agent 2, the technically feasible combinations are as follows:

1   for $q_1 < q_2$ the result is $C_1' < C_2'$
2   for $q_1 = q_2$ the result is $C_1' < C_2'$
3   for $q_1 > q_2$ the options are:
    a $C_1' < C_2'$
    b $C_1' = C_2'$
    c $C_1' > C_2'$

From all combinations of q_1 and q_2, the only outcome potentially consistent with (14) is option 3a, with $q_1 > q_2$ and $C_1' < C_2'$. Agent 1 with the low marginal cost function takes the highest share in total provision, but still produces less than is cost efficient, while agent 2 produces comparatively too much, despite having the lowest share. The intuition here is that, due to his higher marginal cost, agent 2 will under no circumstance be able to match the offer of q_1 on an equal footing but only with a lower offer of q_2. As a result, the exchange ratio $q_2/q_1 < 1$ with the marginal cost of agent 2 higher than of agent 1. With $B_1'(Q) = B_2'(Q)$, it follows from (14) that $q_1 C_1' = q_2 C_2'$. When the average variable cost is proportional to marginal cost, the implication is that the total variable costs of producing q_1 and q_2 are equal in MES. That, however, is a specific case. The general conclusion must be that the low-cost producer may end up with total costs that are higher, equal to, or lower than those of the high-cost producer.

When cost functions are homogeneous but benefit functions differ, with $B_1'(Q) > B_2'(Q)$ the following combinations of q_1 and q_2 with its impacts on marginal costs are technically feasible:

4   for $q_1 < q_2$ the result is $C_1' < C_2'$
5   for $q_1 = q_2$ the result is $C_1' = C_2'$
6   for $q_1 > q_2$ the result is $C_1' > C_2'$

For $B_1'(Q)/B_2'(Q) > 1$, it follows from equation (14) that $q_1 C_1' > q_2 C_2'$. Since marginal cost functions are identical, this implies $q_1 > q_2$ and $C_1'(q_1^*) > C_2'(q_2^*)$, which is option 6. Production is not allocated in a cost-efficient way – that is, the high-benefit agent produces relatively too much; he has higher marginal cost than the low-benefit agent, who produces comparatively too little. The intuition in this case is that, due to his lower marginal benefits, agent 2 will never match the offer q_1 with a higher or equal offer, but rather with a lower quantity q_2, which results in an exchange rate $q_2/q_1 < 1$. Nevertheless, agent 1 will end up with the highest marginal cost. Since the high-benefit agent takes the largest share in output, while accepting the highest marginal costs, he will have highest total costs. Due to his higher benefit function, his payoff still may be highest with $(B_1 - C_1) > (B_2 - C_2)$; however, it is also possible that his total costs are lowest or equal to those of the low-benefit agent.

14.5 Comparing NBS and MES

Table 14.1 provides an overview of the main results that have been derived for NBS and MES.

For the case of homogeneous benefit functions and agent 1 having a lower cost function than agent 2, as well as for the case of homogeneous cost functions and agent 1 having the higher benefit function, we found $q_1 > q_2$ for both NBS and MES. In both approaches, the low-cost agent and the high-benefit agent have the highest share in the production of the public good. However, there can be differences in the discrepancy between quantities. In making the comparison, let us assume that, at the outset, an MES regime is in place and the agents consider a switch from MES to NBS. The planner has the information on the results in the former (MES) market regime and now has the task to calculate the allocation of production and the resulting payoffs under NBS.

In order to derive more definite results than in Table 14.1, we first examine the case in which the two agents have quadratic benefit and cost functions. In this case, agent i ($i = 1, 2$) has total and marginal cost functions:

$$C_i(q_i) = \frac{1}{2} c_i q_i^2 \qquad C_i'(q_i) = c_i q_i \tag{15}$$

and total and marginal benefit functions:

$$B_i(Q) = b_i Q - \frac{1}{2} b_i Q^2 \qquad B_i'(Q) = b_i(1 - Q) \tag{16}$$

As we shall see, the agents' NBS and MES quantities only depend on the ratios of their benefit and cost parameters:

$$g_i \equiv \frac{b_i}{c_i} \tag{17}$$

Let us assume, without loss of generality, that $g_1 > g_2$. We can compare NBS and MES by analyzing (4) and (14). Moreover, since both NBS and MES are Pareto efficient, we know that if q_i is higher (and W_i lower) in one solution, then q_j must

Table 14.1 Summary of results comparison NBS versus MES

Case	NBS	MES
$B_1 = B_2$ and $C_1(q_1) < C_2(q_2)$	$q_1 > q_2$ $C_1' \leq C_2'$ $C_1 \geq C_2$ $(B_1 - C_1) \leq (B_2 - C_2)$	$q_1 > q_2$ $C_1' < C_2'$ $C_1 ? C_2$ $(B_1 - C_1) ? (B_2 - C_2)$
$B_1 > B_2$ and $C_1(q_1) = C_2(q_2)$	$q_1 > q_2$ $C_1' > C_2'$ $C_1 > C_2$ $(B_1 - C_1) > (B_2 - C_2)$	$q_1 > q_2$ $C_1' > C_2'$ $C_1 > C_2$ $(B_1 - C_1) ? (B_2 - C_2)$

be lower (and W_j higher) in that solution. In particular, substituting (15) and (16) into (2a), we find that the Pareto-efficient output levels satisfy:

$$\frac{b_1 Q}{c_1 q_1} + \frac{b_2 Q}{c_2 q_2} = 1 \tag{18}$$

For MES we find, substituting (15) and (16) into (14):

$$\frac{b_1 Q q_2}{b_2 Q q_1} = \frac{c_1 q_1}{c_2 q_2} \tag{19}$$

We can then solve for q_1 and q_2 from (17) to (19):

$$q_i^M = \sqrt{g_i}\left(\frac{\sqrt{g_1} + \sqrt{g_2} + [g_1 - g_2]\left[\sqrt{g_1} - \sqrt{g_2}\right]}{1 + 2(g_1 + g_2) + (g_1 - g_2)^2}\right) \tag{20}$$

For NBS we find, substituting (15) to (17) into (4) and rearranging:

$$\frac{q_1}{g_1 Q - \frac{1}{2} g_1 Q^2 - \frac{1}{2} q_1^2} = \frac{q_2}{g_2 Q - \frac{1}{2} g_2 Q^2 - \frac{1}{2} q_2^2} \tag{21}$$

This means that the welfare-weighted marginal costs of the two agents should be equal, where an agent's welfare weight is given by the inverse of his payoff. Let us now evaluate these welfare-weighted marginal costs at the MES quantities given by (20):

$$\frac{q_i^M}{g_i Q^M - \frac{1}{2} g_i \left(Q^M\right)^2 - \frac{1}{2}\left(q_i^M\right)^2} = \frac{2}{g_i + \sqrt{g_1 g_2}}$$

Since $g_1 > g_2$, the left-hand side of (21) is below the right-hand side at the MES quantities: The ratio of agent 1's marginal cost to his payoff is less than the ratio for agent 2. To achieve equality, q_1 has to rise and q_2 has to fall, so that the left-hand side of (21) rises while the right-hand side falls. Thus, when moving from MES to NBS, q_1 rises while q_2 falls, resulting in lower payoff for agent 1 but higher payoff for agent 2.

To give an economic interpretation to this finding, we elaborate on the two cases presented in Table 14.1. Let $g_1 > g_2$ reflect the case in which benefit functions are identical, and agent 1 has the lowest cost function. Then it is easily seen that MES results in lower marginal cost for agent 1, but equal payoffs. Going from MES to NBS, the increase in q_1 and decrease in q_2 is a reallocation of production reducing the difference in marginal cost and by that improving cost efficiency. As a result, the gain or surplus from cooperation increases while simultaneously the payoff of agent 2 increases and the payoff of agent 1 decreases. Reallocation cannot possibly pass the point at which marginal costs are fully equalized and maximum cost efficiency is attained, as Table 14.1 shows. Here, with inequality of cost functions, NBS is superior to MES in terms of cost efficiency, at the expense of introducing payoff inequality. This is illustrated in the numerical example below. We assume benefit functions $B_1=B_2=Q-\frac{1}{2}Q^2$ and cost functions $C_1=2q_1^2$ and $C_2=8q_2^2$. From (20), the solution for MES is:

$q_1=0.24$; $C_1'=0.96$; $B_1-C_1=0.295-0.115=0.18$;

$q_2=0.12$; $C_2'=1.92$; $B_2-C_2=0.295-0.115=0.18$;

$Q=0.36$; total surplus 0.36.

The outcome for NBS is, from (18) and (21):

$q_1=0.268$; $C_1'=1.07$; $B_1-C_1=0.299-0.144=0.155$;

$q_2=0.097$; $C_2'=1.56$; $B_2-C_2=0.299-0.076=0.223$;

$Q=0.365$; total surplus 0.378.

The numerical example illustrates that, in certain cases, the planner in NBS gives priority to surplus over equality in payoff. In MES, a similar increase in surplus and inequality is not feasible because agent 1 would refuse to make extra costs exceeding his own additional benefits.

In the second case presented in Table 14.1, the condition $g_1>g_2$ is due to homogeneous cost functions and agent 1 having a higher benefit function than agent 2. Here the transition from MES to NBS by way of increasing q_1 and decreasing q_2 increases the gap in marginal costs and raises cost inefficiency, since agent 1 already has the highest marginal costs in MES. Therefore, the surplus created by cooperation is to be lower under NBS than it is under MES; however, the payoff inequality is also smaller – just the reverse of the previous case. The following numerical example illustrates this case. Let the benefit functions be $B_1=2Q-Q^2$ and $B_2=\frac{1}{2}Q-\frac{1}{4}Q^2$, whereas the cost functions are homogeneous following $C_1=C_2=4q_1^2$. For MES, the figures are then, from (20):

$q_1=0.24$; $C_1'=1.92$; $B_1-C_1=0.59-0.23=0.36$;

$q_2=0.12$; $C_2'=0.96$; $B_2-C_2=0.148-0.058=0.09$;

$Q=0.36$; total surplus 0.45.

The outcome for NBS is, from (18) and (21):

$q_1=0.268$; $C_1'=2.147$; $B_1-C_1=0.598-0.288=0.309$;

$q_2=0.097$; $C_2'=0.776$; $B_2-C_2=0.149-0.038=0.111$;

$Q=0.365$; total surplus 0.421.

Going from MES to NBS, generating more equality in terms of payoffs has its costs in terms of a considerable loss in total net benefits, which completely falls on the high-benefit agent 1. In MES, the high-benefit agent would never accept such an outcome.

14.6 Conclusions and policy implications

Many international and global issues, among them climate change, are in essence economic problems caused by international reciprocal negative externalities and uncoordinated exploitation of common pools. Participation of nation-states in a common approach to solve or mitigate the problem can then be analyzed as contributing voluntarily to the production of an international public good. The major problem to be solved through negotiation between sovereign states is how much of the international public good to provide in total and, moreover, how to allocate the production of the public good among participating states.

A usual approach to the allocation problem is the Nash Bargaining Solution (NBS). In this chapter, we have proposed the Market Exchange Solution (MES) as an alternative method to predict the allocation of production effort and the distribution of payoffs. The two approaches are opposed to each other in the underlying view of the economic order. NBS tries to strike a balance between maximizing the surplus from cooperation and sharing it equally in a world of perfect information on cost and benefit functions. In MES, a market mechanism with price signals can detect an equilibrium in which each party maximizes its individual payoff, and information on cost and benefit functions is private. We have compared the two schemes under a regime in which agents have to deliver their contribution to the public good in kind, and production cannot be outsourced. International protocols in which nation-states commit themselves to reduce their emissions with specified amounts within an agreed time span and make no arrangements for international emissions trading are a perfect illustration.

NBS and MES turn out to be both Pareto efficient. In a model with two agents, we found a qualitative similarity in the allocation of production effort: In NBS and MES, the agent with the highest benefit function as well as the agent with the lowest marginal cost function delivers the largest contribution to the public good. Yet the allocations on the frontier of Pareto-efficient solutions are different. With quadratic benefit and cost functions, when a transition is made from an MES regime to an NBS regime, the high-benefit/low-cost agent will have to contribute more, and the low-benefit/high-cost agent is allowed to contribute less. With equal benefit functions, NBS increases total surplus at the expense of introducing payoff inequality in favor of the high-cost agent. With equal cost function, NBS decreases payoff inequality in favor of the low-benefit agent at the expense of reducing the total surplus.

Assessing the two approaches, our view is that when agents, such as countries, are self-interested, MES is better equipped than NBS to predict the allocation of effort and the distribution of gains from cooperation in the shared production of an international or global public good. In MES, basic neo-classical notions are applied to predict the allocation of production tasks. The allocation of contributed shares is based on individual gains expected from the public good; whereas, in NBS, contributed shares are calculated by a planner who proposes more stringent production targets for some of the agents than they would accept in a market setting. It is this feature that makes NBS less suitable as a model of cooperation between sovereign states. An agreement that redistributes the total gain from cooperation to make individual payoffs of participating states more equal may be laudable; it is, however, a different world.

References

Andreoni, J. and Bergstrom, T.C. (1996) "Do government subsidies increase the private supply of public goods?" *Public Choice*, 88: 295–308.

Binmore, K.G., Rubinstein, A., and Wolinsky, A. (1986) "The Nash Bargaining Solution in economic modeling," *Rand Journal of Economics*, 17: 176–188.

Boom, J.T. (2006) *International Emissions Trading: Design and Political Acceptability*, Ph.D. dissertation, Rijksuniversiteit Groningen, Groningen.

Falkinger, J. (1996) "Efficient private provision of public goods by rewarding deviations from average," *Journal of Public Economics*, 62: 413–422.

Guttman, J.M. (1978) "Understanding collective action: Matching behavior," *American Economic Review*, 68: 251–255.

Guttman, J.M. (1987) "A non-Cournot model of voluntary collective action," *Economica*, 54: 1–19.

Helm, C. (2003) "International emissions trading with endogenous allowance choices," *Journal of Public Economics*, 87: 2737–2747.

Hoel, M. (1991) "Global environmental problems: The effects of unilateral actions taken by one country," *Journal of Environmental Economics and Management*, 20: 55–70.

Kryazhimskii, A.V., Nentjes, A., Shibayev, S., and Tarasiev, A. (2000) "A game model of negotiations and market equilibrium," *Journal of Mathematical Sciences*, 100(6): 2601–2612.

Nash, J. (1950) "The bargaining problem," *Econometrica*, 18: 155–162.

Nentjes, A. (1990) "An economic model of transfrontier pollution abatement," in V. Tanzi (ed.), *Public Finance, Trade and Development* (pp. 243–263), Detroit: Wayne State University Press.

Nentjes, A. and Shibayev, S. (2006) "Modeling environmental cooperation on reciprocal emission reduction via a virtual market system," in G. Meijer, W.J.M. Heijman, J.A.C. Van Ophem, and B.H.J. Verstegen (eds), *Heterodox Views on Economics and the Economy of Global Society* (pp. 169–187), Wageningen: Wageningen Academic Publishers.

Nentjes, A. and de Vries, F.P. (2012) *Coordination and Efficiency of Abatement in Negotiated Agreements: How Does it Compare with Direct Regulation and Market-based Instruments?* Stirling Economics Discussion Papers, University of Stirling, Scotland UK (paper presented at the 19th Annual Conference of the European Association of Environmental and Resource Economists, Prague).

Samuelson, P. (1954) "The pure theory of public expenditure," *Review of Economics and Statistics*, 36: 387–389.

Wicksell, K. (1896) "A new principle of just taxation," in *Finanztheoretische Untersuchungen*, Jena: Gustav Fischer.

Index

Page numbers in *italics* denote tables.